COGNITION OF VALUE
IN ARISTOTLE'S ETHICS

COGNITION OF VALUE IN ARISTOTLE'S ETHICS

*Promise of Enrichment,
Threat of Destruction*

Deborah Achtenberg

STATE UNIVERSITY OF NEW YORK PRESS

Published by
State University of New York Press, Albany

© 2002 State University of New York

All rights reserved

Printed in the United States of America

No part of this book may be used or reproduced in any manner whatsoever without written permission. No part of this book may be stored in a retrieval system or transmitted in any form or by any means including electronic, electrostatic, magnetic tape, mechanical, photocopying, recording, or otherwise without the prior permission in writing of the publisher.

For information, address State University of New York Press,
90 State Street, Suite 700, Albany, NY 12207

Production by Christine L. Hamel
Marketing by Patrick J. Durocher

Library of Congress Cataloging-in-Publication Data

Achtenberg, Deborah, 1951–
   Cognition of value in Aristotle's ethics : promise of enrichment, threat of destruction / Deborah Achtenberg.
      p. cm.
   Includes bibliographical references and index.
   ISBN 0-7914-5371-5 (alk. paper) — ISBN 0-7914-5372-3 (pbk. : alk. paper)
   1. Aristotle—Ethics. I. Title.

B491.E7 A245 2002
171'.3—dc21
                                                              2001055011

10 9 8 7 6 5 4 3 2 1

In memory of
Gail and Irving Achtenberg

CONTENTS

Acknowledgments	ix
Abbreviations	xi
Introduction	1
1. Valuable Particulars	13
2. Ethics and Moral Theory	19
3. Ethics and Metaphysics	61
4. The Mean	97
5. Analogy, Habit, Beauty, Unexpectedness	123
6. Emotions as Perceptions of Value	159
Conclusion: Imaginative Construction	179
Notes	191
Bibliography	207
Index	215

ACKNOWLEDGMENTS

I have worked on this book for many years. It has been a solitary project, reflecting interests and concerns that have appeared to be my own. Still, there are some people whose responses to parts of this project have aided or encouraged me.

First, I would like to thank Stewart Umphrey for working with me on previous stages of this work when I was a student at the Graduate Faculty of the New School for Social Research. Thanks also to the organizers of the Conference on the Virtues at the University of San Diego for showing interest in the first essay I wrote on the topics discussed in this book, and to Alasdair MacIntyre for the interest he showed in aspects of my work that relate to his project and Martha Nussbaum for encouraging comments on the original sketch of this project.

Emily Hauptmann's comments on an essay that was a spin-off of this book while it was in progress were insightful and helpful. Charles Young's comments on chapters 2, 3, and 6 were incisive and usefully critical. I wonder if I have responded well enough to them. Alasdair MacIntyre's comments on chapter 3 were thought-provoking. I hope I have answered his questions about that chapter in the other chapters of the book.

I do not think that any author is fully responsible for the contents of his or her work, since I do not think culture works that way. Instead, I think culture creates a work as much as a work contributes to culture. To the extent, though, that an author is responsible for what he or she writes, I, and none of those just mentioned, am responsible for the guiding themes, claims, and intellectual preoccupations in this book. Because I took them to be different enough from those found in other recent books on Aristotle, I set out to write this book, little knowing the number of topics I would have to consider in order to bring the book to what counts for a conclusion.

Thanks to Trina Bertelson and Beth Blankenship at Bold Print, an independent bookstore near my apartment in Reno, for conversations on Sunday afternoons during breaks I took from writing this book. Judy Potter provided me with lovely surroundings in a rental apartment overlooking a wooded canyon and the San Francisco Bay during a sabbatical year I spent working on this project. Thanks, Judy, for helping me have a pleasant year and to the University of Nevada, Reno, for providing me with the sabbatical to work on the book. Thanks to the previous owners of my house on Gordon Avenue in Reno for creating the beautiful setting in which I completed the book and, at the University of Nevada, Reno, to my colleagues in the Department of Philosophy, especially Department Chair, Tom Nickles, and to Bob Mead, Dean of the College of Arts and Sciences, for providing me with the pleasant and well-equipped office that is the other venue in which I worked on this book in its final stages.

Thanks to MP for discussions that have deeply influenced and shaped this book; to the members of Temple Sinai (Reform), especially Rabbi Myra Soifer and fellow members of the Choir and Music Havurah, for providing me with a context in which to lead a religious life; and to the members of SPECTRUM Northern Nevada, especially present and past board members, for moral support and encouragement in political activities that took place during the final stages of this book.

Thanks, finally, in memory, to my mother and father, Gail and Irving Achtenberg, for providing me with models of pursuing difficult projects and thinking in new frameworks.

ABBREVIATIONS

Aristotle

Cat.	*Categories* (Minio-Paluello, 1986)
De An.	*De Anima (On the Soul)* (Ross, 1986)
De Cael.	*De Caelo (On the Heavens)* (Guthrie, 1971)
EE	*Eudemian Ethics* (Walzer and Mingay, 1991)
Gen.Corr.	*Generation and Corruption* (Forster, 1978)
Met.	*Metaphysics* (Jaeger, 1978)
Insomn.	*De Insomniis (On Dreams)* (Hett, 1975)
De Motu	*De Motu Animalium (On the Motion of Animals)* (Nussbaum, 1978)
NE	*Nicomachean Ethics* (Bywater, 1975)
Phys.	*Physics* (Ross, 1973)
Pol.	*Politics* (Ross, 1988)
Post.An.	*Posterior Analytics* (Ross, 1978)
Pr.An.	*Prior Analytics* (Ross, 1978)
Rhet.	*Rhetoric* (Ross, 1975)
Soph.Ref.	*Sophistical Refutations* (Forster, 1978)
Top.	*Topics* (Ross, 1984)

Freud

SE	*Standard Edition* (Strachey, 1920–1922, 1923–1925)

Greek New Testament

Rom.	*Romans* (Metzger and Murphy, 1991)

Hebrew Bible

Deut.	*Deuteronomy* (JPS, 1985)
Gen.	*Genesis* (JPS, 1985)
Isa.	*Isaiah* (JPS, 1985)
Ps.	*Psalms* (JPS, 1985)

Hobbes

Lev.	*Leviathan* (Oakeshott, 1962)

Homer

Il.	*Iliad* (Lattimore, 1951)
Od.	*Odyssey* (Lattimore, 1965)

Kant

CPR	*The Critique of Pure Reason* (Smith, 1965)
DV	*The Doctrine of Virtue* (Gregor, 1996)
GMM	*The Groundwork of the Metaphysics of Morals* (Paton, 1956)
MM	*The Metaphysics of Morals* (Gregor, 1996)

Liddell, Scott, Jones

LSJ	*A Greek-English Lexicon* (Liddell, Scott, Jones, 1983)

Locke

ST	*Second Treatise of Government* (Macpherson, 1980)

Marcus Aurelius

Med.	*Meditations* (Grube, 1983)

Nietzsche

BGE	*Beyond Good and Evil* (Kaufmann, 1966)

Plato

Meno	*Meno* (Burnet, 1974a)
Phdr.	*Phaedrus* (Burnet, 1973)
Rep.	*Republic* (Burnet, 1974b)

Rousseau

DSA	*Discourse on the Sciences and Arts* (Gourevitch, 1986)
DI	*Discourse on Inequality* (Gourevitch, 1986)
ST	*Second Treatise of Government* (Macpherson, 1980)

INTRODUCTION

What is ethical cognition like? That is, when we make (ethical) choices or exercise virtue of character, what kind of cognition is involved? In addition, what is the cognitive component of emotion like? That is, what kind of cognition is involved in our feelings of love, hate, pity, anger, kindness, envy, and so forth?

A simple answer would be that both ethical and emotional cognition centrally involve cognition of value. When we exercise virtue of character, we choose what we appropriately cognize as valuable in some way: to give aid to someone, rather than hurting them; to be friendly to someone, rather than surly toward them; to prevent someone from engaging in actions that maim and destroy ourself or others. When we feel emotion—when we love or hate, when we pity someone or envy them—we are aware of the object of our emotion as valuable in some way: as beautiful or bad, as the subject of suffering or the bearer of positive qualities.

In the early Enlightenment and again in the early twentieth century, this simple answer is rejected. The simple answer has it backward, some then say. Ethical choices or judgments do not involve cognition of value. Instead, value judgments are expressions of emotion. Moreover, emotions themselves are not cognitive—not shaped by how we perceive the world or what experiences we have had of it—but are brute and idiosyncratic. Later, ethics is understood as formalistic or rule-governed. The cognition involved in ethics, on this account, is merely the awareness of the applicability of a universal or a rule to a specific case.

In recent years, a number of philosophers have rejected both emotivism and formalism. There is such a thing as ethical cognition, they say, and it is not merely awareness of the applicability of rules to cases. Instead, it involves a rich awareness of the particular features of complex, concrete situations and the perception of some among those features as salient. Moreover, emotions, they say, are not brute but, instead, are intentional: they are forms of perception, types of rational orientation toward the world, ways of perceiving particular situations.

Such views could be part of a move back to the simple answer just mentioned. For, once we have said that ethical awareness is awareness of salience, we still must ask what is meant by 'salience'. In my view, the best way to spell out what is meant by salient particulars in the ethical realm is particulars that are conducive to or components of some value (or of something valuable). To be salient is to stand out, or even to leap out (as the etymology of the word suggests), to be prominent. To see particulars as salient is to see some of them as more important than others. But, important in what way? For a mathematician, mathematically interesting or unusual or important particulars stand out. For a lawyer, details having to do with liability or right are prominent. It is not enough to say that ethical cognition is cognition of salience. It must be a certain kind of salience. The simple answer looks promising again, with this in mind. What the person exercising virtue of character sees in a situation—what stands out for them or leaps to their mind—is some kind or kinds of value: which health plan will benefit the old, for example; which government agency is unfair in the allocation of opportunities for development; which type of course requirement will most substantially increase students' understanding of the diverse world in which they live.

Similarly, I maintain, we must ask those who say that emotions are forms of perception, types of rational orientation to the world, or ways of perceiving particular situations, what the person feeling an emotion is perceiving or to what part or aspect of the world that person is rationally oriented. Here, too, we would want to include, but not stop at, the idea of awareness of particulars. One can have quite detailed knowledge of the particulars of a certain situation without that knowledge seeming to contribute at all to one's having an emotional reaction to the situation. While, on the other hand, there is at least a common connection between awareness of the value qualities of a situation and certain emotional reactions to it: a detailed perception of decay often leads to a feeling of disgust or revulsion; watching a filmclip of a young girl's near perfect gymnastic performance often leads to feelings of admiration (if not envy); learning in detail how a tyrant devised and carried out his plans to defame and murder his opponents often leads to indignation.

In this essay, I will show that Aristotle holds one version of the simple answer to my opening questions about the cognitive component of ethical virtue and of emotion. In doing so, I will join and add another dimension to the ongoing discussion of the cognitive component of ethical virtue in Aristotle's ethical theory. Recent commentators have pointed to the important fact that Aristotle believes cognition of particulars is more important for ethical virtue than cognition of universals or rules; that the kind of cognition required for ethical virtue is not demonstrative knowledge but cognitive perception or imagination; and that the affective component of ethical virtue is itself cognitive, since emotions are not blind impulses or urges, but have a cognitive component. To these important interpretive claims, I will add another, namely, that, according to Aristotle, the cognitive component of ethical virtue and of emotion is not just perception of particulars, but also perception of something about particulars, namely, perception of their value, that is, perception of them as good or beautiful.

I will give an extended, complex argument for this claim in this essay. Before I do, however, I want to put Aristotle's view in a broader context than the one in which I have just put it. I have just put his answer in the context of one recent line of development of philosophical thought about value and ethics, the one in which there is first the acceptance and then the rejection both of emotivism and of formalism.

To set the new frame I ask whether what is involved in the development of ethical virtue is the achievement of a certain kind of cognition or awareness at all. Perhaps, to the contrary, ethical or emotional development involves not an increase in awareness, but a decrease in, or delay in or suppression of, awareness. Many thinkers have taken this route. Moreover, it is not obvious that they are mistaken in doing so.

Consider, for example, the Roman Stoic philosopher, Marcus Aurelius. Marcus is a case of a philosopher who believes that virtue requires the extinction of emotions rather than their development. According to him, emotions are neutral—neither good nor bad—and virtue requires that one eliminate emotions and despise the flesh. The way he devises for achieving virtue, so understood, is a kind of decrease in awareness: think on the fact that you will die (not on what you could accomplish but on the fact that, no matter how much you accomplish, you, too, will die); think of the meat you long to eat as nothing but the dead carcass of an animal; break the melody you wish to hear down into the notes that compose it; think of the purple robe as sheep's wool dyed with the blood of a shellfish; of sexual intercourse as internal rubbing accompanied by a spasmodic ejection of mucus (*Med.* 6.13, 6.24, 11.2, etc.). My life will inevitably end in death, as Marcus would have us note, but it can involve accomplishment, as well. Meat is the dead carcass of an animal, but is tasty and hearty, too. A melody is more than notes; it is also a whole composed of those notes; a purple robe is more than wool and blood, but a beautiful and symbolically significant piece of clothing; sexual intercourse involves rubbing and ejections, but involves pleasurable sensations and cognitively laden emotions as well. Marcus' method for achieving ethical virtue involves a decrease, not an increase, in awareness. It involves what I will call the 'imaginative deconstruction of wholes'. Wholes, as has been argued at least since Plato and Aristotle (if not since Parmenides and Zeno), are not identical to their parts. A life, a piece of meat, a melody, a robe, and an act of sexual intercourse—each is a whole composed of parts. Deconstruction of such a whole into its parts always leaves out something of what it is to be that whole. For Marcus, we can thus say, ethical virtue involves not an increase, but a decrease in awareness, specifically, a decrease in our awareness of things as parts of larger wholes or contexts.

Consider, for another example, Sigmund Freud. According to Freud, morality originates in the oedipal stage (*SE* 1924, 198). In this stage of development, the boy wants his mother, sexually, and wants his father out of the way. He is aware, however, that acting on his sexual desire for his mother is forbidden and he fears that his powerful father will castrate him if he acts on it. So, he represses, rather than acting on, his sexual instinct. His desire goes into latency. As a result, he is, in later life, unaware of his early childhood attraction to his mother and of the difficult achievement that managing it involved.

All morality originates in this oedipal stage repression, according to Freud, and this in two senses of the term 'morality'. First, morality in the sense of knowing that some of what you want is off-limits comes from this stage. For, though we do not retain conscious awareness of this stage, our superego results from it. Moreover, morality in the sense of the achievement of a flourishing life and of the means to it—what some philosophers have come of late to understand under the heading of 'ethical' rather than 'moral'—comes from this stage, as well. For we cannot act on our every instinct, and so must learn the most economical, or energy-saving, ways of managing those instincts. Repression of those that are off-limits is the most economical way. Repression enables us to continue to function in our lives when we cannot act on our desires. We push those desires and the accompanying awareness of them out of the way, and go on and function in other ways.

The development, through repression, of the superego is for Freud part of the whole process he calls 'structuralization'. Eventually, in addition to mere instinct or id comes superego and ego. This process in Freud is similar to the development of virtue in Aristotle, though Freud has an unfortunate tendency to speak of the acquisition of the ego or of the superego as if it were the acquisition of a faculty rather than the development of a faculty into a settled disposition. Moreover, morality comes from it. So, we can say that for Freud, the development of virtue or morality centrally involves not an increase, but a decrease, in awareness, specifically, the decrease in awareness that Freud calls by the name 'repression'.

With this, we have a new framework for thinking about ethical or emotional development. Some philosophers think the acquisition of ethical virtue involves an increase in awareness and the development of emotion. Others think it involves a decrease in awareness and a suppression or extinction of emotion.

Philosophers who believe ethical virtue requires a decrease in awareness and suppression of emotion do so for different reasons. Marcus and Freud believe this because they believe that our desires and their objects are bad in a certain way—not inherently bad, but obstacles to our flourishing, our acting. For Marcus, desires are neutral. For Freud, they are positive; they fuel all important activity that we do, but cannot always be exercised, due to interpersonal constraints.

Some others believe ethical virtue requires suppression of cognition not because the object of cognition and desire is bad, but because there is something bad or at least limited about cognition itself. Emotion is good, on this account, and awareness is bad. Or, at least, emotion is good and awareness is neutral or ineffective with regard to what is good. Here we might think of Jean-Jacques Rousseau, for example, as well as various books in the Hebrew *Bible*.

According to Rousseau, human beings feel pity and a healthy kind of self-love by nature (*DI* 9). Moreover, our nature, according to him, is prerational. So, prior to the development of reason in us, we are moved both to self-contentment and to acts of kindness toward others. The development of reason, according to him, far from leading to the development of virtue, leads away from it. Virtue is a sublime science of simple souls written in the heart not in the mind (*DSA* 2.61). Simple people, whose reason has not been developed, come to the aid of others in need. Wise people stay secure in their own safety and do not act, even if a murder goes on under their window (*DI* 1.37). Natural human being has a natural strength and vigor, as well, which is ennervated by reflection (*DI* 1). Reflection, according to Rousseau, is a state against nature and the one who meditates or thinks is a depraved animal (*DI* 2.9). Reflection leads away from pity and to the destruction of our naturally vigorous constitution.

Genesis gives us a related picture. The original condition of human beings is an idyllic one. The idyll comes to an end because human beings disobey God by acquiring knowledge of value: they eat of the tree of knowledge of good and evil. In this story, and in many others, we are told that what we need most is not intelligence, but obedience or love or even fear. God's ways are not our ways. His ways are not fully comprehensible:

> For My plans are not your plans,
> Nor are My ways your ways
>   —declares the Lord.
> But as the heavens are high above the earth,
> So are My ways high above your ways
> And My plans above your plans.
>   (*Isa.* 55.8–9)

He makes light before the cause of light (*Gen.* 1.3, 14–18). He makes a human being out of dust (*Gen.* 2.7). He makes rock into a pool of water or a flinty rock into a fountain (*Ps.* 114.7–8). Though incomprehensible, God is the most important being, the being with whom we must be in accord. As a result, our ethical development is not intellectual development, but is affective and voluntary development instead: "You shall love the LORD your God with all your heart and with all your soul and with all your might" (*Deut.* 6.5).[1]

Some other thinkers believe that acquisition of ethical virtue does not require a change in cognition, whether an increase or a decrease, or a change in one's desires, whether development of them or suppression of them. One's desires are brute or instinctual, not formed by our perception of things, but part of our original nature. Virtue requires, instead, alteration of the real situation we are in so that a different way of acting on our desires results.

Thomas Hobbes is such a thinker. He recommends that we direct activation of our basic emotions away from one real object and toward another. Our fundamental, basic, brute emotions are the fear of death and the desire for self-preservation. As a result, our natural state is a state of war of every man against every man (*Lev.* 1.13, 100). With the presence of an all-powerful sovereign, the state of war ends and the citizens acquire a variety of virtues, prime among them being justice. We become just, according to him, because we know that if we do not, the sovereign will use his unlimited power to retaliate. It is in our interest to be just to avoid retaliation by the sovereign and we can count on the other person being just as well for the same reason (*Lev.* 1.15, 115). We become just, then, not by developing our passions—by coming to see that people are not fearful but lovable, for example, or that they are desirable components of our own flourishing life—but by channeling them: once all significant power is in the hands of the sovereign, our brute, ineradicable fear of death is redirected away from every person and to the sovereign, since he is now the most fearful person there is.

There are those, then, who believe that ethical or emotional development requires the development of intellect and emotion and those, on the other hand, who believe that it involves the suppression or channeling of intellect and emotion. Among those in the second group we might usefully look also at Immanuel Kant and Friedrich Nietzsche, since the former recommends that we suppress our emotions and the latter that we suppress our intellect: according to Kant we have a natural inclination to violate the moral law, and virtue is force against that natural inclination; according to Nietzsche, untruth is a condition of life (*MM* 6:380, 1.4).

Aristotle, as I have asserted, is in the first group, the group of those who believe that emotional or ethical development (the two are the same for him) require not suppression but development both of our emotions and of our intellect. Virtue, according to Aristotle, is a settled disposition to choose well. Choice, according to him, is not simply desire, nor is it the sort of faculty that other thinkers might call by the name 'will', but it is deliberate desire.[2] By deliberate desire Aristotle means desire that has been shaped and informed by deliberation. Virtue, then, requires both the development, not the suppression, of emotion and the development, not the suppression, of intellect. Emotions are shaped and developed by deliberation and, more broadly, by practical insight *(phronēsis)* as a whole.[3]

In addition, it is not just any deliberation that informs desire in the case of virtue, but good deliberation, the kind of deliberation that results in a decision for the mean not for one of the extremes. The mean for Aristotle, as I will argue, denotes the good. If so (and with some additional premises), then ethical virtue, for Aristotle, is a settled disposition to desire what one correctly perceives as good. As mentioned above, I will argue in this essay that according to Aristotle, the cognitive component of ethical virtue and of emotion is not just the perception of particulars but also perception of something about particulars, namely, perception of their value. The claim that virtue, for Aristotle, is a settled disposition to desire what one correctly perceives as good is one part of that argument.

By 'value', I mean nothing very rich. Instead, I mean it to be a broad term, one I can use as an umbrella term for various philosophers' notions of what is evaluatively positive and also for an individual philosopher's own various notions of what is evaluatively positive. In the case of Aristotle, there are two principal types of value (if 'type' is the right word, given that 'good' and 'beautiful' do not denote categories for Aristotle). They are the good and the beautiful. Though the two are not the same, they overlap, in a way that I will explain in what follows.[4] When I refer to value in Aristotle, then, I mean to denote the good and the beautiful.

'Good', for Aristotle, means *telos* or *teleion*, as I will argue. A central idea in this essay, thus, is the idea of *telos*. The goal of this essay is not to argue for value realism, however, though increased openness to a certain kind of value realism may be one of its offshoots. In my view, and in Aristotle's as I understand him, value is real, but relational, and its relationality is tied to contexts in such a way that what is valuable in varying contexts itself varies in complex and sometimes unexpected ways.[5] This sort of value realism need not result in the kind of authoritarianism that is often inspired by value realism and that leads many philosophers to reject value realism out of hand.

The goal of the essay is, instead, to discuss the importance of the awareness of a certain kind of relatedness for the development of ethical virtue, that is, for what we may call 'character development' or, simply, 'emotional development'. The type of relatedness I have in mind is the one that a *telos* has to the things whose *telos* it is. Aristotle calls that relationship by the terms *'entelecheia'* and *'energeia'*. The discovery of the importance of awareness of this kind of relatedness for character development is, in my view, one of the great discoveries made by Aristotle, or, to be more accurate, by both Plato and Aristotle, a discovery that has largely been overlooked by contemporary philosophers.[6] For Aristotle, there is a kind of relatedness in which one thing or person is not replaced or destroyed by another, but is developed, enriched, or enabled to flourish. The implications of this view are broad and fundamental. In personal relationships, for example, it implies that the presence of an other need not be a threat to be avoided or guarded against, but may, instead, be an opportunity—an opportunity to fulfill one's own deepest aims. My goal in this essay will be to show that Aristotle holds one version of such a view of ethical virtue and the kind of relatedness that it involves and to point to a crucial component of virtue theory, a component that has been largely overlooked by contemporary virtue theorists and, as well, by modern psychologists, starting with Freud[7] and going up to, but not including, the object relations theorists of the present day.[8]

So we have come around to the question, what is value, a difficult question for us, in our post- or, better, late modern age.[9] Some hold fast to the idea that value is not fact and therefore is not anything at all. Others hold fast to the idea that, since value is not fact, it is, fundamentally, a human creation. For both camps—the camps that used appropriately to be called 'Anglo-American' and 'Continental' but no longer divide up this way—the view that the cognitive component of ethical virtue and of emotion is not just cognition of particulars but of their value is problematic. If value isn't anything at all, we can have no awareness of it. If value is a human creation then creation of value is more cognitively fundamental than awareness of it is.

Aristotle's view of value is not as far from the insight that leads some philosophers to say that value is not fact as might be thought.[10] For Aristotle thinks that evaluation is not mere categorization. 'Good' and 'beautiful' do not name categories according to him. To call something 'good', for example, is not to mention its qualities, its quantity, its time, location, and so forth. Instead, it is to say that it shares in a kind of relatedness in which one thing or person is not replaced or destroyed by another, but is enriched, developed, or enabled to flourish.

This kind of relatedness cannot be defined, Aristotle asserts in *Metaphysics* 9.6. Instead, he says, it becomes clear in different cases by induction, and to be aware of it in different cases is to see an analogy. The claim that awareness of value is awareness of an analogy is not surprising given that, on the most plausible interpretation of *Nicomachean Ethics* 1.6, good is not univocal but is instead an analogical equivocal since good means *telos*. Thus, the cognitive component of ethical virtue and of emotion is not just perception of particulars, for Aristotle, but is perception of a certain recurring relationship between particulars. The virtuous person's practical perception is perception of an analogy. I will argue for this view and also give examples that show what it would mean in practice—examples from ancient ethical theory broadly understood, from the *Nicomachean Ethics* itself and from ordinary practice.

In addition, for Aristotle, good and beautiful are (though differently) principles of wholeness or completeness. Practical perception is, I will argue, perception of particulars as parts of larger wholes. To perceive them as such is to perceive their value. Thus Aristotle can fruitfully be contrasted with Marcus as I have described him. For Marcus, I maintain, the development of virtue requires the imaginative deconstruction of wholes. For Aristotle, to the contrary, it requires the imaginative construction of them. The virtuous person, for Aristotle, sees particulars in the light of the wholes they could compose: the food before me in terms of my overall bodily health; the dangerous action I must pursue in terms of victory in battle; another person in terms of the joint activities we could engage in; my current activities in terms of the life goals I wish to attain; and, in general, every event, situation, and thing in terms of an overall developed and flourishing life.

For Aristotle, our emotions are shaped by these perceptions. As we come to have richer and richer perceptions of how our concrete situation fits into one or another realizable picture of an overall developed and flourishing life, our emotional dispositions change as well. We come to desire, pursue, and take pleasure in those activities, institutions, and people who we see as part of that life and to be averse to those who we see as destructive of it. Virtue does not spring from the suppression of emotions and desires, as suggested by Marcus, Freud, and Kant, but from shaping and developing them by a process of shaping and developing our picture of an overall developed and flourishing life. Nor does virtue result from the suppression of intellect on behalf of value, as suggested by Rousseau, the Hebrew *Bible*, or Nietzsche, but from the development of our intellectual capacity to see value, and to see it in more and more rich and complex ways in the particular situations that confront us.

This is, of course, one of the chief reasons for interest in Aristotle's ethics today. Aristotle asks us neither to suppress our emotions, as certain moralists would, nor to suppress our intellect, as would certain irrationalists. He holds out for us, instead, a picture of a harmonious life, one in which what we want and what we think can, for the most part, be in accord. I will develop that picture in this essay.

First, I will describe the discussions of Aristotle's ethical theory which this essay joins and explain why there is a need to add another dimension to them. Then, I will describe some discussions of Aristotle's ethical theory from which this essay diverges and explain why I feel justified in diverging from them. Then, I will give positive arguments for my own interpretation as well as examples of what Aristotle's view would mean in practice. Finally, I will conclude by discussing some of the strengths and weaknesses of Aristotle's account and some of the implications of my interpretation for contemporary virtue theory as a whole.

These concluding reflections are worth mentioning here at the beginning, so that the reader can see the larger project of which this essay is a part. In my view, as already stated, one central strength of Aristotle's 'imaginative construction' is that it provides an explanation of the fact that ethical virtue results from shaping and developing our emotions and intellect rather than simply eliminating, suppressing, or channeling them.

One central weakness of his account is that it is too broad. It simply is not clear that everything that is appropriate for us to do is something that we can or ought to come to desire. In a politically repressive society, for example, we may have to do many things that we appropriately find undesirable. In such a situation, ethical virtue would, I maintain, require of us that we use some psychological mechanism for putting aside our distaste or aversion rather than that we shape it. Sexual desire provides another example. Though Freud in my view is wrong in supposing that all ethical development results from sexual repression, he is probably right that some of it does.[11] It is plausible that the opposite sex parent (for heterosexuals), and a variety of other people, simply *are* both desirable and off-limits.[12] In such cases, proper emotional development *would* be to somehow put aside, repress, or channel our desires.

Aristotle, as I will argue, presents and explains the view that ethical virtue involves shaping or developing emotions rather than channeling, controlling, or eliminating them. It is not clear, however, that this is the whole story about ethical virtue. It seems more likely that just as we need to learn to shape and develop our emotions, so we need to develop the capacity to distance ourselves from some of them, or to set them aside, or to channel them.

Finally, I will suggest that Aristotle's concept of enriching relatedness, the perception of which enables us to shape rather than simply managing our emotions, is not the last or only word on enriching relatedness. Aristotle's understanding of it is fundamentally hierarchical. If there are other, less hierarchical, kinds of enriching relatedness, they, too, might shape our emotions. I will suggest that this is one of the implicit teachings of twentieth-century developmental psychology, according to which our sense of our self as a self and of an other as other are coterminous and that, therefore, developmental theory is a rich source for our thinking about virtue theory today.[13]

One final note before I begin. I intend, in this essay, to use a variety of approaches to my topic. On the one hand, I will engage in straightforward textual interpretation. When I do that, I will look at a portion of text, give my interpetation of its meaning, and argue for or against the interpretations of others. One strength of my interpretation is that it resolves certain long-standing interpretive problems—namely, the connection between metaphysics and ethics for Aristotle (chapter 3); how to understand the mean so that Aristotle's assertion that ethical virtue is a mean is neither an uninspiring nor trivial one (nor one that implies a certain number of virtuous actions) (chapter 4); and how to understand the distinction between a *logos* and a rule and, having done so, make sense of Aristotle's view that the practically insightful person utilizes a *logos* but not a rule in making choices (chapter 5, section 1).

On the other hand, I will engage in a broader type of interpretation, a type that has less to do with just what Aristotle means and more with how what he means might be construed or framed. To do that, I will utilize a variety of strategies. Sometimes, I will follow out the possible meanings of terms or ways of best conveying their meaning into English. Other times, I will look at a variety of texts from ancient Greek thought to show strains of thought of which Aristotle is best understood as a part. I do this to help open up the meaning of Aristotle's claims. Finally, I will, as I have already done, compare and contrast Aristotle's views with the views of other philosophers and of other thinkers of different types. I will not hesitate to compare thinkers who are usually contrasted and contrast thinkers who are usually compared. Some philosophy today, along with some contemporary social and political thought, is too rigidified, too stuck. In our postmodern age, our age of global communications and the loosening of boundaries, what may turn out to be most important are new syntheses, new combinations, or what I have called a 'new syncretism'.[14] We need to shake things up a bit, in order to recognize that what we think of as *the* history of philosophy is culture-bound and the result of decisions, rather than of mere observation or argumentation. We need to see that it is possible to compare Nietzsche with the Stoics or Rousseau with the Hebrew *Bible* or Aristotle with late psychoanalytic theory. My more specific goal in doing this is to open up a new way of looking at Aristotle, one that will open up for us a new way of looking at ethical theory in general, specifically, in terms of whether different ethical theories center on intellectual development or intellectual suppression and whether they center on emotional development or emotional suppression or management; in terms of whether different ethical theorists feature the imaginative construction or the imaginative deconstruction of wholes; in terms of whether different ethical theorists perceive human interrelation as a promise of enrichment or a threat of destruction or both; and, in general, in terms of the role, for different theorists, of the cognition of value in ethics.

CHAPTER ONE

Valuable Particulars

One group of commentators whose discussion this essay joins includes John McDowell, Martha Nussbaum, Nancy Sherman, and Stephen G. Salkever. McDowell is an early contributor to the discussion. In "Virtue and Reason," he claims that, for Aristotle, the cognitive component of ethical virtue is not knowledge of the applicability of a universal, a set of rules, or a code to a given situation, but perception of particulars as salient in the light of an uncodifiable view of how to live (1979, 331–350). According to Aristotle, McDowell says, the best generalizations about how to behave are only 'for the most part'.[1] This implies that, according to Aristotle, how one should live is not codifiable. Moreover, the universality of law must be supplemented by appreciation of the particular case.[2] We have an uncodifiable view of how to live, however, one which issues in concerns which, due to uncodifiability, cannot be ranked. Instead, one's uncodifiable view of how to live interacts with particular knowledge so that one concern or fact rather than another is seen as salient. According to McDowell, the important cognitive component of ethical virtue is this perception of particulars as salient in the light of one's uncodifiable view of how to live.

In "The Discernment of Perception" (1985) and *The Fragility of Goodness* (1986), Nussbaum joins the discussion. She maintains that, for Aristotle, the cognitive component of ethical virtue is not knowledge of universals or rules, but perception of particulars, that is, recognition of the salient features of complex, concrete situations (1990, 54–105). Though Aristotle does maintain that the person of practical wisdom utilizes a rule or general account *(logos)* in decision making, the rule Aristotle has in mind is not intended to be authoritative for decision making (*NE* 1106b36–1107a2). For, according to her, Aristotle maintains that the standard of excellence is not a universal or rule, but is what the person of practical wisdom would decide and, in addition, the person of practical wisdom does not utilize a universal or rule in making his or her decisions. Instead, the decision requires discernment and the discernment is in the perception of particulars.³ The rule, thus, is not authoritative for decision making, but is instead a mere rule of thumb, a summary of particular past decisions which, because it is such, is useful in guiding us to perceive the salient features of particular cases.

In addition, in "Changing Aristotle's Mind" and in *The Fragility of Goodness*, Nussbaum argues that emotions, for Aristotle, are forms of perception (Nussbaum and Putnam, 1992, 15–16).⁴ They have sorting or discriminatory power, as the accounts of the practical syllogism indicate. They lead or guide perception in situations requiring choice, as we can see from the fact that choice partakes both of intellect and of emotion (it is "desiderative deliberation or deliberative desire") and from the fact that practical wisdom is interdependent with excellence of character (which is in part a disposition concerning emotion) (1986, 308).⁵

In *The Fabric of Character*, Sherman joins the discussion and argues that, according to Aristotle, the cognitive component of ethical virtue is not knowledge of the applicability of rules but is perception of ethical salience and that emotions are intentional states directed at articulated features of an agent's environment through which we come to perceive particular circumstances, to recognize what is ethically salient (1989, chapter 2). For Aristotle, she maintains, ethical theories that begin with the justification of the decision to act begin too late since before making and justifying a decision, one must see that a situation calls for action, that is, one must see that the situation is ethically salient.⁶

Salkever adds his voice to the discussion in *Finding the Mean*. He argues that the cognitive component of ethical virtue is not deductively valid and necessary application of a scientific principle or a rule, but well-informed guessing, resting on a complex perception of the balance of importance and urgency likely to be best for us. Human goods are diverse and competing, as a number of examples indicate. Decisions require not the application of a rule, but the perception of an intelligent balance of the various competing goods (1990, chapter 3).⁷

The extent of the acceptance of this sort of interpretation of Aristotle's view of the cognitive component of ethical virtue and of emotion is indicated by the passing supposition of it in works devoted not specifically to Aristotle but to other, related topics. In their book of philosophical readings on emotion, for example, Cheshire Calhoun and Robert C. Solomon use Aristotle as their prime example of a philosopher according to whom emotions have a cognitive element, one for whom emotions are ways of conceiving particular situations (1984, introduction, part 1). For another example, in his generally positive treatment of Freud, Jonathan Lear criticizes Freud for treating an emotion as a quantity of energy rather than sharing Aristotle's view that an emotion is a rational orientation to the world (1990, 47–51). Lear supports his interpretation of Aristotle by referring to passages in the *Rhetoric* in which Aristotle states that emotions affect the framework through which we view the world, that is, that emotions affect our judgments.

It is not enough, however, to say that the cognitive component of ethical virtue and of emotion is the perception of particulars. People often have knowledge of the particulars of a certain situation without being practically insightful about it or having an emotional reaction to it. One may have even rather detailed knowledge of a situation without being practically insightful about it or emotionally responsive to it. Some additional kind of cognition is required. To denote that additional knowledge, McDowell, Nussbaum, and Sherman use the term 'salience'. We must, according to them, perceive salient particulars or the salience of particulars. Salkever denotes the additional knowledge by the term 'balance'. He maintains that we must perceive the balance of competing goods or that we must perceive the balance of importance and urgency among diverse, competing goods.

Aristotle does not use any term that might easily be translated as 'salience' or 'balance', however. So, we must ask how he would capture and explicate the insight that these terms contain. I maintain, and will argue in the chapters that follow, that, according to Aristotle, what we must perceive in the particulars in each case is their value, that is, we must perceive the particulars as good or as beautiful.

Consider, for example, McDowell's interpretation. According to McDowell, the best generalizations about how to behave are only 'for the most part' according to Aristotle. They are not universals, sets of rules, or codes. Hence the cognition of particulars that is central to ethical virtue according to Aristotle is not knowledge of the applicability of a universal, a set of rules, or a code to particulars. Instead, it is awareness of particulars in the light of our 'for the most part' understanding of how to live. McDowell calls that understanding an "uncodifiable view of how to live." The central cognitive component of ethical virtue according to Aristotle then is perception of particulars as salient in the light of an uncodifiable view of how to live (1979, 331–350).

Why assume, however, that the alternative to universals or rules is an unspecifiable or uncodifiable view? McDowell's arguments for this alternative come largely from Wittgenstein (1979, 336–342). There is some important similarity between Wittgenstein and Aristotle. They both reject the centrality of platonic universals, for example. However, it seems more reasonable to think of Aristotle and Wittgenstein as inhabiting the same broad region of thought regarding the limited usefulness of universals than as having the identical view of it. What if Aristotle thinks that there is a specifiable principle that guides our thought but is not an ordinary universal, rule, or code? In my view, this is exactly what he thinks. The good (i.e., good in general) is not univocal, according to Aristotle, but equivocal by analogy. To know the good (i.e., to know good in general) is to know something universal—specifically, it is to know a certain analogy. However, the analogy is an imprecise analogy, one that shows up differently and unexpectedly in different cases. Hence, we can know the analogy, which is universal, without knowing how good will show up in different cases, that is, how it will be instantiated in different particulars. This is part of what it means to say that good is an analogical *equivocal* (since, of course, not all analogies are equivocal).

I will explain and argue for this interpretation of Aristotle's understanding of the good in the chapters that follow. I will claim that how good is instantiated depends, more significantly than in the case of ordinary universals, on the nature of the particulars in which it is instantiated. Good means completion according to Aristotle, I will argue, and completions of things different in kind are different from each other in unexpected ways. The unexpectedness results from the fact that completion is relative to wholes and wholes according to Aristotle are not reducible to their parts (nor properties of wholes to the properties of their parts).

McDowell's argument is marred as well by insufficient reflection on what Aristotle might mean by 'for the most part'. Why are many claims in Aristotle's ethics true only for the most part? Is it because what we must know if we are to have ethical virtue is uncodifiable or unspecifiable? We cannot simply assume that this is the reason. Instead, as I will argue, Aristotle believes that regarding many of our claims, we have two alternatives: the claims either will be true only for the most part or, if we correct them, they will be universal but so sketchy as to have limited usefulness. This dual possibility is related to the fact that we can know good in its universal aspect without knowing how it will be instantiated in particular cases.

My point is that the fact that many of the claims made in ethics are only 'for the most part'; that the virtuous person's deliberations are not guided by ordinary universals or rules; and that ethics is imprecise, admits of more than one explanation. We need not jump immediately to 'salience' in the light of 'uncodifiability', as McDowell does. Aristotle has, as I will argue, more concrete and detailed reasons for believing that ethical claims are imprecise.

In "Deliberation and Moral Development in Aristotle's Ethics," McDowell works out a new version of his approach to Aristotle's views. We may say that what we perceive or grasp is a universal, he says, so long as we do not say that the perception can be detached from a well-developed psychological or motivational state or that the universal we perceive can be perceived in an act of pure intellect (1996, 23). What the practically wise person grasps or cognizes is doing well, McDowell says.[8] However, there is no blueprint for doing well that can simply be applied, deductively, to cases, first, because there is no blueprint and, second, because what's required for application is not deduction, but discernment of particulars (1996, 21–23).

Between the blueprint picture and the idea of a universal that is not detachable from a certain psychological state, however, there is a lot of middle ground. If a blueprint is a universal whose application to particulars is simple—McDowell describes the application as "straightforward" and "mechanical" (1996, 21)—then McDowell seems on the right track. Aristotle states that we must see what is appropriate to the situation rather than simply applying an art or rule (*NE* 2.2 1104a7–10). This suggests that the application is not simple. The fact that the application is not simple, however, does not imply that what is applied cannot be detached from a certain psychological state.

Instead, it could be a universal whose application in specific cases is complex. It could be, as I have already suggested, that one can grasp the universal without knowing how the universal shows up in particular cases, that one can know the universal without knowing what its instances or applications are like. This could be the case if the universal involved were such that its applications were quite different, one from another, and different in ways that are not predictable or deducible but in ways that can only be known through perception or experience. This is Aristotle's view as I understand it and this interpretation of it fits with his remark in 1.6 of the *Nicomachean Ethics* that knowledge of the good would not contribute much to ones discussions of the particular, human good and, as well, that knowledge of the particular, human good is possible even without the more precise knowledge of the universal good. To live well in general is to live a life that is good overall. To grasp what that would be is to grasp one's good overall. Good is a concept that one can know in its universal aspect without knowing much at all about it in its particular instances or applications. Moreover, it is a concept that one can know, through experience or perception, in its particular instances or applications without knowing anything explicit about it in its universal aspect.

Moreover, on this interpretation it could also be the case that deduction *is* a component of the practically wise person's cognition regarding decisions but that what is more unique to the practically wise person's cognition and what is more complex is not deduction but knowledge of the particular premise of the deduction. One reason for the uniqueness and the complexity is that, as I have already stated, according to Aristotle, good is an imprecise analogical equivocal.

Similarly, Nussbaum's view that the "standard of excellence" is not a universal but is the person of practical wisdom is too extreme. Between the view that the practically wise person consults a simple universal and the view that, instead, we consult the person of practical wisdom there is a lot of ground. Perhaps, instead, we consult a universal—a universal that guides our thought—but still must be sensitive in our discernment of its application to particulars. Moreover, perhaps we consult persons of practical wisdom, according to Aristotle, not because they are, simply, the standard. Instead, we consult them because they are the ones who, because they are sensitive in the discernment of the value of particulars, perceive how the standard shows up in diverse particular circumstances. As a result, they are a standard for us in cases in which we ourselves do not perceive how the standard shows up. This is Aristotle's view as I understand it. According to him, what we must perceive in the particulars in each case is their value, that is, we must perceive the particulars as good or as beautiful. Moreover, value is a universal that we can know in its universal aspect without knowing much at all about it in its particular instances. Good is an imprecise analogical equivocal. Knowledge of its applicability to particulars is complex and requires sensitivity. I shall argue for this view in the chapters that follow.

CHAPTER TWO

Ethics and Moral Theory

Another discussion which this essay joins is the discussion of Aristotle's ethics as an ethical theory that is not a moral theory. One main reason for recent interest in Aristotle's ethics is that it is seen to provide an alternative to moral theories. Bernard Williams, for example, takes this position in *Ethics and the Limits of Philosophy* (1985).[1]

Someone might object, however, and claim that the interpretation presented in this essay does not join the discussion of Aristotle's ethics as an alternative to moral theories but diverges from it. After all, according to this interpretation, the cognitive component of ethical virtue and of emotion for Aristotle is awareness of value and value is understood metaphysically. Isn't one of the hallmarks of moral theory that the moral is connected to the metaphysical?

With Kant's understanding of the metaphysical in mind we must, of course, say 'yes'. However, 'metaphysical' has different meanings in different periods. Much of the antimetaphysical sentiment of our time is better directed toward modern understandings of what it is to be metaphysical, such as Kant's—according to which the metaphysical realm is entirely unconnected to the world of experience—than toward ancient ones such as Aristotle's.

According to Kant, entities such as space and time, freedom and immortality cannot be experienced or known but must be posited to account for the existence and nature of things we do experience and know. Such Kantian arguments, called 'transcendental', move from what can be experienced and known to what cannot be experienced or known but can only be thought. For example, space and time are not features of nature as we experience it but are conditions of the possibility of nature as we experience it. For another example, freedom is not a feature of human action as we experience it—for our experience of human action is of action that is determined by natural laws—but is a condition for the possibility of human action.

For Aristotle, by contrast, understanding begins with perception, imagination, and experience; metaphysical properties and entities—potentiality, actuality, substance, and so forth—are simply the most general features of the beings we perceive, imagine, and experience; our cognition of such properties and entities is cognition of general features implicit in our particular perceptions, imaginings, and experiences and such cognition is knowledge in the strongest sense.[2]

For Aristotle, in other words, metaphysical knowledge *(nous)* is elucidation or articulation of our knowledge of the sensible world since metaphysical knowledge is knowledge of the most general features of that world, while for Kant nature can be known while metaphysical entities cannot be known but can only be thought. For Aristotle, metaphysical properties and entities are the most general features of the world known through perception and experience. For Kant, the perceptible world (appearances) and the intelligible world (things in themselves) are different worlds.

As a result of this general duality, human being is double for Kant as well. Each of us is a natural being *(homo phaenomenon)*, with a physical body, sensations, and inclinations. As such, we are, like the rest of the natural world, determined in our behavior by natural laws. As natural beings we are passive to sense. We are, in addition according to Kant, a moral being with inner freedom *(homo noumenon)*, possessing a faculty of reason capable of spontaneous production of ideas, rather than passive reception of sense, and a will that is free because constrained only by laws grounded in and produced by reason. As phenomenal beings, we are free because constrained only by laws we give ourselves.

According to Kant, the only thing that is good without qualification is the good will (*GMM* 1). To be good, we must will the moral law and treat humanity as an end never merely as a means to ends. Due to our phenomenal nature, however, we are naturally inclined to violate the moral law: "Impulses of nature, accordingly, involve *obstacles* within man's mind to his fulfillment of duty and (sometimes powerful) forces opposing it, which he must judge that he is capable of resisting and conquering by reason . . ." (*MM* 6:380). Virtue is force against those inclinations: "Now the capacity and considered resolve to withstand a strong but unjust opponent is *fortitude (fortitudo)* and, with respect to what opposes the moral disposition *within us*, **virtue** *(virtus, fortitudo moralis)*" (*MM* 6:380). The doctrine of virtue, or ethics, is a doctrine of ends that are duties, namely, to promote one's own perfection and the happiness of others. An end that is a duty does not arise from natural inclination but is "a moral end set up against the ends of inclination, an end that must therefore be given *a priori*, independently of inclinations" (*MM* 6:381). The reason why we must will the moral law and promote ends that are duties is that human beings are beings of a certain unique sort, namely, beings of absolute value (*GMM* 65). They are beings of absolute value because they are free, moral beings, beings whose action is free from contingent influence (*GMM* 61, 64, 65, 77–79).

Kant's understanding of the moral, then, includes the idea of a moral faculty, the will; of force against our inclinations (emotions, desires); and of human beings as beings with a unique, metaphysical quality, freedom, which quality cannot be experienced or known but must be posited and to which we must be responsive if we are to be moral, to have virtue, and to do what is right.

Aristotle's ethics is not, in this sense, a moral theory.[3] He does not make three fundamental claims found in Kant's and in other moral theories: the claim that we possess a special moral faculty beyond or in addition to our faculties for cognition and affect, for example, a will (as in Kant), a conscience or a moral sense, and that our decisions about how to act require the exercise of this faculty; the claim that ethical virtue and appropriate action require not simply that we develop or educate our passions but that we constrain, suppress, or use force against them; and the claim that there exist special moral objects (e.g., freedom in Kant) beyond those objects that we can experience or know, objects to which our special moral faculty must be responsive if we are to have ethical virtue and to act appropriately. Aristotle's ethics can be distinguished from a moral theory on all three counts, as I shall now show.

1

According to Aristotle, ethical virtue requires the harmonious development of faculties of only two types—cognitive faculties and affective ones. It does not require the development of some special moral faculty beyond reason or against emotion—no will toward God, or blind obedience to God, no free will or good will or will of any kind, no moral sense, no conscience.[4]

To prove that Aristotle does not introduce a specifically moral faculty is difficult. We can begin by showing that Aristotle does not introduce such a faculty in the two places where he would be most likely to do so if he were going to—in his discussions of choice *(prohairesis)* and of incontinence *(akrasia)*.

As is well-known, Aristotle defines ethical virtue as the developed capacity for good choice (*NE* 2.6 1106b36–a2).[5] Could choice for Aristotle be a special moral capacity? That is, could choice be some capacity we have beyond or in addition to our faculties for cognition and affect? Aristotle does, after all, carefully distinguish choice from desire. "Those who say it [choice] is desire . . . ," he says, "seem not to speak correctly" (*NE* 3.2 1111b10–12). In addition, choice is, according to him, a capacity the possession of which distinguishes human beings from nonhuman animals: "the other animals share in the voluntary, but not in choice" (*NE* 3.2 1111b9).

In the twentieth century, we have become more than used to claims that the distinguishing characteristic of human beings is our capacity for free agency. Rousseau, in the *Second Discourse*, maintains that free agency is the distinguishing feature of human beings: "Nature alone does everything in the operations of the Beast, whereas man contributes to his operations in his capacity as a free agent. The one chooses or rejects by instinct, the other by an act of freedom . . ." (*DI* 1.15, 148). Kant follows him in this view by supposing, as we have seen, that human beings are divided into an empirically conditioned phenomenal self and a noumenal self—the moral self—which is radically free. We have become accustomed to such claims and practiced in such distinctions since they provide the ground for the division between disciplines—between the natural and human sciences in the nineteenth century or between the sciences and the humanities in our own.[6]

Could choice for Aristotle, then, be a special moral capacity—one that is distinct from desire and intellect and that distinguishes us from nonhuman animals? The answer, of course, is 'no'. Though choice is not simply desire for Aristotle, it is not, for him, some third capacity in addition to intellect and desire. Instead, choice is a capacity that combines a certain sort of intellect with desire. Aristotle defines choice as 'deliberate desire' *(bouleutikē orexis)* (*NE* 3.3 1113a11). He understands deliberation as a specific kind of intellectual activity, namely, the activity of discerning which activities, of those that are in our power, are conducive to our aims. "But we deliberate about things which come about due to us," he says (*NE* 3.3 1112b2–4). Moreover, he goes on, "We deliberate not about ends but about what conduces to ends" (*NE* 3.3 1112b11–12).[7] Choice, for him, is desire that has been shaped and informed by deliberation. It is not a special moral faculty, but instead results from the harmonious development of an intellectual faculty (deliberation) and an affective one (desire).

Theorists who do suppose the existence of special moral faculties often do so in order to explain motivational conflict. We act against our knowledge or desire when we lack the special moral faculty, such theorists maintain. Paul, who, in *Romans*, is one of the first to discuss and centrally utilize a special moral faculty, gives us a paradigm of such conflict: "For I do not do what I want," he says there, "but I do the very thing I hate" (*Rom.* 7.15). He identifies want with what is in the mind and what is hated with what is in the flesh. What is needed to overcome the conflict is the exercise of a specifically moral faculty, which Paul calls 'spirit' or *'pneuma'*. 'Spirit' for him is beyond knowledge and emotion.

Arguably, the Hebrew *Bible* contains similar views, though without consistent mention of a specific faculty. For example, in *Genesis*, obedience to God precedes knowledge of good and bad and is counter to desire: God commands Adam not to eat of the tree of knowledge of good and bad; nonetheless, when Eve sees that the tree is desirable, she and then Adam eat of it; God reproves and punishes them for doing so. Though no faculty of obedience is mentioned in the passage, obedience to God's command is what is called for. Moreover, the passage indicates that obedience does not require knowledge and can counteract conflicting desire. Could it be that Aristotle, too, introduces a special moral faculty in order to explain incontinence?

That some are inclined to think the answer is 'yes' is indicated by the fact that 'weakness of will' or 'moral weakness' are common translations of *'akrasia'*. Their inclination is misguided, however. The term *'akrasia'* simply means 'lack of control' or 'lack of command'. Plato applies the idea of control to character: 'self-control' *(enkratē heautou)*. Anthony A. Long argues that by Aristotle's time, the reference to self is well enough established that Aristotle can elide the reflexive pronoun and assume the term will be heard to imply reference to self: 'lack of self-control'; 'lack of self-command' (1993, 143).[8] In addition to the terminological considerations, and more important for our purposes, in his resolutions of the puzzling phenomenon of incontinence, Aristotle alludes to no faculties beyond our various faculties for cognition and affect.

The puzzling phenomenon that requires account is that of people who seem to act against their knowledge of what is appropriate or good for themselves. Socrates maintains that the phenomenon is illusory. There is no such thing as incontinence, he says. Everyone desires what they believe or know to be good. "Doesn't it seem to you, best one," Socrates asks Meno in the *Meno*, "that all people desire good things?"

After Meno disagrees, Socrates strengthens his question: "Does it seem to you, Meno, that anyone, cognizing that bad things are bad, nevetheless desires them?" (*Meno* 77c1–2; c5–7). Anyone who appears to be acting against their knowledge of what is good, is not really doing so. Instead, they lack the requisite knowledge. Virtue, on Socrates' account, simply is knowledge.

Aristotle rejects Socrates' view that virtue simply is knowledge and substitutes for it the view that virtue requires knowledge but also requires suitable emotional development. In addition, he rejects Socrates' claim that there is no such thing as incontinence:

> Some say it is impossible that someone who possesses knowledge should be incontinent. For it would be strange, so Socrates thought, that when knowledge is present in someone, something else should master it and drag it around like a slave. Socrates was wholly opposed to that view on the ground that incontinence does not exist. For no one, when understanding, acts against what they understand to be best, but they act this way due to ignorance. Now this argument clearly contradicts what is apparent. (*NE* 7.2 1145b21–27)

Though Aristotle rejects Socrates' views, he stays well within the Socratic framework in his own resolution of the puzzle of incontinence. According to Aristotle, the incontinent person does not act against knowledge—at least, not against knowledge that is relevant to the motivation of action. Instead, when someone acts incontinently, one of three situations obtains.[9] It may be that they have knowledge but are not exercising the knowledge they have: "It makes a difference whether the one who does what he should not has knowledge but does not exercise it or does exercise it. The latter seems strange, but it does not seem strange if he is not exercising knowledge" (*NE* 7.3 1146b33–35). It may be that they both have and exercise universal knowledge, but not knowledge of relevant particulars: "they may be using the universal and not the particular premise, for actions are particulars" (*NE* 7.3 1147a2–3). Or they may, when experiencing the passions of spiritedness or of sexual desire, have but in another sense not have the relevant knowledge, like "someone asleep, mad, or drunk" (*NE* 7.3 1147a13–14).

According to Aristotle, then, the incontinent person never acts against active knowledge of particulars, but either acts against knowledge that is possessed but not exercised, knowledge that is not fully possessed, or against knowledge of universals that is not accompanied by knowledge of particulars. In no case does the incontinent person act against knowledge that is active and particular (*NE* 7.3).

Another way to show that Aristotle does not introduce a specifically moral faculty is to ask what the cause of human action is according to him. If Aristotle thinks that action results directly from the exercise of our cognitive and emotional faculties, he has no reason to introduce a moral faculty in addition to our cognitive and affective ones. Aristotle's discussion of incontinence, just recounted, suggests that the cause of action according to him is, we could say, 'knowledge focused on particulars'.

In fact, in the fourth, and most general, resolution of the problem of incontinence, Aristotle indicates that this is his view. Motivational conflict is not conflict between one universal premise and another, he says. For example, in instances of incontinence, it is not the case that one universal premise is overpowered by another. For, emotion does not result from universal premises ('knowledge in the strict sense'). Instead, emotion results from particular premises ('perceptual knowledge').[10] We may, instead, have conflict between universal knowledge on the one hand and particular knowledge on the other. For universal knowledge can be dragged about by the particular knowledge since it is particular knowledge that results in emotion.[11]

In the example Aristotle discusses, he begins with the particular premise, 'This is sweet.' Emotion—specifically, desires—results from the focusing of a universal premise ('Everything sweet needs to be tasted.') on a particular ('this'): if 'everything sweet needs to be tasted' and 'this is sweet.' The result is desire *(epithymia)*, which then leads us to taste the particular sweet thing before us. The conflicting universal premise is not stated but is described as one present in us that would restrain us from tasting. Presumably, he means it would do so if it were focused on a particular. We can suppose the universal premise to be some premise such as, 'Dairy products need to be avoided because they make me ill and uncomfortable' or 'Sweets need to be avoided because they make me fat and tired.' If I am not focusing some such universal knowledge on the particulars before me (for whatever reason), desire does not result and, consequently, does not cause me to act. When desire is present, it "leads us to the object, for desires can move each of the bodily parts" (*NE* 7.3 1147a34–35). Presumably, what is at issue in the conflicting universal premise is not desire but aversion. If I do not focus the premise, 'Dairy products need to be avoided because they make me ill and uncomfortable' on the particular ('this'), then aversion does not result and does not cause me to refrain from acting. As a result, the desire wins out. The causal progression is: universal knowledge; particular knowledge (i.e., we could say, universal knowledge focused on a particular or, as Aristotle sometimes says, perceptual knowledge); desire; and action. For Aristotle, then, we need posit no faculties of soul in addition to cognitive and affective ones in order to account for movement.

Aristotle's *De Anima* account of the causes of human action gives a similar answer but introduces some refinements useful to our inquiry (*De An.* 3.9–11).[12] The simple account is that thought *(nous)* and desire *(orexis)* are the causes of animal movement including human action (*De An.* 3.10 433a9–10, 433a17–18).[13] By thought in this context Aristotle means to include, on the one hand, practical thought *(nous praktikē)* and, on the other, imagination *(phantasia)* (*De An.* 3.10 433a9–12, 433a17–18). By practical thought Aristotle means thought that calculates for the sake of something and thought that is practical (*De An.* 3.10 433a14).[14] He may also mean to include perception (according to *De Motu* 6.700b19–22). By thought that calculates for the sake of something Aristotle presumably means discernment of ends and discernment of the means to or constitutents of ends. By thought that is practical Aristotle presumably means thought that discerns what is to be done (in the face of conflicting or various ends). By perception Aristotle would mean perception of particulars as instances of ends (*De Motu* 6.700b19–22). Practical thought and desire are the causes of human action, according to Aristotle, because "the object of desire is the beginning of practical thought and the last [object of thought] is the beginning of action" (*De An.* 3.10 433a15–17). In addition, whenever it is imagination that produces movement, imagination does not do so without desire (*De An.* 3.10 20–21).

Aristotle complicates the simple, two-cause, account somewhat by saying more strictly that there is one cause of movement, namely, the faculty of desire. He gives three reasons for the conclusion. First, the object of desire causes movement and, due to the object of desire, thought causes movement. This gives causal priority to the faculty of desire over the faculty of thought. Second, if there were two causes of movement, thought and desire, they would have to cause movement by virtue of some one form. Third, intellect does not produce movement without desire since even calculation is accompanied by a type of desire, called 'wish', while a different type of desire, appetite, causes movement even contrary to calculation.

The meaning of the first point is clear. When thought causes movement it does so because desire has taken some object as desirable. Hence, desire precedes thought causally. The meaning of the third point is clear, as well. Intellect never causes movement without desire of some kind, since even calculation, which is the type of reasoning that refers to ends and not to the starting points of action, is accompanied by a type of desire, specifically, by wish, where wish, as we know from the *Nicomachean Ethics*, is wish for ends. (We ought to keep in mind that this claim that desire opposes calculation does not imply that desire opposes all intellect. For, desire results from perceptual imagination and imagination is a type of intellect according to Aristotle in this chapter.)[15]

Aristotle's second point requires more interpretation. What is the 'some one form' by virtue of which a certain thought and a certain desire cause movement? If we can find it, we will have found that which unites thought and desire so that we may appropriately say that there is one cause, not two causes, of animal movement. It is the good or apparent good. Aristotle mentions the good or apparent good in a remark, just following, regarding the fallibility of desire and imagination. "Thus it is always the object of desire that produces movement," Aristotle says, "but this is either the good or the apparent good. And not every one of these, but the practical good" (*De An.* 3.10 27–30).[16] So, when something appears to us to be a practical good, whether it in fact is good or only appears to be good, we move.

Presumably Aristotle's point is more than this, however. For there is no particular reason for him simply to assume that there is one rather than two causes of animal movement. Instead, we might rather hope that he has noticed in the phenomenon of the causality of animal movement that desire and thought do not act independently, but as a unit. If he has, he could explain what he has noticed by maintaining that, in actual desire, thought and desire are not separate. Nicely, Aristotle does make a claim of this sort in *De Anima*. In actual desire the faculty of desire and the faculty of perception are the same—in fact, perceiving the object as good, taking pleasure in it, and desiring it all are activities of the same faculty, the faculty of perception: "To be pleased or pained is to activate the perceptual mean toward what is good or bad as such. And avoidance and desire, when at work, are this. And the faculty of desire and of avoidance are not different, either from one another or from the faculty of perception; but their being is different" (*De An.* 3.7 431a10–14). He also says there that sometimes in desire, appearances take the place of percepts: "To the thinking soul appearances are like perceptions; and when it asserts or denies [that they are] good or bad it flees or pursues [them]" (*De An.* 3.7 431a14–16).[17] As a result there is a similar causal unity in cases in which we receive an appearance of, rather than perceiving, an object to be good.[18] Presumably, then, Aristotle's second point is that in actual desire, thought and desire are the same.[19]

With this in mind, Aristotle complicates his account of animal movement including human action a second and final time. The causes of movement are one in form but more than one in number. This final interpretation includes and combines the first interpretation, that the causes are two (thought and desire), and the second, that the cause is one (the faculty of desire or, better, the practical good). In form, the cause is the practical good. In number, however, the cause is double, the practical good and the faculty of desire (the former unmoved and the latter moved). He can make both of these claims since in actual desire the faculty of desire and the practical good are not different but are the same. For, according to Aristotle, the soul is somehow all the beings (*De An.* 3.8 431b20–21). More specifically, in actual perception, perception and the objects of perception are the same—namely, the same in form (*De An.* 3.8 431b20–432a1) and, as we know (*De An.* 3.7), desire is an activity of perception.

If we put together this conclusion—that, in actual desire, desire and the practical good are the same—with the conclusion we just reached, that in actual desire, thought and desire are the same, we can conclude that the causes of animal motion, including human action, are one in form. In actual desire, desire and thought are one and, in addition, desire and its object, the practical good, are one—one in form, in both cases, though more than one in number.

Thought, as cause of motion, can be practical thought or imagination. Practical thought, as we have seen, includes calculation for the sake of something (discernment of ends and discernment of the means to or constituents of ends) and practical thought in the narrow sense (discernment of what is to be done) and probably also perception (common perception of particulars as ends). Imagination has three types, perceptual imagination *(phantasia aisthētikē)*, calculative imagination *(phantasia logistikē)*, and deliberative imagination *(phantasia bouleutikē)*, which parallel the three relevant types of practical thought. All animals have perceptual imagination, Aristotle says. Only human beings have calculative and deliberative imagination. Presumably Aristotle mentions imagination as a cause of animal movement at this point because, according to him, there is no desire—and hence no action—without imagination (*De An.* 3.10 433b28–29).

We can reasonably conclude that, for Aristotle, imagination is not propositional. For it can take the place of perception in producing pleasure and desire according to him and the common perception of something as good is like, and therefore not identical to, assertion and denial: it is like it, in that imagining something as good has a double structure like the double structure of assertion and denial (1. imagining something 2. as good; 1. asserting something 2. is good); it is different than it since imagining something as good is not propositional (to imagine something as good is not to assert that it is good) (*De An.* 3.7 431a14–15, 8–11 with 3.6 430b26–30).

As previously mentioned, practical thought supplements calculation since calculation discerns ends or goods and the means to and constituents of those ends or goods, while ends can conflict and are various. How does practical thought supplement calculation? By comparing different ends and their value, and by synthesizing different ends into combined ends and comparing the combined ends and their value. Aristotle understands deliberative imagination in a similar way. According to him, to determine what is to be done one must compare the value of different valuable particulars and combine the images of different valuable particulars into one unified image of them all:

> Perceptual imagination, as we have said, is found in all animals while deliberative imagination only in those that are calculative. For whether one shall do this or that is at once a task requiring calculation. And one must measure by one [measure], for one pursues what is greater. This implies that one is able to make one image out of many. (*De An.* 3.11 434a5–10)

To paraphrase: though calculation and calculative imagination are required, they are not all that is required for one's decisions about what one will do. Calculation is not the whole of practical thought nor is calculative imagination the whole of the imagination relevant to action. For we pursue what is greater (i.e., better or more desirable) and so must have one measure. But this—to have one measure of the various valuable particulars—requires that one have the ability to combine many images of valuable particulars into one, unified image of them. That is, one must have the faculty called 'deliberative imagination'.

Moreover, once we have this unified image of various valuable particulars, it will be the source of our motivation, the source of our action. We are moved, according to Aristotle, by the last object of practical thought. Depending, however, on the larger whole of which an object of thought is an imagined part, we may in one case be moved to pursue a certain object and in another case moved to avoid it. This is so even if the thing in question is something good, even if it is a practical, achievable good. Since goods conflict and are various, a practical good may, when imagined as part of one larger whole, cause us to experience desire and engage in pursuit while, when imagined as part of another whole, cause us to experience aversion and engage in avoidance. The larger, unified image of which our image of a particular, practical good is a part is, then, the source of our motivation, the source of our action.

This conclusion supports my general interpretation of cognition of value in Aristotle's ethics since I have asserted and will argue in what follows that, according to Aristotle, when one has ethical virtue one is motivated not simply by whatever good is at hand but by a realizable picture of an overall developed and flourishing life and by the image or perception of particular goods as being a part of that larger picture. All of us are motivated by thought of and desire for 'some one form', namely, the practical good (or, the apparent practical good).

In his accounts of human action, then, Aristotle gives us detailed accounts of the capacities required for human action. The accounts include a variety of cognitive and affective capacities characterized in a variety of ways but do not include any capacities other than cognitive and affective ones. Importantly for our argument, they do not include any capacities we might call 'moral' capacities—that is to say, no capacities beyond our ordinary cognitive and affective ones. Instead, human action is caused by our desire for particular practical goods which desire includes, as a unified constituent, thought of those particulars as practical goods. The types of desire include wish and appetite. The types of thought involved include practical thought (including perception, calculation, and practical thought in the narrow sense) and practical imagination (including perceptual, calculative, and deliberative imagination). In the best cases, human action is caused by deliberative imagination and not just by perception and perceptual imagination or calculation and calculative imagination. By means of perception and perceptual imagination, we discern valuable particulars. By means of calculation and calculative imagination, we discern in addition the means to and constituents of valuable particulars. By means of deliberative imagination, we combine our images of competing and various valuable particulars into one, unified, whole image. When a particular is seen as valuable for us as a constituent of this larger whole, then it is the cause of our action, the source of our motivation.

2

Though Aristotle does not believe that human beings have a special moral capacity, there would still be ground for calling him a 'moral theorist' if he maintained that our acquisition of ethical virtue requires not simply that we develop or cultivate our emotions, but that we constrain them, channel them, or use force against them. Does Aristotle hold such a view? After all, according to him, one main difference between human beings and the other animals is that human beings possess *logos* and, in their actions, obey it, while nonhuman animals neither possess nor can perceive *logos*, and so, in their actions, simply obey their passions (*Pol.* 1.5 1254b22–24, 7.12 1332b5). He even goes so far as to state that human beings can act against their nature and their habits and obey *logos* if they are persuaded that to do so is better (*Pol.* 7.12 1332b6–8).

The answer, of course, is that Aristotle does not hold the view that virtue requires forcing ourselves to act against our emotions. Instead, he believes that emotions can be developed or cultivated so that we can act on them rather than against them. To see that this is his answer, however, one must see clearly what these two alternatives are.

One alternative is that emotions are brute feelings, impulses, or urges that we will have no matter what we believe, no matter how we perceive the world, and no matter what experiences of the world we have had. On this alternative, emotional development does not centrally feature some kind of general cognitive development but requires, instead, what might best be called 'emotional management'. For example, the brute impulse could be held down or dammed up. Or, it could be allowed to flow but channeled away from one object and toward another.

The second alternative is that emotions are not brute feelings, impulses, or urges but are, instead, in part constituted and in part directly caused by our beliefs, perceptions, or experiences. On this alternative, emotions are cognitive or intentional and need not simply be managed but can be developed or cultivated. Since emotions are in part cognitively or intentionally constituted, emotional development centrally features cognitive development. In fact, we may say that emotional development on this account in part is cognitive development of some kind—that emotional growth involves growth in awareness or sensitivity—though the process of development may not itself be a strictly intellectual one.

Aristotle takes the second alternative. Ethical development at its best according to him is not control of our emotions, suppression of our emotions, or force against our emotions. Good action that results from forcing ourselves to act in accord with our reason and against our emotions is not virtuous according to him but merely continent. The distinction between virtue and continence is crucial to Aristotle's ethical theory. Both virtue and continence are good since neither the virtuous person nor the continent person as a result of emotion acts against reason. The continent person, however, has opposing emotions while the virtuous person does not, and has desires and pleasures that oppose reason but does not allow himself to be led by them. The virtuous person, to the contrary, lacks opposing desires and pleasures and instead desires and takes pleasure in good activities themselves. We shall come back to this alternative later.

Kant, Hobbes, and Freud take the first alternative, the emotional management alternative, according to which emotions are brute impulses that must be held down or dammed up or allowed to flow but channeled away from some and toward other objects. To speak less metaphorically, emotional management includes, for example, preventing activation of an emotion or directing activation away from some and toward other real objects. I say 'real object' to point out that what is involved in emotional management does not involve changing how we feel by changing our general understanding, that is, changing the nature of an emotion by changing its intentional object. Instead, the nature of the emotion remains the same and the emotion is felt in relation to a different actual object.

Kant is an example of a philosopher who recommends the first kind of emotional management, that we prevent, or lessen, activation of certain emotions. That he recommends emotional management is not surprising since according to him emotions are brute rather than cognitive: "feeling is not a faculty whereby we represent things, but lies outside our whole faculty of knowledge . . ." (*CPR* A 801a). For Kant, virtue is a kind of fortitude or constraint. Human beings are naturally inclined to violate the moral law and to take pleasure in doing so. Virtue is the capacity to resist or conquer these natural inclinations.

The claim that Kant diverges from Aristotle in this way may seem at odds with the views of contemporary interpreters who have usefully pointed out that though Kant grounds morality in reason, not in emotion, nonetheless development or training of our emotions is a moral duty according to him and that, in this respect, Kant's views are closer to Aristotle's than often suggested by recent interpreters. For example, in *Making a Necessity of Virtue*, Nancy Sherman mentions the

> growing acknowledgment that in later works, such as *The Doctrine of Virtue*, Kant recognizes the duty to develop emotions as a part of our duties of virtue. We have a duty to habituate empirical character and, in some sense, a duty to diminish the merely accidental natures of our nature. Our agency extends deeply to the cultivation of our passional selves. (1997, 125)

What is at issue in this section of this essay, however, is not whether both Kant and Aristotle importantly feature development or training of emotions in their moral or ethical theories. Instead, what is at issue here is what that development or training is like. Put differently, the question is whether the modification of emotions called for might best be called 'cultivation', 'development', or 'shaping' on the one hand or, alternately, might best be called 'management', 'suppression', or 'control'. In my view, **Aristotle opts for the first and Kant for the** second option.

Kant's general remarks bear this out. As mentioned in the introduction to this chapter, according to Kant we are, due to our phenomenal nature, naturally inclined to violate the moral law: "Impulses of nature, accordingly, involve obstacles within man's mind to his fulfillment of duty and (sometimes powerful) forces opposing it, which he must judge that he is capable of resisting and conquering by reason . . ." (MM 6:380). Virtue, according to him, is force against those inclinations: "Now the capacity and considered resolve to withstand a strong but unjust opponent is fortitude *(fortitudo)* and, with respect to what opposes the moral disposition within us, virtue *(virtus, fortitudo moralis)*" (MM 6:380).

These general remarks by themselves do not establish my claim, however, since they can be misleading, as Kant himself points out. It is not the case according to Kant that our best relation to inclination always is resistance to it or fortitude against it. Instead, cases of resistance or fortitude make the nature of virtue most perspicuous. Virtue is a type of strength according to Kant and "Strength of any kind can be recognized only by the obstacles it can overcome, and in the case of virtue these obstacles are natural inclinations, which can come into conflict with the human being's moral resolution . . ." (DV 394). Inclinations do not always conflict with moral resolution or principle, however, but sometimes coincide with it. Hence, sometimes we must resist inclination and other times allow it. Emotional health will involve tendencies of both kinds.

In his discussion of sympathy for the feelings of others, Kant mentions both of these tendencies. Sympathetic joy and sadness are sensible feelings of pleasure or displeasure at another's feelings of joy or pain. We are naturally receptive to such sympathetic feelings. Receptivity to them is natural and unfree. Willing them is not natural and is free. We have a duty, called the 'duty of humanity', to will such feelings in cases in which they will help us promote the welfare of another person. When I cannot help the other person, I ought not feel sympathetically even though the other person is suffering and I am naturally receptive to sympathetic feelings for their suffering (DV 456–457).

Between receptivity to feeling and actual feeling lies will. By exercising it, I can prevent or allow feeling to be experienced. In the case of sympathetic feeling, I am receptive to the feeling by nature. Through will, I determine whether I will experience the feeling or not. I have a duty to experience the feeling in cases in which I can promote the welfare of the other person supposing that the feeling will aid me in promoting her or his welfare. I ought not experience the feeling in cases in which promotion of the welfare of the other is not possible.

In the case of the sensible feeling of sympathy for others' joy and suffering, then, one whose emotion is appropriately trained will allow activation of the emotion in some cases and prevent it in others. In each case, it is will that is responsible for appropriate response, allowing it in some cases and preventing it in others. Will is necessary because our natural responsiveness does not by itself result in instances of appropriate response.

Kant's discussion of sensible affect and passion in general is instructive as well. In the case of sensible affect and passion in general, what is required according to Kant is apathy (moral apathy). For, sensible affect (e.g., anger) precedes reflection and sensible passion (e.g., hatred), is a desire that, because we have given ourself up to it, has become a lasting inclination (*DV* 408). One precedes reflection and the other is entrenched; neither is responsive to principle (*DV* 407–408). Moral apathy is a specific type of absence of affect that results when feelings arising from sensible affect "lose their influence on moral feeling" or respect for law because respect for law is "more powerful than all such feelings" (*DV* 408).

The emotionally healthy person will, then, hold down sensible affect and passion. That is, to speak less metaphorically, the emotionally healthy person will prevent or lessen their activation. Sensible affect and passion are brute. We do not prevent or lessen their activation by understanding their objects in a different way. Instead, their force is weakened by a more powerful force (respect for law). One power (respect for law) overpowers another (sensible affect or feeling). It is necessary to overpower sensible affect and passion because they are types of brute natural responsiveness and do not by themselves necessarily result in instances of appropriate response.

The kind of emotional modification called for by Kant, then, is a type of management, suppression, or control. Virtue according to Kant is not a type of developed natural responsiveness. Instead, natural emotional responsiveness is brute and virtue is the fortitude, strength, or will to withstand it. In addition, though virtue or strength is most manifest when exercised to withstand natural emotional response, it can be exercised as well to allow such response. For example, we exercise will both when we allow ourselves to feel sympathetic joy or sadness and also when we prevent ourselves from feeling it. Moreover, we prevent ourselves from feeling an emotion not by cultivating the emotion to make it more responsive or reflective. Instead, according to Kant, we prevent ourselves from feeling emotions that are fundamentally intellectually nonresponsive, or minimize the extent to which we feel them, by utilizing a stronger power to overpower them. For example, anger and hate are nonreflective according to Kant—anger because it is hasty, hate because it is entrenched. The power of each is minimized when it is overpowered by the stronger power present in respect for law.

Hobbes is another philosopher who opts to understand emotional maturity not as emotional development or cultivation but, instead, as emotional management or control (in his case, primarily social control). Specifically, Hobbes recommends a type of emotional management that fits into our second type, namely, that emotion be allowed to flow but channeled away from one object and toward another. Or, to speak less metaphorically, what he recommends is not that we change or perfect a person's basic emotions but that we accept them as given and instead change the real situation persons are in so that basic emotions are felt toward one real object rather than another.

According to Hobbes, passions—desires and aversions—are brute.[20] We value things—take them to be good, evil, or contemptible—because we desire them or are averse to them, rather than desiring or being averse to things because we take them to be good, evil, or contemptible:[21] "But whatsoever is the object of any man's appetite or desire, that is it which he for his part calleth *good:* and the object of his hate and aversion, *evil;* and of his contempt, *vile* and *inconsiderable*" (*Lev.* 1.6, 48).[22] 'Good', 'evil', and 'contemptible', he goes on, are relative to the person using them, rather than signifying something about the things to which they are applied: "For these words of good, evil, and contemptible, are ever used with relation to the person that useth them: there being nothing simply and absolutely so . . ." (*Lev.* 1.6, 48–49). Desires and aversions, then, are not types of perception of good or evil that result in movement toward the things perceived to be good and away from those perceived to be bad. Instead, 'good' and 'evil' signify desires and aversions and desires and aversions simply are bodily movements toward and away—small bodily movements called 'endeavour' (small in comparison with walking, speaking, striking, etc.):

> These small beginnings of motion, within the body of man, before they appear in walking, speaking, striking, and other visible actions, are commonly called ENDEAVOUR. . . . This endeavour, when it is toward something which causes it, is called APPETITE or DESIRE. . . . And when the endeavour is fromward something, it is generally called AVERSION. These words, *appetite* and *aversion*, we have from the Latins; and they both of them signify the motions, one of approaching, the other of retiring. (*Lev.* 1.6, 47)

Not only are our natural passions brute according to Hobbes, they are also naturally constituted in a way that is detrimental to social cohesiveness. As a result, social life requires that emotions be managed or controlled, since, being brute, they cannot be developed or cultivated. Our basic natural passions are the fear of death and the desire for self-preservation.[23] Because in our natural state we perceive others to be equal to us in power and prudence, we are naturally distrustful ("diffident"):

> From this equality of ability, ariseth equality of hope in the attaining of our ends. And therefore if any two men desire the same thing, which nevertheless they cannot both enjoy, they become enemies; and in the way to their end, which is principally their own conservation, and sometimes their delectation only, endeavour to destroy, or subdue one another. (*Lev.* 1.13, 98–99)

As a result of our distrust, we are naturally warlike: "Hereby it is manifest, that during the time men live without a common power to keep them all in awe, they are in that condition which is called war; and such a war, as is of every man, against every man" (*Lev.* 1.13, 100). Nature, Hobbes says, "dissociate[s], and render[s] men apt to invade, and destroy one another . . ." (*Lev.* 1.13, 100). War, in his description, is the necessary result of our natural passions when left uncontrolled. He describes war as "that miserable condition of war, which is necessarily consequent . . . to the natural passions of men, when there is no visible power to keep them in awe, and tie them by fear of punishments to the performance of their covenants, and observation of . . . laws of nature . . ." (*Lev.* 2.1, 129).

As a result, the first function of society is to establish an all-powerful sovereign who will channel our natural passions. Rather than eliminating or softening our self-interested desire for self-preservation (through changing our views of what sort of thing really is fearful, for example, or of what sort of thing really is desirable), we accept desires of that sort as given and redirect them by constructing a commonwealth that will be understood to be the means to satisfying them. The reason why men, despite their natural love of liberty, introduce "that restraint upon themselves in which we see them live in commonwealths, is the foresight of their own preservation, and of a more contented life thereby . . ." (*Lev.* 2.17, 129). Rather than eliminating or softening our fear of death (perhaps, again, through changing our idea of what sort of thing is fearful or what sort of thing is noble), that is, rather than eliminating or softening the fear that leads us to be warlike toward others, the fear is redirected by instituting a sovereign who will be understood to be the center of all power, the object of all fear. It is that fear of death, now redirected, which makes us social. It is that fear, redirected, which makes us virtuous. For Hobbes, virtues do not result from the development or cultivation of our natural passions. Instead, virtues are contrary to our natural passions. Virtues result from redirected terror:

> For the laws of nature, as *justice, equity, modesty, mercy,* and, in sum, *doing to others, as we would be done to,* of themselves, without the terror of some power, to cause them to be observed, are contrary to our natural passions, that carry us to partiality, pride, revenge, and the like. And covenants, without the sword, are but words, and of no strength to secure a man at all. (*Lev.* 2.17, 129)

We become just, according to Hobbes, not because we come to see that people are not fearful but lovable, for example, or that they are intrinsically desirable components of our own flourishing life. Instead, we become just, according to him, because we know that if we do not, the sovereign will use his unlimited power to retaliate. It is in our interest to be just to avoid retaliation by the sovereign and we can count on the other person being just as well for the same reason (*Lev.* 1.15, 115). Virtue is not cultivation of emotion but redirection: once all significant power is in the hands of the sovereign, our brute, ineradicable fear of death is redirected away from every person and to the sovereign, since he is now the most fearful person there is.

Freud is another thinker who understands emotional development as a type of channeling and control with the father playing roughly the same role in relation to the son for Freud that the sovereign plays in relation to the citizen for Hobbes. For Freud, similarly to Hobbes, our actions are caused by desires or "drives" that are basically noncognitive. There are two fundamental types of drive, sexual drives (drives for sexual satisfaction) and ego drives (drives for self-preservation) with sexual drives the more basic or original of the two (1923b, 180–182).[24] Drives are internal stimuli that press for elimination or satisfaction, internal tensions, or excitations that press for release (1915, 84–87).[25] They are relatively independent of their object (1915, 90–91). For example, at first, sexual drives are directed to oneself (in the early autoeroticism or normal narcissism of the oral and anal stages). When they become too great, they are directed to another person (an 'object'): "whence does that necessity arise that urges our mental life to pass on beyond the limits of narcissism and to attach the libido to objects? The answer which would follow from our line of thought would once more be that we are so impelled when the cathexis of the ego with libido exceeds a certain degree" (1914, 66). We do not desire the other because we intrinsically value her. We value her because she can satisfy our drive. In this case and in the others, the characteristics of the object are relatively unimportant so long as the object can satisfy our drives: "[object] becomes attached to [drive] only in consequence of being peculiarly fitted to provide satisfaction" (1915, 87–88). The object can be oneself or another person; it can be a person of our own or the other gender; if the object of our drive is another person and that other person is not or ceases to be available, we can redirect the drive to someone else. "The object is less closely attached to the drive than was at first supposed; it is easily exchanged for another one, and moreover, an instinct which had an external object can be turned round upon the subject's own self" (1923b, 181).

In lived experiential terms, sexual desire for Freud is relatively impersonal. We begin by satisfying it on ourselves. When the intensity of the desire becomes so great that we can no longer satisfy it in this way, we find another person who can satisfy our desires. Our tie to that person is relatively loose and is determined by whether the person offers the satisfaction we seek. If he or she does not, we can shift the desire to someone else.

Emotional health for Freud is, in part, learning to manage these drives, that is, to direct them to objects that will provide us with satisfaction. At first, autoerotism is appropriate. Later, when our drives become intense enough that autoerotism can no longer satisfy them, it ceases to be a healthy focus, and drive toward an object becomes stage-appropriate. Emotional health is appropriate management of our drives. Emotional illness is blocked or fixated drive.

Managing drives to attain satisfaction is not all there is to emotional health for Freud, of course. The world is not, according to him, constructed so that imagined or needed satisfaction by means of an object is always ours for the taking—even when the desired object is present. Some objects, though desirable, are not available to us. In fact, the attempt to attain sensual satisfaction by means of present objects often conflicts with our drives for self-preservation (ego drives). A boy learns this at an early age, according to Freud. He desires his mother, but his father stands in the way. The boy becomes his father's rival. Then out of fear of him—fear of punishment, ultimately fear of castration—the boy suppresses his desire for his mother and comes to identify with his father (1923a, 33–32). All morality comes out of this oedipal stage recognition by the boy that his mother, though desirable, is off-limits: "In this way the Oedipus-complex proves itself, as has already been suggested on an historical basis, to be the origin of morality in each one of us" (1924, 198).[26] Morality, then, results from a primal act of management (or, more accurately, from a complex and continuing series of acts of management), an act of suppressing his desire for what he cannot have.

Two senses of the ethical can be discerned among Freud's concerns. On the one hand, he is concerned about morality in the sense just mentioned, namely, learning to restrict our desires for what does not belong to us. Like the citizen who becomes just out of fear of the all-powerful sovereign, the boy becomes moral according to Freud out of fear of his powerful father. The process is complex. He feels fear. He suppresses, or to speak technically, 'represses', his desire and checks the aggressiveness that aims to support it. He identifies with his father (i.e., wants to be like him), with the powerful one who has and protects what the boy desires and cannot have. He takes in the image of his father (specifically, he introjects it) as an ideal ('ego ideal') and as a developed mental faculty or 'structure', called the 'conscience' or 'superego' (1917, 168–169; 1923a, 35–37).

On the other hand, Freud has a eudaimonistic ethical conern. For Freud, drives provide the energy for all important human endeavor. If drives are blocked, our activity is restricted and stunted. When they are allowed to flow, they generate all important activity. We live a good life; we are active; we flourish (to borrow a term from Aristotle interpretation), when we allow drives to attain satisfaction.

This points to the necessity of what Freud calls 'sublimation'. A flourishing life requres drive satisfaction. The satisfaction of some drives, however, is prohibited. Some desires that as a result are blocked still can aid us in living a good life, however, if they are redirected from the desired object and toward another. If you cannot have the woman you want, your desire for her, since it is relatively independent of its object, can be redirected into cultural, political, or creative activity. The desire can be 'sublimated', in Freud's terminology. That is, it can be made sublime. In sublimation, the object is changed and the aim is changed as well, from sexual satisfaction to release of some other sort (1923b, 181).

Even affection for others, according to Freud, at its core is sexual drive—that is, desire for one's own satisfaction by means of an object. There is no fundamental social drive according to Freud, no "herd instinct." Social drive is sexual drive with a changed aim, not in the way aim is changed from sexual aim to some other kind of aim in sublimation—from sexual to artistic satisfaction, for example—but change from sexual satisfaction to a close approximation to sexual satisfaction. Love and friendship are, according to Freud, aim-inhibited sexual impulses or drives: "They have not abandoned their directly sexual aims, but they are held back by internal resistances from attaining them; they rest content with certain approximations to satisfaction and for that very reason lead to especially firm and permanent attachments between human beings" (1923b, 183). A wide variety of affectionate ties falls under this heading according to Freud: "To this class belong in particular the affectionate relations between parents and children, which were originally fully sexual, feelings of friendship, and the emotional ties in marriage which had their origin in sexual attraction" (1923b, 183).

The others types of affection, that between siblings and group members, similarly do not originate from a more primary social drive. They stem, instead, from hostile rivalry, rivalry that due to fear is channeled into identification. An older child, for example, sees the younger as a rival for the parents' love and affection and would like to put the younger one out of the way. He sees that he cannot act on his hostility without retaliation since the parents love all the children equally. So he is forced to identify with the other children (1921, 119–120). The relation of group members—in church, army, society— is similar. "Thus social feeling," Freud says, "is based on the reversal of what was first a hostile feeling into a positively-toned tie with the nature of an identification" (1921, 121). Affection between siblings and group members, then, is rivalry for love caused by fear to change its course.

It is clear, then, that for Freud sex drive is basic. Friendship or affection is not the origin of sexual desire, but is a substitute for it, a substitute drive with a second-best aim.[27] I do not desire someone because I am fond of her. Instead, I am fond of someone, or love her, because what I really want, namely, sexual satisfaction with her, is prohibited and fondness or love, a close approximation, is permitted. Affection or love *is* sexual drive, but with an inhibited sexual goal.[28] Similarly, in the case of sibling or group affection, what I really want, parental love, which as just indicated at its core is sexual, is dangerous as a result of which I identify with others whose drive is similarly imperiled.

For Freud, then, emotional development involves management of two types. The first type of emotional management is allowing and aiding desires to find needed satisfaction. The second type is checking or channeling desires and impulses whose satisfaction, though preferable, is prohibited: repression, sublimation, or aim-inhibition of prohibited desires; reversal of hostile impulses that stem from prohibited desire. This type of management is the origin of the moral. We are moral and social if we appropriately manage drive through the oedipal stage:

> Religion, morality, and a social sense—the chief elements in the higher side of man—were originally one and the same thing. According to the hypothesis which I put forward in *Totem and Taboo* they were acquired phylogenetically out of the father-complex: religion and

moral restraint through the process of mastering the Oedipus complex itself, and social feeling through the necessity for overcoming the rivalry that then remained between the members of the younger generation. (1923a, 37)

Emotional growth for Freud, then, is the mastery or management of sexual drive and has two basic types. We flourish if we are able to manage drive in such a fashion as to achieve our sexual aims. We are moral and social if we appropriately manage drive in the oedipal stage. Desire is a given, then, for Freud. In emotional development, it is managed, not cultivated or made reflective.[29]

For Kant, Hobbes, and Freud, then, emotions are, in one way or another, brute, and emotional development is not a process of making emotions more reflective or more cognitively responsive. Instead, for each of them, emotional development is not, strictly speaking, development, but a type of management. For Kant, emotions are a type of brute natural receptivity that is not responsive to principle. Their exercise sometimes is and sometimes is not appropriate and can and ought to be allowed when appropriate or, when not appropriate, resisted or constrained by an overpowering stronger force of will or respect for law.

For Hobbes, desires and aversions are not evaluations or responses to evaluations. Instead, 'good' and 'bad' signify desires and aversions which are themselves types of small bodily movement. Emotional development does not involve changing a person's view of what sort of thing is, for example, fearful or desirable. Instead, it involves accepting as given that we are fearful of death and desirous of self-preservation and delectation, and redirecting our fears and desires by altering real objects in the world so that different ones become most fearful and most desirable to us.

For Freud, drives are stimuli that press either for release or satisfaction. They are not directed to objects due to intrinsically valued characteristics of the object but due to the usefulness of the object in satisfying our private desire. As a result, desires are relatively independent of any one type of object (self/other, male/female, this person/that person) and emotional health is emotional management: either allowing or aiding desires in attaining satisfaction when permitted and needed; or repressing, inhibiting, or channeling desires whose satisfaction is prohibited.

For Aristotle, to the contrary, emotions are not brute but cognitive.[30] Specifically, as I will argue in chapter 6, emotions for him are types of perception or appearance of particulars as good or bad (specifically, of particular persons doing or suffering good or bad). When we perceive or receive an appearance of particulars of the specified type as good we feel pleasurable emotions (confidence, desire, admiration, friendship, etc.). When we perceive or receive an appearance of particulars of the specified type as bad we feel painful emotions (fear, aversion, pity, hatred, etc.). Emotions are in part caused and in part constituted by the relevant perceptions or appearances.

In addition, emotional development at its best according to him is not control of our emotions, repression of our emotions, overpowering of our emotions, or force against our emotions. Good action that results from forcing ourselves to act in accord with our reason and against our emotions is not virtuous according to him but merely continent. "The incontinent person," he says, "knowing that what he does is base does it due to emotion while the continent person, knowing that his desires are base, does not follow them due to *logos*" (*NE* 7.2 1145b12–14). The incontinent person is one in whom reason and emotion conflict and in whom emotion determines what is done counter to what is best; the continent person is one in whom reason and emotion conflict and in whom reason controls emotion to such an extent that it is reason that determines what is done and the person acts for what is best. The very word for continence, '*enkrateia*', means 'control'.

As we have seen in this chapter, the distinction between virtue and continence is crucial to Aristotle's ethical theory. Both virtue and continence are good since neither the virtuous person nor the continent person as a result of emotion acts against reason. The continent person, however, *has* opposing emotions while the virtuous person does not, *has* desires and pleasures that oppose reason but does not allow himself to be led by them. The virtuous person, to the contrary, lacks opposing desires and pleasures and instead desires and takes pleasure in good activities themselves. The state of the virtuous person, the best state, is one in which desires and reason are in accord. The virtuous person's emotion, according to Aristotle, "speaks with the same voice as reason on everything" (*NE* 1.13 1102b28). Virtue, for Aristotle, is a type of accord, continence a type of control. The virtuous person does not act well because opposing emotions are under control. Instead, the virtuous person does what he wants to do. The virtuous person's desire and reason have the same object.

As a result, it is not surprising that when Aristotle defines virtue as a settled disposition to choose well, he goes on to define 'choice' as 'deliberate desire'. For Aristotle, virtue is both a settled disposition to deliberate well and to desire what one has decided upon: "Choice will be deliberate desire for things that are in our power. For when as a result of deliberation we have decided, we desire in accord with our deliberation" (*NE* 3.3 1113a10–12). In virtue, deliberation and desire have the same object.

Similarly also for the attainment of ethical virtue. We attain ethical virtue according to him through doing acts of the virtue to be attained. Eventually, acts of the virtue that we do without having the virtue lead to acquisition of the virtue (i.e., to acquisition of the particular disposition that is that virtue). The criteria for having acquired the virtue, specifically, for not simply doing just acts but doing them justly, for not simply doing moderate acts but doing them moderately, include that we choose the acts and choose them for their own sake (*NE* 2.4). Given that choice is deliberate desire, attainment of an ethical virtue, then, involves both emotional modification, since we come to desire the acts in which we are engaging, and intellectual modification, since we come to desire them deliberately. Attainment of an ethical virtue does not simply involve emotional modification—for example, suppression of emotion, overpowering of emotion, or channeling of emotion—but involves intellectual modification as well.

Deliberation, according to Aristotle, involves a true apprehension of an end or good as well as correctness about what is constitutive of that good or instrumental to it (*NE* 6.9 1142b31–33). Since the choice of the acts is choice of them for their own sake, the correctness is about only what is constitutive of the good. In other words, once we have attained a virtue, when we are engaging in acts of a particular virtue, we desire those acts and correctly believe that the acts are themselves good.[31] It is because we cognize the acts as good that we come to desire them since, as I have asserted in the first section of this chapter and will argue in chapter 6 on emotion, perception of particulars of a certain sort as good is pleasure and pleasure, according to *De Anima*, leads to desire.

Spelling out these claims and drawing a picture of the role of cognition of value in Aristotle's ethics are among the main aims of this essay. Suffice it here to claim, with more complete argument to come later, that for Aristotle acquisition of a virtue is not acquisition of a developed capacity or tendency to suppress emotion, to control emotion, or to channel emotion but is acquisition of a developed capacity or tendency to experience emotion and desire accordingly with one's cognition of value.

Contrast this with Kant, Hobbes, and Freud. For Kant, desire and intellect are in harmony only in cases in which virtue involves will allowing experience of an emotion, not in cases in which will resists or constrains experience of an emotion. For Hobbes, in the development of virtue, neither the emotion nor its general cognitive content or accompaniment are modified (e.g., fear and the belief that death and what leads to death is most fearful). Instead, states of affairs are changed (a commonwealth is constructed, an all-powerful sovereign instituted) so that the emotion will be directed toward a different real object. For Freud, like Kant, even in cases of emotional health, emotions and intellect, more specifically drives and ego, are in harmony only when drives are permitted to attain satisfaction. They are out of harmony when satisfaction of drives is prohibited.

For Aristotle, in sum, emotions are fundamentally cognitive and emotional development centrally involves cognitive development. Emotional development is not development of the capacity to manage basic and brute emotions—to control them, overpower them, suppress them, force them—but is development of the capacity to experience emotion and cognition in accord. Accordant affective and cognitive experience is a result of the fact that, as I will show, emotions are themselves types of cognition for Aristotle, specifically, perception or appearance of certain types of particulars as good or bad. Because of this fact, namely, the fact that emotions are a type of value cognition, emotional development can be understood really to be a type of development—or cultivation or shaping—and not merely a type of management. For Aristotle, the acquisition of ethical virtue is not simply a process of forced emotional modification but is, instead, a process that makes emotions more deliberate or reflective, more responsive to principle or *logos*, and, most importantly, more responsive to value.

3

For Aristotle, value is not a special moral object beyond those we can experience or know to which our special moral faculty must be responsive if we are to have virtue and act appropriately. For him, awareness of value is simply a cognitive matter. Value is cognized by our two faculties for nondiscursive awareness, intellectual insight *(nous)*, and practical insight *(phronēsis)*, or, as Aristotle often says more simply, value is perceived.[32] It is cognized by emotion as well, since emotion for Aristotle is not brute but is itself a type of perception of value, specifically, perception of the value of certain types of particulars.[33]

Moreover, for Aristotle, perception of value is not perception of entities or properties that transcend the world we experience and know. Instead, it is perception of the most general features of that world. Specifically, it is perception of a certain kind of relatedness, namely, the internal relation he calls *'entelecheia'* or *'energeia'* and that we might call 'development', 'completion', or 'fulfillment' (as I will argue in this section). 'Good', for Aristotle, simply means 'development', 'completion', or 'fulfillment'. We will have to complicate the account more than that—for example, to accommodate 'good' both as substantive and as predicate—but let us begin with the simpler claim: 'good', for Aristotle, means *'entelecheia'* or *'energeia'*.

To see this, let us begin with Aristotle's discussion of good as an analogical equivocal.[34] For Aristotle, good is equivocal because a variety of persons, things, or states of affairs are appropriately called 'good' though what it is for them to be good is not the same from case to case. When the name 'X' is common to different things but the account of their being X *(logos tēs ousias)* differs, X is equivocal (*Cat.* 1.1a1–6).[35]

Though good is equivocal, it is not merely ambiguous. Some equivocals are merely ambiguous. Sharp is an example. It is equivocal since it is appropriate to call different types of things 'sharp' though what it is for them to be sharp differs. A note is sharp because it is too high. A knife is sharp that is capable of efficient cutting. Sharp is merely ambiguous, however, because there is no connection between what it is to be sharp in one case ('too high') and in another ('capable of efficient cutting') (*NE* 5.1 1129a26–31).[36]

Good is a nonambiguous equivocal because there is a connection between what it is to be good in one case and in another. The two main types of nonambiguous equivocals for Aristotle are focal equivocals *(pros hen)* and analogical equivocals *(kat' analogian)*.[37] In each case, a certain type of relatedness is crucial. In the case of focal equivocals, different things are appropriately called 'X' because they have perhaps different relations to some one thing (*Met.* 4.2 1003a33–b10, 7.4 1030a34–b3, 11.3 1060b31–61a3). In the case of analogical equivocals, different things are appropriately called 'X' because they have the same relation to perhaps different things (*NE* 1.6 1096b28–29; *EE* 1.8 1218a30–33).

For example, healthy is, according to Aristotle, a focal equivocal. What it is for a body to be healthy is not the same as what it is for medicine to be healthy or exercise to be healthy. A healthy body is one with an active and stable disposition to be affected in such a way that it both is preserved and flourishes. Healthy medicine and exercise, on the other hand, are medicine or exercise that result in a healthy body. Healthy is a focal equivocal because one account of what it is to be healthy (healthy body) is included in all the other accounts of what it is to be healthy (healthy medicine, healthy exercise). Different things are appropriately called 'healthy' because they have perhaps different relations to some one thing, namely, a healthy body (*Met.* 4.2 1003a34–b1, 11.3 1061a5–7; *EE* 7.2 1236a17–20).

Good, on the other hand, is an analogical equivocal. Different things are appropriately called 'good' according to Aristotle because they have the same relation to perhaps different things. This view is important for our purposes because it implies that perception of value is perception of a certain sort of relatedness. Moreover, as I will show, it is a sort of relatedness that itself cannot be defined ahead of time but must be seen.

A passage in *Nicomachean Ethics* 1.6 shows us that good is an analogical equivocal. The passage occurs after the argument that good is equivocal not univocal. Aristotle asks what type of equivocal good is and can be interpreted to claim in response that good is not a focal or ambiguous equivocal but an analogical one: "But, how is it said? For it does not seem at least to be like those which are equivocal by chance. But is it by all being from one or aiming toward one? Or, rather, is it by analogy? For as sight is in the body, so mind is in the soul, and another in another" (*NE* 1.6 1096b26–29). Aristotle prefers the third alternative, that good is an analogical equivocal, as we can see from the fact that he says "or, rather" and gives what appears to be a short argument by example for that alternative ("For as sight is in the body, so mind is in the soul, and another in another.")[38]

A passage in the *Eudemian Ethics* 1.8 discussion of the equivocity of the good probably is intended as a similar argument by example for the analogical equivocity of the good: "And the statement that all things aim at some one good is not true. For each thing stretches out for its own good, the eye for sight, the body for health, and similarly another thing for another" (*EE* 1.8 1218a30–33).[39] Good is not a focal equivocal, the passage suggests, since it is not the case that all things aim at some one good. Instead, good is an analogical equivocal, since one thing aims at one good and another at another.

'Analogy', or *analogia* in Greek, means 'same *logos*' or 'same relationship'. To say that good is an analogical equivocal is to say that different things, persons, states of affairs, and so forth, are appropriately called 'good' because they are relata of a specified relationship. What is the relationship? The examples Aristotle uses in the *Nicomachean Ethics* 1.6 and *Eudemian Ethics* 1.8 passages just quoted are examples of the internal relationship Aristotle calls '*entelecheia*' or '*energeia*'. That is, they are examples of the relationship that obtains between a *telos* and the things of which it is the *telos*. As sight is the good or *entelecheia* of the body so mind is the good or *entelecheia* of the soul *(NE)*; as sight is the good or *entelecheia* of the eye so health is the good or *entelecheia* of the body *(EE)*.

For example, we know from *Physics* 7.3 that health according to Aristotle is a virtue of the body and that virtues, both of body and of soul, are *teleiōseis* (completions): "for virtues are completions *(teleiōseis)* and vices departures *(ekstaseis)*; thus, they are not alterations *(alloiōseis)" (Phys.* 7.3 246a27–b3).⁴⁰ We know from *De Anima* 2.1 that (the eye's capacity for) sight is a type of *entelecheia* or completeness according to Aristotle since according to him there are two grades of *entelecheia* (i.e., of development of matter into form), related to each other as knowledge, understood as the potential to know, is to knowing: "completeness *(entelecheia)* is said in two ways, as knowledge and as knowing" and, we can add, as sight and seeing *(De An.* 2.1 412a10–11). The relationship by virtue of which sight and health are analogous, then, is the relationship that a *telos* has to the things of which it is the *telos*, namely, *entelecheia* (or, in its process form, *'teleiōsis'*).

The good of anything is its *telos*. A good is a *telos*. The relationship by virtue of which things are good is *entelecheia* or *energeia*. The process or state of having achieved good is *teleiōsis*. (I say the relationship is not just *entelecheia* but *entelecheia* or *energeia* because *energeia* and *entelecheia* are close equivalents for Aristotle: "The term *'energeia'* which is connected to *'entelecheia'*, has been extended to other things for the most part from motions" *(Met.* 9.3 1047a30–31).

Corroborating passages are easy to find. In the immediate beginning of *Nicomachean Ethics* 1.7, the chapter just following the discussion of the equivocity of the good, Aristotle states very clearly that the good of each practice and craft is its end *(telos):* "What, then, is the good of each [practice and craft]? Or is it that for the sake of which the rest is done? In medicine, this is health; in strategy, victory; in housebuilding, a house; in another, another; and in every practice and choice it is the end *(telos).* For all the rest is done for the sake of this" *(NE* 1.7 1097a15). More general support is available in the *Metaphysics* where Aristotle regularly identifies good with the end *(telos)* or the for the sake of which *(hou heneka):* "The remainder are causes as the end, that is, the good *(to telos kai t'agathon)* of the others" *(Met.* 3.2 996a23); "everything which is good by itself and due to its own nature is an end . . ." *(Met.* 5.2 1013b25).⁴¹

Moreover, since for Aristotle, the terms *'entelecheia'* and *'energeia'* are close equivalents and they name the relationship that obtains between a *telos* and the things of which it is the *telos*, Metaphysics 9.6 provides further corroboration. In it, Aristotle says that *energeia* cannot be defined but must be seen by analogy. What we mean by it, Aristotle says, is clear in different cases by induction:

> What we mean is clear by induction from particular cases and one must not seek a definition of everything but also see *(synhoran)* the analogy—that as that which is building is to that which is capable of building, so that which is awake is to that which is asleep, and that which

is seeing to that which has its eyes shut but has the capacity to see, and that which is separate from matter to the matter, and that which is unwrought to that which is wrought up. Let *'energeia'* be determined by the first part of each of these differences and 'the potential' by the second. But all things are not said in the same way to be in *energeia* but by analogy—as a first thing is in or to a second so a third is in or to a fourth; for some are as movement is to potentiality and others as substance to a certain matter. (*Met.* 9.6 1048a35–b9)[42]

Aristotle makes clear in the passage that *energeia* is analogical. He also makes another important claim, namely, that *energeia* cannot be defined but must be seen in different instances by analogy. His reason for the second claim is that "all things are not said in the same way to be in *energeia* but by analogy."[43] In other words, 'in *energeia*' is not a relationship that is the same in different cases but is a relationship that differs in different cases. Some relationships are the same in different cases (e.g., the relationship that obtains between two and four and between five and ten). Others are different in different cases.[44] *Energeia* is a relationship that is different in different cases. If *energeia* were a relationship that is the same in different cases, it would not be equivocal any more than double or 'to the left of' are equivocal.

As a result, *energeia* is universal in one respect and particular in another. It is universal in that a variety of things, persons, and states of affairs can share in it. It is particular in that what it is to share in it is different in different cases. As a result, one can, regarding good, grasp the universal without knowing what its instances will be like. The instances are quite different, one from another, and different in ways that are not predictable or deducible but in ways that can only be seen or perceived. Good is an analogical equivocal but the analogy is an imprecise analogy not a precise one.

Confirmation of the analogical nature of *energeia* is found in *Physics* 1.7 where Aristotle asserts that the second term in the *energeia*/potential relation is analogical (specifically for the case in which the relation is between substance and matter). Using the term "underlying nature" for the matter, Aristotle says that it is knowable by analogy: "The underlying nature is knowable by analogy. For as the bronze is to the statue, the wood to the bed, or the matter and the shapeless before receiving shape to any thing which has shape, so is the underlying nature to substance, that is, to the 'this-what' or being" (*Phys.* 1.7 191a7–12).

For Aristotle, then, value is not some special moral object beyond those that can be known by our cognitive and affective faculties. Instead, value is a certain kind of internal relatedness that we know by the rational process of induction from particular cases. More specifically, we know value in different cases by seeing the recurrence of that kind of relatedness in a variety of situations. Awareness of value is not exercise of some special moral responsiveness on some special non- or suprarational moral object. It is, instead, awareness of the recurrence of a specified relationship—a relationship that we can grasp universally without knowing ahead of time what its instances or applications will be like. It is, to put the point differently, awareness of a specified analogy.[45]

The analogy is the relationship that obtains between different *telē* and the things, persons, or states of affairs whose *telē* they are. What is that relationship like? To put the question differently, what is a *telos*?[46] *Telos*, for Aristotle, means end or goal, completion, fulfillment, or full development. It is one of the four causes, the four answers to the question why, discussed in the *Metaphysics*. It is Aristotle's fundamental discovery or invention. There is efficient cause, or the source of motion; material cause, or the matter; formal cause, or what Aristotle calls by the unusual phrase the 'what was being'; and final cause, or *telos* which he refers to as the 'for the sake of which'.

How shall we understand *telos*? I have previously proposed that by '*telos*' Aristotle means constitutive limit.[47] Limits are of two kinds. Some are destructive or harmful. They destroy what they limit or harm it. Others are constitutive. They are constitutive of what they limit being, more fully or securely, what it already is. They are constituents or components of its flourishing.[48] As the edges of a table not only limit the table, but constitute it, so a virtue such as courage not only limits activity of a certain type but allows it to be, fully, what it is, not only limits emotion of a certain type but allows it to be, fully, what it is. *Telē* are in contrast with limits that are not constitutive: split the table with an ax and the new limits will not constitute, but destroy, the table; engage the enemy recklessly and you will not engage the enemy at all, but be defeated by him or her. Limits differ; not all limits are destructive or harmful. Those that constitute an action or thing are beneficial; they are its *telē*.

For further illustration, consider an example from a skill, namely, playing the lyre. Is putting your finger on the first string halfway down constitutive of lyre-playing? Sometimes it is, and sometimes it is not. Sometimes pressing the first string halfway down is lyre-playing; other times, it makes noise. The virtue of lyre-playing (and a virtue is a first-stage *telos*—or, more precisely, first-stage *teleiōsis* or *entelecheia*) is the developed capacity to play the lyre well. Having and exercising the virtue limits what one can do when playing the lyre (one must press the strings in the appropriate places, not other places, and must press them in a certain manner and at certain times, not other times, etc.). However, by observing those limits in playing the lyre, what results is that one actually plays the lyre, rather than making noise. The virtue of lyre-playing constitutively limits one's activities in lyre-playing. By contrast, having an injury to one's hand limits what one can do when playing the lyre (one must press the strings in a certain manner, for example, and not in others). In this case, when one observes these limits in playing the lyre, the result is that one plays the lyre badly, or not at all, or makes noise. These limits constrain one's lyre-playing. They destructively or harmfully limit one's activities in lyre-playing.

For another skill example, in skiing, sometimes leaning forward will enable you to ski—will be a constituent of skiing—and other times it will cause you to fall.[49] Sometimes speeding up will enable you to ski and other times slowing down will do so. When you fall, you cease to ski, so in that case, leaning back or speeding up, leaning forward or slowing down, is not constitutive of, but destructive of, skiing. When it is the cause of continued skiing, it is not only that, but also a constituent of skiing; it is a component of the *telos* (viz., skiing). Or, put another way, then it is a component of what it is to be skiing.

This latter phrase shows the connection between form and end in Aristotle's metaphysics, and explains why he uses the unusual coinage, the 'what was being' *(to ti ēn einai)*, as a substitute for form. The 'was', here, is an imperfect, and commentators disagree on just how to take it. They agree, however, that it refers to repeated action. I propose that the 'what was being' means what something was being all along.[50] When you leaned forward and fell, your intent or aim was not to fall, but was to lean forward and ski. Leaning forward was intended to be skiing; but, sadly, or sometimes comically, it was not. When you leaned back and skied, your intent was fulfilled or completed; your leaning back was skiing all along; it was a constituent of skiing; skiing is what leaning back, along with the other movements made, was being.[51]

The virtue of skiing (and, again, virtue is a first-stage *telos*, *teleiōsis*, or *entelecheia*—in English, first-stage completion or development) is the developed capacity to ski well. Having and exercising the virtue limits what one can do when skiing (one must, as just indicated, in some cases lean forward and not back and in others lean back and not forward or to the side, one must in some cases speed up not maintain speed or slow down, and in other cases slow down not maintain speed or speed up, etc.). When one observes the limits that virtue prescribes, what results is that one skis, rather than falling. The virtue of skiing constitutively limits ones activities in skiing. Being tired also limits what one can do when skiing (when tired, one may only be able to lean forward, not back, or may only be able to ski slowly, and not speed up; one may only be able to stand tall, not flex one's knees). In this case, when one observes these limits on what one can do when skiing, the result is that one skis badly, or not at all (due to a fall, e.g., or simply to coming to a halt due to lack of appropriate power). These limits constrain one's skiing. They are destructive or harmful to it.

Telos, then, is not a kind. To talk about *telos* or completion is not to distinguish things into kinds or categories, but to distinguish potential from development within kinds or across them. *Telē*, in fact, may be very different in kind, as we can see from the example of courage, where the *telos*—courageous activity—may in one case have running forward as a constitutive feature, in another case running around, in another retreating. Just as in playing the lyre the *telos* may sometimes involve depressing the string and other times releasing it, so on the battlefield courageous activity may sometimes involve running forward, and other times running back. *Telos*, then, is relative—not, as we might say, subjective, but relative to the context and to kind. As Aristotle says, completions of things different in kind are themselves different (*NE* 10.5 1175a22–23).

Let us consider the ethical example, courage, in the same manner as we have looked at the two skill examples. Having and exercising the ethical virtue called 'courage' limits what one can do when engaging an enemy on a battlefield (in some cases, one must go forward and not back, in others back and not forward, etc.). When one observes the appropriate limits—the limits prescribed by virtue, as varied as they may be—one will actually engage the enemy, that is, push the enemy back, say, or avoid enemy fire. The virtue of courage constitutively limits engagement of the enemy. When one does not observe the limits prescribed by courage, one will not engage the enemy at all but will be defeated by him or her. For example, if one tends always to go forward, recklessly, one will not engage the enemy, but be pushed back or killed by him. Or, if one tends always to go back, in cowardly fashion, one will not engage him at all. Recklessness and cowardice do limit one's actions in engaging the enemy—the reckless one must generally go forward and not back; the cowardly one must generally go back and not forward. The limitations are destructive or harmful ones, however. Recklessness and cowardice constrain one's engagement of the enemy; they are harmful or destructive of it.

Because '*telos*' means constitutive limit, we can translate it, and its variants, '*entelecheia*' and '*energeia*', by a family of terms that themselves mean, or pertain to, constitutive limitation: 'completion', 'development', or 'fulfillment', as well as the more usual translations, 'end' and 'goal'.[52] These terms do not designate kinds or categories. They signify instead enrichment of things according to their kind or category.

That Aristotle thinks *telos* means constitutive limit is indicated by the contrast he draws between acquisition or realization of a *telos* and the acquisition of a new quality, that is, between *teleiōsis* (completion) and *alloiōsis* (alteration).

For example, it would be absurd, Aristotle says in the *Physics*, to suppose that the coping or tiling of a house is an alteration and not a completion, or that in receiving its coping or tiling a house is altered and not completed.[53] So also with virtues and vices and with the things that possess or acquire them: "for virtues are completions and vices departures;" Aristotle says, "thus, they are not alterations" (*Phys.* 7.3 246a27–b3). Being tiled is to a house, we may say, as receiving virtue is to a human being. In being tiled a house does not lose the characteristic of being a house, that is, cease being able to do what houses as such do, namely, provide shelter; instead, it becomes a more complete house, that is, one more fully or securely able to provide shelter. Similarly, in acquiring a virtue such as courage, a human being does not lose the characteristic of being a human being, that is, cease being able to do what human beings are peculiarly able to do, namely, to act; instead, courageous human beings are more fully or securely able to act, since they face their fear and, in the face of it, act anyway. In being tiled, a house is not altered but developed. Similarly, in acquiring virtue, a person is not altered but is developed. By contrast, in fading from white to beige, a house loses the characteristic of being white; the house is altered since the white color is destroyed and replaced by a different color. Similarly, in becoming tan from exposure to the sun, a human being loses the characteristic of being pale; the human being is altered since the pale color has been destroyed and replaced by the dark one.

For another example, according to Aristotle in *De Anima*, neither the change from the capacity for knowledge to the possession of it, nor from the possession of knowledge to the exercise of it, is alteration.[54] Alteration is the destruction of something by its contrary, while both coming to know and exercising knowledge are examples of change into self, that is, fulfillment *(eis hauto gar hē epidosis kai eis entelecheian)*, or into dispositions or nature (*De An.* 2.5 417b2–16). Change into self, that is, fulfillment, or disposition or nature is not alteration—or, if we decide to call it that, then we must correct for having done so by making a strong distinction between two very different kinds of alteration.[55] The idea that change into fulfillment *(entelecheia)* is change into self provides further support for the claim that *telos* means constitutive limit.

These examples show us two kinds of change for Aristotle—change in which the subject of the change is destroyed and replaced and change in which the subject of the change is preserved and enriched. A *telos* is a principle of preservation or enrichment. A being that achieves its *telos*, that achieves *entelecheia* or *energeia*, will be preserved or enriched. Of course, enrichment or fulfillment cannot be achieved in just any way. Some activities or relationships stand in the way of it. Too much water, for example, will destroy a plant, rather than enabling it to grow. The appropriate amount of water will allow it to grow and bloom. Once again, we are led to the idea of *telos* as constitutive limit: a *telos* does not destroy and replace what it limits but, instead, is constitutive of it.

To claim that virtue is developed potential is to locate it at the second grade in the well-known Aristotelian distinction of potential into two grades (*Met.* 9.1–2; *Phys.* 7.3). There is simple potential, and then there is developed potential or *hexis*. Simple potential is the capacity to act or be affected. Developed potential or *hexis* is the capacity to act or be affected well: "again what are called 'capacities' are capacities either of simply acting or being affected, or of acting or being affected well" (*Met.* 9.1 1046a16). This is spelled out as follows: "one kind is the capacity for being affected"; "another kind is the disposition *(hexis)* to be unaffected by change for the worse or by destruction" (*Met.* 9.1 1046a11; 13). Virtue is such a *hexis;* that is, it is a disposition to be unaffected by change for the worse or by destruction. In the *Physics*, Aristotle makes this point both about virtue and about vice. Virtue puts what possesses it in a good condition with regard to its proper affections, where by proper affections he means affections by which something is naturally produced or destroyed. Putting this together with the *Metaphysics* passages just discussed, we can conclude that what Aristotle means when he says that virtue puts what possesses it in a good condition is that virtue puts what possesses it in a condition of being unaffected by what destroys it and affected by what produces it. Vice, on the other hand, we can conclude, puts what possesses it in a bad condition with regard to what affects it: a condition of being affected by what destroys it and unaffected by what produces it (*Phys.* 7.3 246b8–9, 17–20 with *Met.* 9.1 1046a11, 13).

For example, bodies maintain themselves and grow by taking in nutriment. Nutriment consists in hot and cold, wet and dry elements. Bodies take these in in different mixtures and proportions. When a body is disposed to take in hot and cold, wet and dry in a mixture and proportion both in relation to itself and the environment that preserve it and enable it to grow into and stay at its mature form, it has virtue—the bodily virtue called 'health'. When it tends to take them in in a mixture and proportion that cause it to be stunted or to die, it has the bodily vice (or, better, defect) called 'disease' (*Phys.* 7.3 246b3–20).

Let us consider this bodily example, health, in the same manner in which we looked at the ethical example and the two skill examples.[56] Having and activating the bodily virtue, health, limits what a body can do when maintaining itself and growing (it must take in hot and cold, wet and dry in a certain proportion and not another). When a body does observe the limits prescribed by health, it will actually be maintained and grow. The virtue of health constitutively limits maintenance and growth. Having and activating the bodily vice, disease, also limits what a body can do when maintaining itself and growing (it must take in hot and cold, wet and dry in a certain proportion and not another). In this case, however, when a body observes these limits on what it can do when maintaining itself and growing, the result is that it it is not maintained or does not grow, but is stunted or dies. These limits constrain the body's activity. They destructively or harmfully limit it.

The idea of *telos* as constitutive limit or as principle of preservation or enrichment is crucial to Aristotle's ethics and to his political theory in general. It provides for a kind of relatedness between things or people in which one thing or person does not destroy, harm, or replace another, but enables the other to be what it is, to develop, or flourish. Development *(teleiōsis)*, as we have seen, is not the same as alteration *(alloiōsis)* in which one quality is destroyed and replaced by another. Instead, it is a fulfillment or completion, an enrichment of what already is. It is change into self. It is the more complete attainment of something's own goals. *Telos* as constitutive limit or as principle of preservation or enrichment also is a kind of relatedness in which one thing or person is not forced by another, constrained by another, or destroyed by another. Force, for Aristotle, is action contrary to something's nature. "'By force'," he says, "is the same as 'contrary to nature'" (*De Cael.* 3.2 300a23–24).[57]

For example, as I have argued, emotional development (i.e., ethical virtue), is not, for Aristotle, the developed capacity to control, overpower, repress, force, or extinguish those of our emotions that are not concordant with our goals. Instead, it is the developed capacity, or disposition, to experience emotions concordantly with what we appropriately take to be our goals. A courageous person, for example, is more able to achieve his own aims on the battlefield since he does not fear trifles and is not fearless of major dangers (*NE* 3.7 1116a3, 3.6 1115a25). He is neither so fearful nor so fearless as to be prevented from achieving his own battlefield aims. If he tends to feel fear all the time, he will not achieve his battlefield aims because his fear will lead to retreat even when retreat is not conducive to his aims. If he tends not to feel fear any of the time, then he will not reach his battlefield goals since he will charge ahead even in the face of obstacles that will prevent him from attaining those goals. If, in distinction from these two extremes, he instead tends to feel fear when he perceives a real obstacle to his battlefield goals and not to feel fear when there is no real obstacle to those goals, then he will be more likely actually to achieve those goals. Courage, then, is not the disposition to control or repress fear but is the disposition to feel fear concordantly with goals correctly or appropriately understood. The courageous person is better able to attain his own goals.

In addition, courage has to do with fear. Fear is "a certain pain or disturbance [resulting] from the appearance of a future destructive or painful evil" (*Rhet.* 2.5 1382a21–22). A person's attainment of courage is not an alteration of that person (although it may involve some alterations). It is not the destruction of that person's fear and replacement of it with another emotion. Instead, it is a development, enrichment, or fulfillment of that person's tendency to feel fear. Fear is pain that results from an apparent or imagined evil. Courage is a tendency to feel that pain when the appearance or imagining actually reaches its mark. That is, it is a tendency to feel that pain toward actual evils. Courage, then, constitutively limits fear. When one has courage, one's fears reach their own internal goals.

Similarly, a moderate person is more able to do the actions she aims at in general, since, for example, she simply does not desire food and drink to an extent that would be detrimental to health and fitness nor, for example, is her desire for food and drink so low as to be detrimental to them (*NE* 3.11 1119a16). Disease and poor physical condition lead away from the achievement of a person's own goals. Moderation is not the developed capacity or disposition to suppress or control one's desires for food, drink, or sex. Instead, it is the developed capacity or disposition to desire them when they are concordant with what one correctly takes to be one's goals. A moderate person is not one who tends never to desire food, drink, or sex (nor, obviously, one who tends to desire them all the time) but, instead, is one who tends to desire them when they are concordant with what she understands, correctly or appropriately, to be her goals.

Ethical virtue, then, is not a disposition to destroy or force our emotions. Instead, it is a disposition to experience emotions concordantly with what we appropriately take to be our goals and to experience emotions concordantly with their own internal goals. Ethical virtue, as a result, is an example of *telos* as constitutive limit; of a kind of relatedness between things in which one thing does not destroy, harm, or replace another, but enables the other to be what it is, to develop or flourish; of development *(teleiōsis)* as fulfillment, completion, or enrichment (rather than alteration—*alloiōsis*—as destruction and replacement); of preservation or enrichment rather than force or constraint; or change into self, or change into something's own goals, or change into something's nature.

For a second example of *telos* as constitutive limit, friendship, at its best, is not, for Aristotle, one person's use of another person as an object to fulfill the first person's own aims. Instead, friendship, at its best, is a relationship of mutual development and flourishing, that is, a relationship between two persons in which each is a constituent of the other's development and flourishing. This mutual development and flourishing is not present in the two deficient kinds of friendship— friendships of pleasure or of utility. In each of the deficient kinds, one person loves another for the sake of attaining some benefit from him or her, some enjoyment or some practical use. In friendships of the best kind, however, one loves the other for his or her own sake, not simply for some good for oneself that one gets from him or her (*NE* 8.2–4). In this kind of friendship, each person is better able to develop his or her character, that is, to acquire virtue, and, in addition, to act virtuously or be happy. A certain training in virtue results from living together with those who are good, Aristotle says (*NE* 9.9 1170a11). Moreover, it is difficult for even the good or virtuous person to be active *(energein)* alone, leading a solitary life, without friends (*NE* 9.9 1170a5–6). In a friendship, I am limited in what I do by my relationship to my friend. However, in the best friendships, the limitation is not a destructive or harmful one. The limitation does not constrain me but, instead, enables me to be, more fully, what I already am, for in friendship, I am more fully able to develop virtue, to be active and happy. The limitations of friendship are enabling. They enable me to develop. Friendship limits without constraining.

For a third example of *telos* as constitutive limit, just government is not, for Aristotle, a form of regrettably necessary bondage or constraint on our nature, as it is for Hobbes, Locke, or Rousseau. Instead, for Aristotle, just government is a form of rule in which the rulers aim at and to some extent achieve the development of our nature, that is, virtue and happiness. For Hobbes, as we have seen, social virtues are contrary to our natural passions, and the first function of government is to institute an all-powerful sovereign so that our terror and awe of him will force us to acquire social virtues (*Lev.* 2.17). For Locke, our natural or prepolitical state is a state of perfect freedom some of which, in political society, we must give up in order to acquire security (*ST* 2.4, 9.123). Rousseau believes that my original, presocial nature is good and that social interaction is always some kind of deformation or slavery. When we enter social life, we become slaves and lose our goodness: "As he [man] becomes social and a Slave, he becomes weak, timorous, groveling, and his soft and effeminate way of life complete the enervation of both his strength and his courage" (*DI*, 1.11, 146). Government and civilization are bondage according to him:

> While government and laws provide for the safety and well-being of assembled men, the sciences, letters and arts, less despotic and perhaps more powerful, spread garlands of flowers over the iron chains with which men are burdened, stifle in them the sense of that original liberty for which they seemed to have been born, make them love their slavery, and turn them into what is called civilized peoples. (*DSA* 1.9, 4–5)

For Aristotle, in contrast to Rousseau, just government is not a form of bondage but is, instead, to be contrasted with bondage. Unjust governments are those in which the rulers rule for their own good, as a master does in relation to a slave. Just governments, by contrast, are those in which the rulers rule for the good—that is, what we might call the 'full development'—of the citizens (*Pol.* 3.6 1279a17–21). The human good, according to him, is virtue and happiness, that is, it is the development and exercise of our species-specific capacities for emotion and cognition. Cities come into existence for the sake of mere life, according to Aristotle, but they stay in existence and have as their most fundamental aim the good life, that is, a life in which we both develop and exercise those capacities (*Pol.* 1.2 1252b27–30). In a just government, then, we are limited without being constrained or forced. Instead, the government and laws of a just regime enable us to develop. In a just government, the laws are limitations without being chains. They are enabling limitations.

The examples of friendship and government indicate that the idea of *telos* as constitutive limit and of *entelecheia* and *energeia* as constitutive relatedness extend to include the idea of mutually constitutive relationships. I cannot develop and flourish without you; you cannot develop and flourish without me. Some of what I am is accessible to me only in relation to you; some of what you are is accessible to me only in relation to you. Only together can each of us attain our ends. The best friendships are examples of this kind of mutually constitutive relationship. "The friend," Aristotle says, quoting the proverbial remark, "is another self" (*NE* 9.4 1166a31). Similarly, in the political realm, I attain my fullest development and happiness only together with others in political society. "Human being is by nature political," Aristotle says in a now famous remark (*Pol.* 1.2 1253a2–3), a remark to be contrasted with

Hobbes's claim, quoted in section 2 of this chapter, that nature dissociates ("It may seem strange to some man, that has not well weighed these things; that nature should thus dissociate, and render men apt to invade, and destroy one another . . ." [*Lev.* 1.13, 100]). I cannot develop and flourish without other citizens in a city; they, too, cannot develop and flourish without other citizens in a city. Some of what each of us is is accessible to us only in the relationships with each other that the city provides. Political relationships, we may say then, are mutually constitutive. Both friendship relationships and political relationships are, then, examples of *telos* as constitutive limitation and, more specifically, of mutually constitutive relatedness. We have seen three examples, then, of *telos* as constitutive limitation: ethical virtue, friendship, and just government.

These examples of constitutive limitation and constitutive relatedness make it evident that there are two important kinds of relationships for Aristotle—relationships in which one thing or person is replaced, harmed, or destroyed by another and relationships in which one thing or person is preserved, developed, enriched, or enabled to flourish. The latter type of relationship is what value is for Aristotle. Moreover, awareness of this relationship either obtaining or not obtaining among particulars (in part) constitutes our emotions and motivates our actions. Adequate awareness of this relationship obtaining or not obtaining among particulars is, for Aristotle, the central cognitive component of ethical virtue.

We can say, then, in summary that for Aristotle value is not some special moral object beyond those that can be known by our ordinary cognitive and affective faculties. Instead, for Aristotle value is among the most general features of the world that we do experience and know. It is a certain kind of internal relatedness that we know, first, by the rational process of induction from particulars and, then, by seeing the recurrence of that kind of relatedness in a number of varied situations (i.e., by seeing an imprecise analogy). It is enriching, rather than destructive, relatedness. It is constitutive, rather than constraining, limitation. It is, of course, in addition Aristotle's central discovery: final cause, Aristotle's most fundamental contribution to the line of thought about the nature of things that was initiated by the Milesian materialists.

Conclusion

Aristotle's ethics is not, then, a moral theory in three important senses, senses derived from reflection on a paradigmatic moral theory, namely, Kant's. Aristotle does not believe that ethical virtue requires the development of a special moral faculty in addition to reason or against emotion such as a will, a conscience, or a moral sense. Instead, for Aristotle, ethical virtue requires the accordant development simply of cognitive and affective faculties. He does not maintain that ethical virtue requires suppression, constraint, or control of our emotions. Instead, for him, it requires the development or cultivation of emotion. He does not argue that value is a special moral object that cannot be experienced or known but only posited to account for what can be experienced or known. Instead, for him, value is a type of internal relatedness known through induction and by awareness of an inexact analogy.

CHAPTER THREE

Ethics and Metaphysics

Another discussion this essay joins, as chapter 2 makes clear, is the discussion of the relation between ethics and metaphysics for Aristotle. Among recent commentators, that discussion has centered on whether Aristotle's ethics has or does not have a metaphysical *foundation*. Foundationalism, in recent philosophic terminology, has to do with epistemology, specifically, with justification. The recent discussion regarding the supposed metaphysical foundation of Aristotle's ethics centers on Terence Irwin's claim that the argument of the ethics requires for its justification appeal to principles outside ethics, principles found in metaphysics, physics, and psychology. A group of commentators, including Timothy Roche, Sherwin Klein, and Alfonso Gomez-Lobo, have argued that it does not. They claim, instead, that the ethics is dialectically grounded, pointing to arguments in the ethics and showing that their premises are reputable opinions, requiring no extra-ethical supplementation. These commentators' arguments are persuasive (Gomez-Lobo 1989; Irwin 1978, 1980, 1981, 1985, 1988; Klein 1988; Roche 1988).

Still, this essay makes extra-ethical principles, principles discussed and argued for in metaphysics, physics, and psychology, crucial to Aristotle's ethics. For example, *telos* and *energeia*, Aristotle's most fundamental metaphysical principles, are featured in this essay though they are neither argued for nor much discussed in the ethics. Someone might object to this and maintain that a principle such as the metaphysical principles *telos* or *energeia* cannot be crucial to Aristotle's ethics nor awareness of them to ethical virtue. For, as just mentioned, such principles are neither argued for nor much discussed in the ethics. Moreover, Aristotle distinguishes ethics from metaphysics. Ethics is imprecise, according to Aristotle (*NE* 1.3, 1.7, 2.2) where by 'precise' he means 'prior' or 'fundamental' (not resting on something underlying) (*Pr.An.* 1.27 87a31–33). Metaphysics, by contrast, is first philosophy (*Met.* 11.4 1061b19). It is precise and deals most with what is prior (*Met.* 1.2 982a25–26). The most prior or fundamental principles, *telos* and *energeia*, from the most prior or fundamental study, metaphysics, cannot be crucial to Aristotle's ethics if ethics is to remain an imprecise branch of study.

Moreover, the objection might continue, in this essay you bring in metaphysical principles when Aristotle, to the contrary, shies away from them. For example, according to the argument of this essay, the central cognitive component of ethical virtue for Aristotle is awareness of the value of particulars where 'value' denotes the good and the beautiful both of which, according to this essay, are understood by Aristotle in terms of *telos* and *energeia*. In contrast, whenever Aristotle begins to approach a metaphysical principle or topic (or principles from other precise branches of study, e.g., physics or psychology), he redirects his discussion on the grounds that discussion of such principles is not needed for ethics's practical goal. Roche makes this objection against Irwin's foundationalist interpretation of Aristotle's ethics. He points out that whenever the argument of the ethics approaches an issue that falls within the sphere of another science, Aristotle redirects the course of the discussion on the grounds that such questions are not appropriate to the argument. This essay, then, reverses Aristotle's procedure, rather than representing it. For it adduces metaphysical principles where Aristotle explicitly shies away from them.[1]

Though the objections do not hold up, there is an element of truth in them. For though the argument of the ethics does not require for its justification appeal to extra-ethical principles, the argument of the ethics does require appeal to such principles for a different reason. I want to steer a path between the two poles of the recent discussion of the connection between Aristotle's ethics and his metaphysics, physics, and psychology. One pole is the pole according to which the argument of the ethics requires appeal to metaphysical, physical, and psychological principles for its justification. The other is the pole according to which because the argument of the ethics is dialectical, appeal to principles found in metaphysics, physics, or psychology is not required by it. I want to maintain that the argument of the ethics requires appeal to metaphysical, physical, and psychological principles (and topics and arguments) not for its justification but for its full elucidation or articulation.

Charles Taylor has said, recently, that "Ontological accounts have the status of articulations of our moral instincts. They articulate the claims implicit in our reactions" (1989, 8). It is something very much like this claim that I wish to make about the relation between ethics and metaphysics for Aristotle. What metaphysics can provide for ethics is not justification but, instead, full understanding. As Aristotle suggests in *Posterior Analytics*, we "know better" or, more precisely, "know more" *(epistatai mallon)* when we know from what is prior (*Post. An.* 1.9 76a18–19).[2] Such full understanding is not necessary for the practical goal of ethics. Nor does such full understanding hold out the promise of correcting mistaken claims that might be made in ethics. Instead, consideration of the relevant metaphysical, physical, and psychological principles, topics, and arguments is for its own sake. It is an instance of the activity Aristotle calls '*theōria*' or 'contemplation'. Aristotle's ethics can then be read throughout on two levels: it can be read in terms of its own imprecise but fully justified claims, and it can be read in terms of the more precise metaphysical, physical, and psychological principles and arguments consideration of which gives the ethics greater articulation or depth.

Someone could object to such a double reading on the grounds that, for Aristotle, the imprecision in ethics is ineliminable. I maintain, to the contrary, that for Aristotle there are two types of imprecision in ethics and though one type is ineliminable, the other type can be, and to an extent is, eliminated. Moreover, I maintain that even the type of imprecision that is ineliminable is caused in part by a connection between principles of ethics and principles of metaphysics rather than a separation between them. Specifically, the connection is 'being an instance of'. Some principles of ethics are instances of a metaphysical principle, namely, of *telos* or *energeia*, metaphysical principles that are themselves imprecise and equivocal (as I have argued in chapter 3, section 3). That is to say, because some principles of ethics are *telē* or *energeiai* (or variants thereof), and because *telos* and *energeia* are imprecise and equivocal, some principles of ethics are ineliminably imprecise. There are double grounds for reading the ethics on two levels, then: first, because a more precise, metaphysical, argument for some ethical claims is possible; second, because the ineliminable imprecision in ethics is explained by appeal to metaphysics.

Aristotle's comments on the imprecision of ethics are of two kinds: those that have to do with the necessary imprecision due to the subject matter of ethics and those that have to do with the imprecision due to the kind of inquiry ethics is, namely, a practical inquiry the goal of which is good practice rather than precise knowledge. The eliminable imprecision in ethics is the imprecision due to the type of inquiry ethics is. Many of the claims in the ethics are *that* claims rather than *why* claims or *what is it* claims. "One science is more precise than another science and prior to it," as Aristotle points out in the *Prior Analytics* passage previously referred to, if "the same science concerns the 'that' and the 'why', not the 'that' separately from the 'why' . . ." (*Pr. An.* 1.27 87a31–33).[3] A correct and fully justified claim *that* something is true is less precise than a claim *that* and *why* it is true. Some *that* claims in ethics are made more precise when they are supplemented by *why* claims.

Moreover, when we know *what* something is we know *why* it is. As Aristotle says in *Posterior Analytics* 1.31, "The universal is valuable because it makes clear the cause" (*Post. An.* 1.31) or, in 2.2, "to know what it is is the same as to know why it is" (*Post. An.* 2.2 88a5–6, 90a31–32). For example, what is a harmony? An arithmetical ratio between high and low. Why does the high harmonize with the low? Because an arithmetical ratio holds between the high and the low (*Post. An.* 2.2 90a19–21).

A simple example of this in the ethics is the claim that (final) good is equivocal. We see *that* (final) good is equivocal from the fact that the accounts of what it is to be good in the case of different final goods are different. Aristotle's examples are honor, practical insight *(phronēsis)* and pleasure. Presumably he means something like the following: honor is (a final) good because it befits virtue; practical insight is good because it attains the truth; pleasure is good because it feels good. But, we want to know more. We want to know *why* different (final) goods are appropriately called 'good' even though the accounts of what it is to be good in each case are different.[4] That is, we want to know *why* (final) good is equivocal. Aristotle does not tell us. Nor does he, here or anywhere in the ethics, say *what* (final) good is (though, of course, he does eventually say what human final good is). The answer to the *what* question would provide the answer to the *why* question: good means *telos* (or some variant of it) and *telos* is equivocal. (We know that *telos* is equivocal according to Aristotle in part from passages such as one found in his discussion of pleasure previously discussed in chapter 2, section 3: "things different in kind are completed *[teleiousthai]* by different things" [*NE* 10.5 1175a22–23].)[5] What is good? *Telos*. Why is good equivocal? Because good means *telos* and *telos* is equivocal.

If the general line of argument I am laying out is correct (and I will argue for it in more detail in what follows), it is as a result possible to make Aristotle's ethics more precise than it is—first, by supplementing *that* claims with *why* or *what is it* claims and, second, by demonstrations of roughly the following form:

1. Good means *telos* (or some variant thereof).
2. X is a *telos* (or, is *teleion*, is a *teleiōsis*, etc.).
3. Therefore, X is good.

Since good means *telos* or its variants, when we see something as good, then, we are seeing it as a *telos* or as *teleion* or a *teleiōsis*, and so forth. We may not be articulately aware of what we are seeing, any more than a person who sees various items as circles may be articulately aware of the criterion on the basis of which he or she is selecting certain items out and collecting them together. Aristotle would say that the universal is in the perceptions, though we may have the perception more than once and still not know the universal (*Met.* 1.1 980a27–981a7). Ethics stays with true and justified but less articulated claims about the human good to a great extent. Still, those claims can be made more precise and are made more precise, to an extent, in Aristotle's extra-ethical writings. In the rest of this chapter, I will spell out these interpretive claims in greater detail.

1

Aristotle discusses the imprecision due to the subject matter of ethics in *Nicomachean Ethics* 1.3 and 2.2. I will quote the two passages in full:

> Our inquiry will be adequate if its degree of clarity is in accord with the subject matter. For we must not seek precision similarly in all accounts any more than in all the products of the arts. Now, fine and just things, which political science investigates, have much difference and wandering, so that they are thought to be by convention only and not by nature. Goods, too, have this sort of wandering, since many have experienced harm due to them. For some previously have been ruined due to wealth and others due to courage. It is necessary, therefore, to be content when speaking about and from such things to indicate the truth coarsely and in outline, and when speaking about and from such things as are for the most part, to conclude such things as well. It is necessary in the same way also to accept each of the things said. For it belongs to the one who has been educated to seek as much precision in each genus as the nature of the thing admits. For it is evidently similar to accept persuasive arguments from a mathematician and to demand demonstrations from a rhetorician. (*NE* 1.3 1094b11–27)

> But this must be agreed on beforehand, that the entire account of actions must be stated in outline and not precisely, just as we said at the beginning that the accounts demanded must be in accordance with the matter. Matters concerning actions and the beneficial, like matters of health, have no fixity. And when the general account is this imprecise,

the account of particulars is even more imprecise. For they do not fall under any art or rule, but the agents themselves always must consider what is appropriate *(ton kairon)*, as is the case also in medicine and navigation. (*NE* 2.2 1103b34–1104a10)

These passages clearly have to do with the imprecision due to the subject matter of ethics. In the first, Aristotle prescribes the degree of clarity or precision that fits the subject matter: "Our inquiry will be adequate if its degree of clarity is in accord with the subject matter. For we must not seek precision similarly in all accounts. . . ." He also speaks of limitations on precision due to the nature of the things discussed: "For it belongs to the one who has been educated," he says, "to seek as much precision in each genus as the nature of the thing admits." In the second passage, Aristotle reiterates the first view: "the entire account of matters of practice must be given in outline and not precisely, just as we said at the beginning that the acounts demanded must be in accordance with the matter." In these passages, Aristotle prescribes a degree of imprecision in ethics that corresponds to the nature of the subject matter ethics discusses.

In the first passage Aristotle discusses three central parts of the subject matter of political science, fine things, just things, and good things. After a general comment on imprecision, he begins his specific remarks by asserting that fine and just things exhibit what he calls "difference" *(diaphora)* or "wandering" *(planē)* by which, presumably, he means variety or fluctuation. As a result of the variety or fluctuation, fine and just things are thought *(hōste dokein)* to be fine or just by convention only, not by nature.

'*Hōste dokein*' can mean either 'so that they seem' or 'so that they are thought', with the former allowing that fine and just things seem to be fine and just only by convention to Aristotle and the latter suggesting that they seem so to other people but not to Aristotle. We know from 5.7, however, that Aristotle does not think all just things are just only by convention since he there divides political justice into the portion of it that is conventionally just and the portion that is naturally just (*NE* 5.7 1134b18–19). As a result, we are justified in translating '*hōste dokein*' as 'so that they are thought'. In this passage, then, Aristotle follows his own principle, enunciated in his discussion of pleasure six books later, that we should state not only the truth but also the cause of error so that we will produce conviction in the true view (*NE* 7.14 1154a22–23). The reason that people mistakenly think fine or just things are fine or just only by convention, he explains, is that fine and just things exhibit variety or fluctuation.

Good things, too, he goes on, exhibit this kind of fluctuation. He gives two examples of goods—wealth and courage—to support his claim: we can see that things that are good fluctuate from the fact that people experience harm due to those things; for example, though wealth and courage usually are good, people are sometimes harmed by them. The wandering, in this case, is the fluctuation of wealth and courage which, though they generally are good, may also sometimes be harmful or bad since people are sometimes harmed as a result of them. By wandering, therefore, Aristotle means the fluctuation of something between good and bad. Courage can lead me to fight a hopeless battle. Wealth can be used for unlimited increase of possessions, rather than for the acquisition of the type and number of possessions that will lead to a good life. Aristotle's point is that the difference between courage or wealth in one case and another is not just a difference in our conventional beliefs about courage and wealth but is in fact a difference found in the things—wealth and courage—themselves: in one situation or context they really are good; in another they really are bad. Aristotle here argues for realism about value—about the fine, the just, and the good—but for realism of a contextual or relational type.[6]

This leads to two results for our inquiry, according to Aristotle. First, when we are speaking about and from such things—that is, when speaking about fine, just, and good things or from premises about fine, just, and good things—we will not be able to do more than indicate the truth coarsely and in outline. Second, when speaking about things that are 'for the most part' (e.g., courage or wealth, since they are good only 'for the most part') or from premises about things that are 'for the most part', our conclusions will only be 'for the most part' as well. We can expect, then, that Aristotle's political inquiries (including inquiries into ethical topics) will have a coarse or outline quality and that they will include 'for the most part' conclusions—including conclusions that some practice or quality is good, fine, or just only 'for the most part' as well as other types of 'for the most part' conclusions. We ought to accept imprecision of this sort, however, since it results not from some inadequacy on the part of the one who engages in the political inquiry, but from the nature of the subject matter of politics itself, that is, from the fact that it is about fine, just, and good things.

When we think about Aristotle's politics, candidate examples of 'for the most part' conclusions come easily to mind. Polity is the best form of government for most actual situations, Aristotle says, though when it is possible, aristocracy is better. Monarchy is generally bad, though in those rare cases in which it is possible (when a city's population includes some one person who far surpasses others in virtue), it is very good. Property qualifications for office are good in one type of government, oligarchy, but not in another, polity. Some types of communal property are good, while other types are not. In some regimes, elections are good; in others, offices are for life. The imprecision here does not result from a faulty imprecision on Aristotle's part, Aristotle would say, for it is in the nature of the things politics considers to be imprecise. All these things fluctuate from good to bad depending on the larger context of which they are a part.

When we think about Aristotle's ethics, however, examples seem harder to come by. The definitions of happiness and virtue are claims that are always true, not for the most part true. Moderation is always a mean between immoderation and insensibility, anger between irascibility and unirascibility. Play is good but not the best life. Contemplation is better than any other type of virtuous activity. And so on. What Aristotle has in mind about ethics is not immediately clear. This is a problem, of course, since the comments on imprecision occur in the ethics itself. More specifically, the 1.3 passage on imprecision currently under consideration occurs just before Aristotle defines the human good (NE 1.3–1.8). What, then, does he have in mind?

What we have to go on here are the examples Aristotle gives—of two goods, wealth and courage, sometimes also being harmful. Our account of them must be imprecise in a certain way. In what way exactly? Aristotle gives us two possible ways. Either the account must be a rough, outline account or it must be one that involves claims true only 'for the most part'. The latter seems the obvious answer, but I shall argue that the other is true for Aristotle as well. Consider courage. For the most part, courage is good. Sometimes, however, it is not, as we see from the fact that "many have experienced harm due to" it.

What is striking about this example is that it seems very un-Aristotelian. We can suppose that he means something like the fact that courage can lead us confidently and unaware into danger. Courageous people are wont to rush ahead, and damn—or just not think about—the consequences.

One who acts in this way, however, is not a person with courage as Aristotle understands it. Instead, it is what Aristotle calls 'natural courage' that can be harmful in this way, the 'courage' that is nothing more than passion—spiritedness *(thymos)* or desire *(epithymia)*—applied to all situations whether appropriate or not, in other words, the courage that is a passion and not a mean. A person is not brave because, driven by their spiritedness, they rush into danger without seeing the perils that lie ahead; nor are they brave if desire impels them forward (NE 3.8 1116b33–1117a2). The 'courage' due to spiritedness is better called 'natural courage', Aristotle says, and would become courage in the strict sense if choice and 'the for the sake of which' were added to it

(*NE* 3.8 1117a4–5). That is, spiritedness is the uncultivated counterpart of courage. It becomes courage if the spirited passion is shaped and informed by deliberation regarding the means to, and components of, an appropriate end (since deliberation is the component of choice that the spirited person lacks). The courageous person experiences and acts on the spirited passion only when it is appropriate to do so, not as a matter of course.

Note what has happened in this paragraph. We begin with one of the two types of imprecision mentioned by Aristotle in the 1.3 passage and, by resolving it, we end up with the other. We begin with natural courage or spiritedness, the courage that is for the most part good but that has led many into harm. We end with courage in the strict or full sense, the courage that is a disposition to experience the spirited passion and act on it when appropriate, but not when it is not. Courage so defined is defined universally, not just for the most part, but, as a result, is defined in a sketchy way. The definition is general and, in a frustrating way, lacking in detail. We have understood it, to use Aristotle's terms, coarsely and in outline.

Wealth is similar. For the most part, wealth is good. Still, many have been harmed by it, for example, by accumulating it beyond what is beneficial. According to Aristotle, the goal of economics is not wealth understood as property without limit. This is wealth in a sense, but not genuine wealth. Genuine wealth is constituted by the goods that are necessary for life and useful for community in the household and the city (*Pol.* 1.8 1256b26–31). We know that the city, according to Aristotle, comes into existence for the sake of mere life and stays in existence for the sake of a good life (*Pol.* 1.2 1252b29–30). To say that wealth is constituted by goods necessary for life and useful for the household and city, then, is to say that wealth is comprised of household and city goods sufficient for a good life. So Aristotle says, "sufficiency of such goods for a good life is not limitless" (*Pol.* 1.8 1256b31–32). Once again, we have moved from one type of imprecision to another—from a 'for the most part' claim (wealth is for the most part good) to a universal claim that is sketchy or coarse (wealth is constituted by goods sufficient for a good life). Each claim is correct; each is imprecise.

Is it far-fetched to suppose that in the passage from 1.3 Aristotle uses 'courage' and 'wealth' in seemingly un-Aristotelian fashion? Not at all. In fact, it is likely. These early chapters of Book 1 are preparatory, introductory. Moreover, Aristotle proceeds in a similar way in his 1.5 discussion of pleasure. There he considers whether pleasure is the human good and decides that it is not, since pleasure is slavish and suitable for cattle. We know that later Aristotle will give us a more refined account of pleasure and will maintain that the type of pleasure referred to in 1.5, bodily pleasure, is only a part and not the best part of pleasure as well as claiming that it is a mistake to confuse bodily pleasure with pleasure as a whole. His early discussion of pleasure, therefore, is in a sense un-Aristotelian.

For, the 'for the most part' imprecision in the case of each example is dealt with by introducing the concept of the good. In the case of courage, the 'for the most part' imprecision of natural courage is replaced by a universal but sketchy and coarse account of courage as a mean. The mean, as I will argue in the next chapter, refers to the good. In the case of wealth, the 'for the most part' imprecision of wealth understood as property without limit is rectified by a more genuine understanding of wealth as possessions sufficient for the human good, a definition that is universal, though again sketchy.

Why are different types of good things imprecise in this way? Because, good is a certain sort of equivocal. Good is not a certain *type* of thing or activity. That is to say, it is not simply by virtue of being of a certain *type* (a certain quality, quantity, time, place, etc.) that a thing or activity is good. Instead, a thing or activity of a certain type is good if by virtue of being of that type it is instrumental to or constitutive of completion of some kind. A tendency to rush ahead is good only for the most part; a tendency to rush ahead when doing so will lead to victory and to refrain from rushing ahead when doing so will put victory at risk is universally good.

In the second passage, from 2.2, Aristotle reiterates his view that good things—'the beneficial' *(ta sympheronta)*—involve difference or wandering—'no fixity' *(ouden hestēkos)* (NE 2.2). Since general accounts of what is good are like this, accounts of particulars are even more imprecise, for as a result of the lack of fixity of the general account, particulars do not fall under any art or rule and agents must, instead, consider in each case what is appropriate.

It is easy to misread Aristotle and simply say that according to him, practical philosophy is imprecise because it has to do with particulars. Particulars are not fixed. They vary and fluctuate. Therefore, practical philosophy is imprecise. That, however, is not Aristotle's point in this passage. Instead, his point is that in practical philosophy, it is because the general account is imprecise that the account of particulars is even more imprecise. As just explained, good is imprecise because to be good is not to be a certain *type* of being. Instead, a thing of a certain type is good if, by virtue of being of that type, it is instrumental to or constitutive of completion of some kind. Because the good in general is imprecise in this way, particular goods are imprecise as well.

To see the import of this, consider geometry. Application of geometry to particulars is imprecise, as anyone who has been involved in carpentry or building knows. Corners are not quite right angles. Or, even if they are, they may cease to be when the weather changes or the earth shifts. So, descriptions of the geometric features of tables, counters, rooms, and buildings are imprecise. Still, there are rules, applicable in the same way in every case, for whether a countertop is square, the walls are perpendicular to each other or at a right angle to the floor. Moreover, it is generally fairly easy to tell whether the particulars involved meet the criteria specified in the rule. The account of particulars will still be imprecise, however, since it will often be the case that particulars almost meet the criteria, but not quite, or that they meet them at one time, but can be expected to cease meeting them later.

In the case of what is beneficial in human practical affairs, there is imprecision due to the fact that someone's actions are not completely good or to the fact that their action or character may cease to be good or cease to be as good as they were. However, there is an even greater source of imprecision in the case of beneficial human action, namely, that the very same action that is good in one context may be bad in another. Rushing ahead toward the enemy in one case may be good and the courageous thing to do, while in another case, it may be foolhardy or reckless instead. 180 degrees is always a right angle and if the angle becomes greater or smaller, it ceases to be a right angle. Rushing toward the enemy is not always courageous and good, and retreating, in many circumstances, is not cowardly or bad.

Practical affairs are imprecise, as the 2.2 passage points out, because there is no art or rule by which to decide how to act. That there is no rule for deciding how to act does not, however, indicate that there is no way at all to decide how to act. Though the amount of anger or money called for by a specific situation cannot be specified by a rule, one can, instead, see what is appropriate (or suitable or proper) to that situation—*ton kairon*. This is part of what Aristotle means when he says that the decision is in the perception (*NE* 2.9 1109b23).[7]

Ho kairos (what is appropriate to the occasion) is, for Aristotle, the good in the category of time. Good is said in as many ways as being, according to Aristotle, for example, in the category of substance, the god and mind, in quantity, the measured, "in time, *kairos*" (*NE* 1.6 1096a23–27).[8] Aristotle confirms this understanding of '*kairos*' as a type of good by defining it, in the *Prior Analytics*, as 'needed time' *(chronos deon)* and then associating the needed with the good, specifically, with the beneficial *(ophelimon)* (*Pr. An.* 1.36 48b35–37).[9] Moreover, '*kairos*' is a term used sometimes simply to stand for the appropriate or good in general (*Met.* 8.3 1043b23–25).[10]

The identification of *kairos* with good and the claim that in practical decisions we cannot apply a rule but must look to what is *kairos* suggest that practical decision making for Aristotle is imprecise because the good is imprecise: practical decisions are not the same from situation to situation because the good is not the same; the good is not univocal but equivocal by analogy since, as we have seen, good, for Aristotle, means *telos* or *entelecheia*. Our decisions, then, require not the application of a rule to the situation at hand, but perception of a certain kind of relatedness, specifically, of completion, development, or fulfillment.

The ineliminable imprecision due to the subject matter of ethics, then, has a cause and it is not simply that the subject matter of ethics is particulars. Instead, it is caused by the fact that the subject matter of ethics is the *value* of particulars. If we say that certain types of things are fine, just, or good, our assertions are only true for the most part. For fine, just, and good things exhibit variety and fluctuation. If we replace our limited assertions with universal ones—things of these types are fine, just, or good when they are a mean—our assertions, though universal, are sketchy. Similarly, since our general account of good is imprecise, our account of particular goods is even more imprecise.

The ineliminable imprecision due to the subject matter of ethics is caused, then, by the part of metaphysics to which ethics is connected, namely, to the good understood as *telos* (and its variants and close equivalents). As a result, we have reason to read ethics on two levels, the ethical and the metaphysical. For the ineliminable imprecision in ethics is explained by appeal to metaphysics. As a result, reflection on metaphysical principles, on what they are and what they are like, results in a deeper, more articulate, understanding of ethical claims.

2

Aristotle discusses a second kind of imprecision in ethics, the imprecision due to the type of inquiry ethics is, in *Nicomachean Ethics* 1.7:

> One must recall the things said before and not seek precision similarly in all things, but the precision that accords with the subject matter in each case and the degree that is appropriate to the inquiry. For a carpenter and a geometer seek the right angle differently as well; the carpenter seeks it as far as is useful for his task, while the geometer seeks what and what sort of thing the right angle is, since he is a contemplator of truth. One must act the same way in other cases, then, so that digressions not become more important than the task at hand. Nor must one demand the cause similarly in all cases, but it is sufficient in some cases to exhibit the 'that' beautifully, for example, concerning

principles, and the 'that' is a first and a principle. Some principles are seen by induction, some by perception, others by a certain habituation, and others in other ways. (*NE* 1.7 1098a26–1098b4)

It is commonly and, as I will argue, incorrectly assumed that this passage is a second discussion of the kind of imprecision discussed in 1.3, the imprecision due to the type of subject matter ethics involves. Myles F. Burnyeat, for example, states about this passage, "The search for a satisfactory specification of happiness and the good for man has just been completed, and Aristotle is reflecting on the extent to which he should claim precision and proof for his answer: it has the status of 'the that' merely, and, being general, no more precision than the subject matter allows." He does not mention the imprecision due to the kind of inquiry engaged in (1980, pp. 70–73). Klein cites this passage as an example of subject matter imprecision and says in explication of it, "Aristotle believes that ethical rules or principles can, at best, be only generally or roughly true (*NE* 1094b11, 1098a26–33) because the subject matter is variable (changeable), i.e., capable of being otherwise" (1988, 63). Irwin discusses the 1.3 passage but does not even mention the 1.7 passage in his discussion of why according to him ethics cannot be a demonstrative science (1981, 201–206). Stephen G. Salkever, in his discussion of the necessary imprecision of social science according to Aristotle, cites both passages dealing with the imprecision due to the subject matter of ethics but does not cite the 1.7 passage on the imprecision due to the type of inquiry engaged in (1990, 93–94).

There is some scholarly divergence, however. Roche sees that this passage on imprecision, unlike the other two passages, has as its point that the reason that ethics, and political science more generally, is imprecise is that its goal is action of a certain type, not theory:

> The branch of philosophy under which Aristotle places his inquiry in the *Ethics* is *politikē*. But *politikē*, according to Aristotle does not even belong in the same general area of knowledge as metaphysics: *politikē* is a *practical* science, the goal of which is to evoke certain types of conduct, while metaphysics is a *theoretical* science, the goal of which is a true and precise account of reality. . . . (1988, 54)

Roche mentions this passage as part of his argument, against Irwin, that ethics does not have a metaphysical foundation (1988, 54–55). As mentioned earlier, though Roche is in my view right to suggest that appeal to metaphysical principles is unnecessary to justify claims made in ethics, nonetheless appeal to them could be, and I think is, necessary for full articulation of and understanding of claims made in ethics.

Theodore James Tracy notes in the most unambiguous way, that there is a type of imprecision in ethics that results from the type of inquiry ethics is and, as well, that it is eliminated in other inquiries. According to Tracy, for Aristotle, the precision of each type of inquiry *(methodos)* is limited by the purpose of the type of inquiry: "He holds that each discipline should consider the matter and form of its objects only up to a certain point, i.e. in so far as necessary for its purpose." Ethics has a practical, not scientific, goal. Its goal is "the practical guidance of human action" rather than "a profound scientific analysis of it." Hence, though precision regarding moral excellence and moral activity is possible, it is left to Aristotle's more technical scientific treatises: "The *Nicomachean Ethics*, therefore, deliberately refrains from discussing the nature of moral excellence in all its physiological and psychological details, leaving these to the more technical scientific treatises (e.g., the *Physics*, the biological works, the *De Anima, Parva Naturalia, De Motu Animalium*)" (1969, 223–225).

Still, in the most recent and detailed discussion of Aristotle's methodology in ethics, Georgios Anagnostopoulos argues that both the inexactness due to the subject matter of ethics and the inexactness due to the goals of ethics are probably ineliminable, the former because it is based on the nature of the subject matter itself (1994, 339–340), the latter because if we change the goal of a discipline we no longer have the same discipline since things that have a function or goal are defined in terms of their function or goal (1994, 354–355). Moreover, he finds this result to be highly problematic since, following Plato we can say that "it is more important to know exactly how things are about matters of conduct, about what we must do or be" than about subjects assigned to theoretical disciplines since the consequences of having inexact knowledge about matters of conduct "can . . . be grave: we may be led astray and harmed" (1994, 356).

Roche, Tracy, and Anagnostopoulos agree that ethics for Aristotle involves 'inquiry imprecision' but disagree on the broader implications of this. Roche believes it implies a justificatory independence of ethics from metaphysics; Tracy that despite the inquiry imprecision involved in ethics, more profound scientific analysis of human action and virtue is possible and carried out at least in part in other works; Anagnostopoulos that it is logically impossible for Aristotle to make ethics more precise and that this result is ethically problematic. In this section, I shall argue for a position similar to Tracy's.

It is important to note that in the passage from 1.7, Aristotle mentions two different types of imprecision in ethics and that, though in it he does refer to the imprecision due to the type of subject matter involved in ethics, what he actually discusses is a second imprecision to which ethics is subject, the imprecision due to the kind of inquiry at hand, namely, practical inquiry, the goal of which is not contemplation but good action. We must seek, he says, "the precision that accords with the subject matter in each case" (the first imprecision) "and the degree that is appropriate to the inquiry" (the second). He goes on to explain the second imprecision by comparing ethics to carpentry:

> A carpenter and a geometer seek the right angle differently as well; the carpenter seeks it as far as is useful for his task, while the geometer seeks what and what sort of thing the right angle is, since he is a contemplator of truth. One must act the same way in other cases, then, so that digressions not become more important than the task at hand.

As the carpenter inquires about the right angle only to the degree that is useful to his task, not to the degree required by the theoretical nature of geometry and not so far as to ask about it *what sort of thing it is*, so practical inquiry ("other cases") is limited by its task. The limitation is further explicated: "Nor must one demand the cause similarly in all cases, but it is sufficient in some cases to exhibit the 'that' beautifully, for example, concerning principles, and the 'that' is a first and a principle." As the carpenter need only know *that*, say, the angle-sum of a triangle is equal to two right angles, since that is all that is required for his productive task of building a table or house, so the student of politics need only know *that*, say, virtue comes from habit, since that is all he needs for his task, namely, the practical task of becoming good or of making the citizens good. As the carpenter need not know *why* the angle-sum of a triangle equals two right angles (the cause, the proof) for his productive task, so the student of politics need not know *why* virtue comes from habit for his practical task. We can name the practical task, though Aristotle himself does not name it in this passage, since he does name it elsewhere. In 2.2 and 1.9, he makes it clear that the task is to become or make the citizens good: "the present inquiry is not for the sake of contemplation like the others (for we inquire not in order to know what virtue is but in order to become good, since otherwise the inquiry would be of no benefit)" (*NE* 2.2 1103b26–29); "political science bestows most of its care on making the citizens of a certain character, namely, good and capable of beautiful deeds" (*NE* 1.9 1099b29–32).[11]

There is further support for the claim that the imprecision due to the type of inquiry ethics is is the eliminable imprecision of *that* claims in comparison with *why* claims or *what it is* claims. Let us look first at a variety of discussions of *that* claims versus *why* claims.

'That' claims vs. 'why' claims: As mentioned in the introduction to this chapter, according to Aristotle in the *Posterior Analytics*, a science is more precise than another science and prior to it if that same science concerns the 'that' and the 'why', not the 'that' separately from the 'why'.[12] Practical inquiry, like carpentry, is imprecise inquiry which asserts *that* certain claims are true, not precise inquiry which asserts *why* they are true. (Or, more precisely, practical inquiry is largely like carpentry, staying away from more precise claims about cause as much as possible.) As Aristotle says in the *Metaphysics* (somewhat obscurely but clearly enough for our purposes), "For the end of contemplative inquiry is truth while the end of practical inquiry is action. For even if they consider how things stand, practical people do not contemplate the cause in itself, but what is in relation to something and now. But we do not know truth without the cause" (*Met.* 2.1 993b20–24).

Another passage in which Aristotle states that discussion about cause is to be avoided in practical philosophy is one of two passages in the *Nicomachean Ethics* in which he describes the desired student of politics. He begins by asking whether the inquiry he and his listeners are engaged in is one from or to principles: "But let it not escape us that there is a difference between arguments from principles and to principles. Indeed, Plato did well when he puzzled at this and sought whether the way is from principles or to them, just as one seeks in the stadium whether the way is the one from the judges to the finish or back again" (*NE* 1.4 1095a30–b1). The reference to Plato suggests that what Aristotle is asking so far is whether ethics is a demonstrative ('from principles') or dialectical ('to principles') inquiry, that is, is it (to use the terminology of *Top.* 1.1–2) an inquiry whose premises are true, primitive, immediate, and causal or one whose premises are reputable opinions from which conclusions that are true, primitive, immediate, and causal may be derived. He goes on and answers the question in what follows: "For it is necessary to begin from the known, but this is said in two ways. For some things are known to us and others known simply. Perhaps then it is necessary for us, at least, to begin with the things known by us" (*NE* 1.4 1095b2–4). Ethics utilizes, then, the procedure typical of dialectic, beginning with what we know and moving toward what can be known in itself or simply. Aristotle continues by discussing the desired student:

> Hence, the one who is to listen sufficiently to speeches concerning the beautiful and just and in general concerning political subjects must have been brought up in beautiful habits. For the 'that' is the principle and if it should appear sufficiently, there will be no additional need for the 'why'. Such a person either has such principles or can get them. (*NE* 1.4 1095b4–8)

Here Aristotle uses the term 'principle' in a way different than he uses it in the beginning of this passage, where it means 'first principle', that is, as stated above, one that is true, primitive, immediate, and causal. Here Aristotle shifts to the principles at the other end—to what is first for us not what is first in itself, to the 'that' not the 'why'. David Ross, in order to make the distinction between types of principle evident in his translation itself, translates *'archē'* in this part of the quotation as 'starting point' rather than what he uses in the earlier portion of the passage, namely, 'principle'. The one who has been brought up in beautiful habits will have 'starting point' principles—or, if not, will be able to get them.

The passage is routinely understood by recent interpreters so that the 'that' is a starting point and the 'why' is the fleshed-out definition of the human good in which the ethics culminates. The problem with this understanding of the passage is that Aristotle says that a student who has been appropriately reared will have the 'that' and so will have no need in addition of the 'why'. We would not want to say that the well-reared student will not need the fleshed out definition of the human good. For, if we did, we would be saying that no one who is a suitable listener to Aristotle's lectures on ethics will need the knowledge in which they culminate.

To preserve contemporary interpretations, we could say, alternatively, that the students will not need the 'why' at the beginning of the lectures.[13] The argument could go as follows, 'The well-reared student will have the "that." Full articulation of the "that" would lead to the "why" in which the ethics culminates.' A relevant comparison would be to a discussion of how to define circles. For someone to be an appropriate participant in such a discussion, they must first see *that* some figures are circles. They are then prepared to move to knowledge of *what a circle is*.

This is a true and important claim about the well-reared student (that their knowledge of *that* claims prepares them for future knowledge of *what* and *why* claims) and is one we will need to come back to. However, it is not Aristotle's point in this passage. Aristotle does not say that the well-reared student will not need the 'why' at the beginning. Instead, on the most plausible interpretation, Aristotle says that (1) the well-reared student has, or easily can get, knowledge of some starting points, namely, knowledge of some *that* claims; (2) knowledge of these starting points (or, ease of attaining knowledge of them) will eliminate the need a student otherwise would have for knowledge of certain *why* claims; (3) inquiry aiming at knowledge of those *why* claims would be digressive since we must begin with what is known to us. According to Aristotle, the well-reared student will have or easily be able to get starting points (viz., *that* claims) and, as a result of having them, will not need the 'why' in addition.

It is more plausible to maintain that knowledge of the *why* claims is not needed by ethics at all and that the well-reared student's knowledge of the *that* claims for some reason eliminates a need he otherwise would have for knowledge of those *why* claims. This interpretation implies that ethics is going to stay on the level of the 'that' (or, more precisely, stays on the level of the 'that' as much as possible). Can this interpretation be squared with Aristotle's suggestion that ethics is a dialectical inquiry starting with what is known to us ('starting points', 'thats') and moving toward what is known in itself ('principles', 'whys', 'whats')?

It can if we make two suppositions: (1) the 'why' the student's fine upbringing will eliminate the need for is not the fleshed-out definition of the human good in which ethics culminates; (2) ethics moves in the direction of but intentionally stops short of knowledge of certain first principles. In accord with these suppositions, let us say that the 'why' the student will not need in addition will be causal explanations of a variety of claims made in ethics including causal explanations of propositions that comprise some of the premises of ethical argumentation and, in addition, the causal explanation of the fleshed-out definition of the human good that is the conclusion of ethical argumentation. The inquiry is a dialectical one because it begins with what is known to us, moves *in the direction of* what is known in itself, though it does not go all the way to those first principles.

In other words, the starting points for argument to the answer to the question, what is the human good, will be propositions that assert *that* something is true without asserting *why* it is true. Someone who has been well reared (the meaning of this will be explicated in chapter 5, sections 2–6) will understand *that* certain claims are true and, as a result, will not ask *why* they are. Ethical inquiry culminates in a fleshed-out answer to the question, What is the human good? The answer is a *that* claim not a *why* claim—as it must be if ethics is to remain imprecise. Ethical inquiry can be supplemented by appropriate *why* claims (as well as appropriate *what* claims). When it is, the movement to what is known in itself is complete. Once that movement is complete, demonstration can take place. Ethics, then, is the first part of an at least two-part dialectical movement to first principles; once the first principles are reached, demonstrative knowledge can proceed from them.

The well-reared student's knowledge of *that* claims, then, is preparatory for knowledge of *why* and *what* claims. However, that future knowledge is achieved outside of ethics itself and not all those who are prepared will want or need to seek it, just as recognition of circles is preparatory for defining them though some of those who recognize circles will have no desire or need to define them.

It seems likely that what Aristotle is suggesting in the 1.4 passage as a whole is the psychologically acute claim that often people who ask why a claim is true are those who do not know or accept that it is true. An example from the ethics itself will both show this and, as well, provide an example of a proposition in the ethics that stays at the level of the 'that' and not the 'why'. (Our first example, mentioned in the introduction to this chapter, was the claim *that* final good is equivocal.) The example is the important claim that virtue comes from habit.

Though Aristotle gives two causal arguments that virtue is not by nature (since nothing that exists by nature can form a habit contrary to its nature and since regarding things that come to us by nature we first acquire the potentiality and later exhibit the activity), both his arguments that, instead, virtue comes from habit are noncausal. We know that virtue comes from habit, first, from what legislators do, namely, make citizens good by instilling good habits in them. We know that virtue comes from habit, secondly, from the fact that this is how every virtue, as well as every art, is both produced and destroyed. Aristotle does not tell us what goes on in, say, our souls during the habituation process that causes us to become virtuous as a result of doing virtuous acts. Nor does he tell us, say, what is true about the nature or form of our soul or the nature or form of virtue such that habituation in the sorts of acts that virtue requires results in a settled and developed disposition to do those sorts of acts. It is likely that giving an account of these things would take a good amount of time. So, from the standpoint of the purpose of ethics—to become good or make the citizens good—it is better to utilize claims that rely on experience rather than on causal reasoning: 'virtue comes from habit, for statesmen make their citizens good from habit', 'virtue comes from habit, for all the virtues and vices as well as the arts come from like habits' (*NE* 2.1 1103a19–1103b2). If we are aware from experience *that* statesmen make their citizens good from habit, then we do not need, for practical purposes, to know why.

Note, though, that someone who had been raised so that he or she had never had the experience of a repeated act done out of self-discipline or shame or the discipline of others eventually resulting in a disposition to do that type of act without being disciplined or shamed into doing it but instead doing it because one enjoys doing it—such a person might simply not accept the claim that a virtue comes from habit. Why would anyone ever, this person might ask, come to enjoy facing danger or limiting their food intake? Why not, instead, immediately when one can avoid danger and eat whatever is pleasant? Note how easily one slips from the question whether something is true (whether people acquire virtue from a like habit) to the question why. A person who has had the experience is less likely to ask the question why though in fact it is an interesting and difficult question.

To be more certain about the view that ethics stays on the level of the 'that' not the 'why' as much as possible, we need more examples from the ethics of 'that' claims not accompanied by 'why' claims. So far, we have seen two: the claim that virtue comes from habit and the claim that final good is equivocal (discussed in this chapter's introduction).

Another argument that stays on the level of the 'that' rather than the 'why' is an argument for the central claim that contemplative activity is perfect happiness. We say the gods are blessed and happy. What do the gods do? *Action (praxis):* As the following examples show (and all others would show), a life of actions would be trivial and unworthy of the gods. It would be absurd to suppose they do just acts such as making contracts and paying debts. Brave acts—facing fears and dangers because doing so is beautiful? Generous acts? To whom? It would be absurd to suppose they have money or things of that sort. It would be gross to praise them as temperate since they do not have bad desires. *Nonaction:* We all suppose that they live. Therefore, they are active and do not sleep like Endymion. *Production:* If we take away from a living being action and, even more, production . . . *Contemplation:* what remains other than contemplation? (*NE* 10.8 1178b7–21).

Of course, we know that Aristotle has an extended argument for the claim that the god is a contemplator elsewhere. In the *Metaphysics*, the god is defined as thinking of thinking *(noēsis noēseōs)*. The god must be active but must not move, since motion involves potentiality and therefore imperfection (*Met.* 12.7, 12.9). Moreover, the object of the god's activity must not be something other than the god, since then the god would be dependent and not perfect (*Met.* 12.9). Similarly, the object of the god's activity must not be better than the god, since then again the god would not be perfect (*Met.* 12.9). Hence, the god must be the object of the god's own activity. Pure thought *(noēsis)* is action without motion or any kind of imperfection. Hence, the god is pure thought of pure thought *(noēsis noēseōs)* (*Met.* 12.9).[14]

Two things are evident when we compare these two arguments. First, it is clear that the *Metaphysics* argument is the more precise argument in Aristotle's sense. For it both utilizes primary principles (perfection/completion, activity, potentiality) and, in addition, it explains why: Why is god a contemplator? Because god is perfect and contemplation is perfect activity. The *Nicomachean Ethics* argument does not utilize primary principles. Instead, it utilizes claims about what is bad (gross, bad, trivial), namely, feeling fear, having bad desires, sleeping rather than doing anything, producing things—claims which, according to Aristotle, are true but not primary. It also does not explain the cause by virtue of which god is a contemplator. The god cannot do a number of bad actions and the only type of action that is left after those have been mentioned is contemplation. Aristotle does not even explain the cause by virtue of which production, according to him, is bad (viz., because it involves matter which is imperfect). It is apparent to any well-reared Athenian that making things is laborious and to be avoided if possible. Surely, the god does not engage in laborious activity. Much less does Aristotle explain the cause by virtue of which the god's activity is contemplation (because it is pure activity involving no matter or imperfection).

Second, it is reasonable to suppose that, for Aristotle, each argument is valid and sound (supposing we allow for an enthymematic quality). The *Nicomachean Ethics* argument utilizes his audience's correct intuitions or perceptions about what is good and what is not and, from them along with a valid argument by elimination form, comes to his conclusion. The *Metaphysics* argument is not better due to validity or soundness. It is not 'more correct'. Instead, it is more fundamental and, as a result, explanatory. When we think about it, we can articulate his audience's correct intuitions (correct according to Aristotle, anyway). They all have to do with good and bad, where good means complete or perfect and bad incomplete or imperfect. The *Metaphysics* argument does not correct the *Nicomachean Ethics* argument. It does not correct the perceptions on which it is based (any more than the definition of 'circle' corrects the perceptions of circles on which it is based). Instead, it articulates them more fully. It gives them depth.

Someone might argue against my view that ethics stays away from discussions of cause as much as possible by adducing a passage from the *Eudemian Ethics* and interpreting it to say that the study of cause is just as relevant to ethics as to any other domain. To the contrary, I maintain that the passage at issue, read in context, does not provide a basis for refuting the position being maintained in this section, but instead supports the position exactly. The relevant passage, out of context, is the following:

> And in every inquiry, arguments said philosophically are different than arguments said non-philosophically. As a result, we must not deem theoretical study of the sort that makes evident not only the 'what' but also the 'why' to be a digression even for the student of politics. For such [a way of proceeding] is the philosophical [way of proceeding] in every inquiry. (*EE* 1.6 1216b35–39)

By itself, this passage does seem to refute my view that in political science, Aristotle thinks we should stay away from discussions of cause for the most part. However, the 'even' in "we must not deem theoretical study of the sort that makes evident not only the 'what' but also the 'why' to be a digression even for the student of politics" suggests that Aristotle's claim needs to be seen in context. For it could imply that we do in fact have reason to see discussions of cause as digressive for the student of politics, but that Aristotle wants us to know that even for this student, such discussions are not entirely digressive. What Aristotle says next gives support for this interpretation:

> Nevertheless, there is need for much caution in this. For since to say nothing at random but with argument is to seem philosophic, some people often escape notice when they give arguments foreign to the subject being discussed and vain (and at one time they do this due to ignorance and at another due to imposture), as a result of which it happens that even people who are experienced and able in practice are captured by these people who neither have nor are able at constructive or practical thought. And this happens to them due to lack of education. For it is lack of education concerning each subject to be unable to distinguish arguments appropriate to the subject from those that are foreign to it. (*EE* 1.6 1216b40–17a9)

Here Aristotle indicates that, though introducing theoretical discussion, including discussion of cause, into political study is not always a digression, still it must be done with caution. For, it is easy to find that in introducing it, one has in fact digressed and that experienced and practical people, who, Aristotle seems to suggest, have constructive and practical thought, will be led to digress by people who do not have it. Aristotle goes on in the final portion of the passage to claim once again that it is beneficial to distinguish discussions of the 'why' from discussions of the 'that':

> It is fine, too, to distinguish separately the statement of cause and what is demonstrated, both due to what was just said, that it is unnecessary in regard to all things to attend to arguments but often rather to attend to phenomena (while now when people are not able to resolve [an argument] they are compelled to trust what has been said), and because often something that seems to have been proved from argument is true but is not true because of the cause stated in the argument. For it is possible to show truth through falsehood, as is clear from the *Analytics*. (*EE* 1.6 1217a10–17)

He gives, here, two reasons for separating the two topics. First, sometimes it is better to consider phenomena than argument. For, when people cannot fully resolve something that seems problematic in an argument, they are compelled to accept the argument. Second, one can argue for a true conclusion but adduce the wrong cause for the conclusion's being true.

Presumably Aristotle's point in the first case is that when an experienced or practical person cannot find a resolution to something that seems problematic in an argument, they are as a result forced to give up their belief in a true claim the truth of which they found through consideration of phenomena. They are aware, from practical experience, that a certain claim is true. However, the argument, though seemingly problematic, indicates that the claim is not true. Hence, they are in a position in which they must give up a claim that they have good practical, experiential, phenomenological reason to hold, because the argument suggests that they should.

A simple example from the history of philosophy would be Zeno's arguments that motion and plurality are impossible. It is hard to resolve the problems involved in Zeno's arguments. Still, ought one thus to give up one's experientially based belief that motion and plurality are in fact possible?

An example from Aristotle's ethics would be the claim that virtue comes from habit. Suppose, again, that someone who had not been brought up in beautiful habits asked the question, Why would repeated experiences of facing fear or of denying oneself some desirable food or drink result in their coming to take pleasure in doing such unpleasurable acts? (The claim might be something more like the following: "If I never see another football field again, it will be too soon.") A person who is cognizant, from experience (either their own or that of others), of the fact that doing such acts repeatedly often does result in a disposition to do them with pleasure may find they have no answer. The fact, however, that they have no answer, does not mean that their experiential claim is false. Clearly, resolving the problem will take some time—more time, to paraphrase, than is useful for the purposes of ethics.

Another example relevant to ethics would be a parent who is experienced and able at the practical task of childrearing. Suppose that this parent's childrearing technique involves some discipline and punishment. Suppose someone argues that children are by nature good and so one ought to raise them by leaving them alone and allowing their natural goodness to come out. The parent may find it difficult to argue against this view, and so might be inclined to give up the successful technique. It would be more difficult if the parent involved shared the view—one that is perhaps false—that children are naturally good. It would be even more difficult if the one making the argument added the claim that childrearing techniques that involve discipline and punishment imply the claim that children are evil by nature. If so, the able but concerned parent might respond, then I must stop raising my children in this way since I certainly do not believe they are evil by nature.

Aristotle's second point is an interesting one. It is of course true that one can argue for a true conclusion but adduce false causes for its being true. One example Aristotle gives of this is: 'A human being is a stone. A stone is an animal. Therefore, a human being is an animal' (*Pr. An.* 2.11 53b30–35).

A slight variation on the last example will show the importance of this second point. Suppose again a parent who is experienced and able at childrearing whose childrearing technique involves some discipline and punishment. Suppose someone comes along and argues that discipline and punishment are good childrearing technique since children are naturally evil and discipline and punishment constrain their natural evil. The parent, appalled at utilizing a technique intended for evil creatures since he or she does not believe children are evil creatures, abandons the technique and begins just letting the children follow their impulses, since this seems more suited to creatures who are not evil. In this case, one could argue that the conclusion is true, but that a false cause is adduced for it being true, since, one could argue, children are not evil but undeveloped by nature and discipline and punishment are sometimes appropriate as an aide in their development. Aristotle's point, plausibly, is that a bad argument for a true claim might lead a practical person to give up the claim due to disagreement with the argument.

In further support for the claim that the imprecision due to the type of inquiry ethics is the eliminable imprecision of *that* claims in comparison with *why* claims or *what it is* claims, let us now look at discussions of *that* claims versus *what is it* claims.

'That' claims vs. 'what is it' claims: If we go back to the *Nicomachean Ethics* 1.7 passage regarding inquiry imprecision, we recall that Aristotle says, "A carpenter and a geometer seek the right angle differently as well; the carpenter seeks it as far as is useful for his task, while the geometer seeks what and what sort of thing the right angle is, since he is a contemplator of truth." The carpenter, here used as an analogue to the student of political science, does not inquire into what something is. Are there examples in the ethics in which Aristotle could discuss what something is but does not? Are there, as a result, more examples of imprecision in the ethics that Aristotle does not eliminate in the ethics but could or perhaps does eliminate elsewhere? To see that the answer is 'yes', we need only consider the various well-known passages in which Aristotle redirects his discussion away from metaphysics and from other branches of study such as physics and psychology on the grounds that the precision provided by them is more than is needed for our purposes.

For example, after discussing the equivocity of the good in 1.6, Aristotle says that a more precise account of it is more appropriate to another part of philosophy: 'Perhaps, though, these subjects must be left for now since precise treatment of them would be more appropriate to another [part of] philosophy' (*NE* 1.6 1096b30–31). The subject he has been considering in the chapter as a whole is the good—not the human good but good in general, what it is, or, as he puts it, "the universal good" *(to katholou beltion)*. He concludes that good is equivocal, moreover, that it is analogically equivocal as he argues briefly by example. The examples used suggest, as I have shown, that good is eqivocal by analogy because good means *telos* and *telos* is equivocal by analogy. If so, the other part of philosophy to which the precise treatment is deferred is metaphysics, specifically, the part of metaphysics in which *telos* is discussed, namely, Book 9 of the *Metaphysics*. In the ethics, Aristotle never gives the more precise account of what the good is. The more precise account is possible, however, and is carried out there.

In the *Nicomachean Ethics* 1.13 discussion of the human soul, Aristotle asserts that we students of politics ought to study the soul but only to the extent sufficient for our purpose of making the citizens good and obedient to the laws (*NE* 1.13 1102a9–10) or of engendering human happiness (*NE* 1.13 1102a14–15): "Then the student of politics must study the soul and must study it for the sake of these things and to the extent sufficient for what is sought. For greater precision perhaps is more laborious than belongs to the matters at hand" (*NE* 1.13 1102a23–26). He proceeds to discuss the rational and irrational parts of the soul and the type of virtue that is appropriate to each part. He does not discuss what the soul is or what it is like any further. He gives a more precise account of what the soul is and is like, of course, in *De Anima*, where he defines it and discusses its various powers. He also gives a more precise account of how virtue completes both the emotional and intellectual parts of the soul in *Physics* 7.3 (*Phys.* 7.3 246a10–248a9). Arguably, either or both of these passages provide the more precise account here alluded to. The more precise account, then, is possible and is carried out.

In *Nicomachean Ethics* 10.4, Aristotle discusses what pleasure is, as part of his discussion of whether pleasure is the human good. His aim in the chapter is, first, to show that the best activity is the activity of the best faculty in relation to the best of its objects and thus to show that the best life as he describes it in the rest of the ethics is also the most pleasant life. By doing so, he defeats the hedonist by, in effect, being a better hedonist than the hedonist. To do so, he must distinguish pleasure from movement. "We have discussed movement precisely in another place," he says (*NE* 10.4 1174b2–3), and then goes on to say that pleasure is and movement is not complete at every moment since the place from which and the place to which give movements their form. The more precise account of movement is found in *Physics* 3.1–3. There, he says what movement is, namely, actuality of potential just as potential (*Phys.* 3.2 202a7–8). He could have argued more precisely: 'Movement is actuality of potential just as potential. What is actual just as potential is not complete. Hence, movement is not complete'. Such an argument is more precise, because it explains *why* movement is not complete. But, the first premise is so precise as to be digressive in virtually any audience.

In *Nicomachean Ethics* 10.8, as part of his argument that the contemplative life is the best human life, Aristotle puts off the discussion of intellectual insight *(nous)*, the faculty we utilize in contemplating, to another place. The practical life is good in a secondary way, since it has to do with emotions and the body, and its virtues have to do with our composite nature as well. The virtue that belongs to the contemplative life, does not: "The virtue of intellectual insight *(nous)* is separated [from the composite].[15] Let us speak only to this extent about it. For to treat it precisely would be more than belongs to what is at hand" (*NE* 1178a22–23). This passage is part of the passage discussed earlier regarding the god as contemplator. An account of it would follow the same lines as that account. It would lead us to Book 12 and to related sections of the *Metaphysics*.

The imprecision due to the type of inquiry ethics is, then, can be, and in part is, eliminated. It is eliminated by supplementing *that* claims found in ethics by *why* claims and *what is it* claims found in metaphysics, physics, and psychology. As a result, it is once again evident that ethics can be read on two levels: it can be read in terms of its own imprecise but fully justified *that* claims and it can be read in terms of the more precise *why* and *what is it* claims found in metaphysics, physics, and psychology, claims the consideration of which gives Aristotle's ethics greater articulation or depth.

3

The goal of this chapter is to show that, according to Aristotle, the argument of the ethics requires for its full articulation appeal to extra-ethical principles found in metaphysics, physics, and psychology. Support for the claim has come from examination of the two types of imprecision in the ethics. One type, the imprecision due to the type of inquiry ethics is (practical inquiry the goal of which is good practice rather than precise knowledge), is not eliminated in the ethics, but can be eliminated by appeal to principles found in metaphysics, physics, and psychology.

The other cannot be eliminated but is explained in part by appeal to principles found in metaphysics. In each case, appeal to the relevant extra-ethical principles gives greater articulation and depth to the argument of the ethics.

As we have seen, however, Anagnostopoulos draws different conclusions, ones that conflict with the argument of this chapter: that the inexactness due to the goals of ethics is probably ineliminable; that this is highly problematic because we might be led astray and harmed by inexact knowledge of what we must do or be. It is important to respond to these two conclusions.

Regarding the first, Anagnostopoulos considers two alternative ways of overcoming the imprecision, either by making two distinct disciplines out of ethics, one that is practical and imprecise and one that is theoretical and precise (1994, 361), or by making the ethics itself precise which is impossible, according to him, since ethics then could not achieve its practical goal and ethics is defined in terms of its goal (1994, 354, 355). There is a third alternative, however, which Anagnostopoulos does not consider, namely, that the more precise account is found in a variety of Aristotle's other disciplines—specifically, in metaphysics, physics, and psychology. We can suggest, then, that the analogy 'ethics is to some other study as carpentry is to geometry' is filled out not by mention of one other study but three. The fact that this three-part study is not called 'ethics' or 'higher-order ethics' need not be significant.

The reason ethics is made more precise in three sciences rather than one, I suggest, is that ethics answers the question, What is the human good? Good is defined as *telos* and its variants. Hence a more precise account of the human good is one that includes a more precise account of good, an account found in the *Metaphysics*, particularly in the discussions of the transcategorial division of being into *dynamis* and *energeia* (*energeia* being a close equivalent of *telos*). Human being is a natural being whose form is its soul. Hence more precise discussion of human being is found in physics and psychology. Human good is not a genus since 'good' is not generic but transgeneric. Hence the more precise account of human good would be found not in one but at least two other disciplines—at least one (and, it turns out, two) for 'human' and one, the one in which transgenerics are discussed, for 'good'.

Anagnostopoulos's second conclusion is fundamentally mistaken. He believes that imprecision in ethics is highly problematic since if our knowledge about matters of conduct is 'inexact', we might be led astray or harmed. This concern would have merit if imprecise knowledge were incorrect in some way but the examples we have looked at do not suggest any such incorrectness. For example, for Aristotle the imprecise argument that god is a contemplator, is (allowing for enthymemes) valid and sound. It simply is not fundamental and explanatory. What we lack, when we lack the *Metaphysics* argument that god is a contemplator, is not truth understood as correspondence. Instead, what we lack is truth understood as full understanding. When Aristotle says in the *Ethics* or the *Metaphysics* that practical philosophy does not seek knowledge or truth but good action, he means 'knowledge' in the strong sense: not merely a conclusion drawn from a valid argument with true premises but from a valid argument with true premises that are fundamental and explanatory. In addition, he means 'truth' in the sense of the full understanding of something.

In *Metaphysics* 9.10, Aristotle distinguishes between two kinds of truth. One who thinks the separated is separated or the combined is combined has the truth regarding things that are composite. The opposite of this sort of truth is error (*Met.* 9.10 1051b2–5). For example, one who thinks the wood is white when the wood in fact is white has the truth, one who thinks the diagonal of a square is incommensurable since it is incommensurable has the truth (*Met.* 9.10 1051b20–21). With regard to noncomposite things, truth is contact *(thigein)* and saying *(phanai)* and the opposite is not error but ignorance where ignorance is noncontact (*Met.* 9.10 1051b23–25). Aristotle contrasts 'saying' *(phasis)* with 'assertion' *(kataphasis)* (*Met.* 9.10 1051b24–25). In the case of composite things, we make assertions: the wood is white; the diagonal is incommensurable. To assert is to say something about something. In the case of noncomposite or primary things, assertion is not possible, only a mere saying is. A saying indicates that we have taken the thing in, touched it, grasped it, contacted it. The opposite of that is simply not to have taken it in, not to have grasped it. For, Aristotle says, it is not possible to be in error either about the 'what it is' or about noncomposite substances or actualities but only to intuit *(noein)* them or not to intuit them (*Met.* 9.10 1051b25–32).

The claim that perfect happiness is contemplation is an assertion—a true assertion, according to Aristotle. Therefore, the more and less precise arguments for it have the truth in that sense. To say that the more precise argument has the truth and the less precise does not must mean, then, that the more precise argument involves the grasp of some primary or noncomposite principles—some 'whats'—the grasp of which is lacking in the less precise argument, namely, as I have said, the principles actuality, potentiality, and perfection/completion.

Further evidence for the claim that the imprecision that results from the fact that ethics is inquiry with a practical goal does not lead to incorrectness, falsehood, or error of some kind is Aristotle's claim that the one who has experience rather than knowledge in the strong sense is more not less able in practice than the one who has knowledge: "On account of this, some who do not know, especially those who have experience, are more practical than others who know; for one who knew that light meats are digestible and healthy, but did not know which sorts of meat are light, would not produce health, but one who knows that chicken is light and healthy is more likely to produce health" (*NE* 6.7 1141b16–21).[16]

The one who knows *that* chicken is light and healthy is more likely to produce health than the one who knows *why* (light meats are healthy because they are digestible). Though he lacks precise knowledge (knowledge of cause), the practice will be well-guided by the knowledge he has. Hence, greater precision does not imply greater correctness.[17] Knowledge of the 'that', then, will not harm us or lead us astray.

In addition, the *Eudemian Ethics* passages on the 'what' and the 'why' suggest a concern that is in a way the opposite of Anagnostopoulos's concern, namely, they suggest Aristotle's concern that certain types of pursuit of precise knowledge itself can lead us astray or harm us. Though, as we have seen, Aristotle has this concern, his grounds for it are importantly different than the grounds some others have for concern about the relation between theory and experience. His is not the concern of someone who believes that theory is so unlike experience that theoretical study destroys experiential knowledge and perception. Such a view is found in middle and late modern critiques of early modern theorizing such as the critiques given by Rousseau and Nietzsche and their followers. Early modern theory is an appropriate object of such attacks since according to it the world we experience is radically unlike the world theoretically and thus correctly understood.

For Aristotle, to the contrary, theory at its best does not correct experience but articulates it. So the dangers Aristotle sees sometimes accompanying theory are a different type. They are, first and crudely, dangers involved in the application not of good but of bad theorizing to experience, as in the example mentioned in the *Eudemian Ethics* passage of being influenced to change one's practice as a result of someone adducing a false cause. Secondly and more generally, they are the result of routinely accepting theory over experience, argument over phenomena, in cases of apparent conflict between them. Instead, according to Aristotle, theory and experience must harmonize. For, according to him, as we have seen, philosophical accounts must include not just arguments, but also explanations of how things appear to us (*NE* 1.8 1098b9–12, 7.14 1154a22–25).

Finally, Anagnostopoulos's ethical concern about ineliminable imprecision would have merit, in addition, if 'imprecise knowledge' were not based on argument. However, the examples we have looked at, such as the claim that virtue comes from habituation or that god is a contemplator, do not lack argument. This is crucial. To say that ethics is imprecise or that ethics stays as much as possible with *that* claims rather than *why* claims is not to say that ethics avoids argument. It is not to say that, in ethics, we tell people what is good without giving reasons for our assertions. Aristotle gives arguments—arguments he thinks are valid and sound—that virtue comes from habit and that god is a contemplator. What he does not give are fundamental and explanatory arguments. For Aristotle, ethics is fully justified. Hence its lack of precision is not ethically harmful.

Anagnostopoulos's two concerns, then, are not well-founded. The imprecision due to the type of inquiry ethics is can be, and at least in part is, eliminated in three other disciplines, metaphysics, physics, and psychology. Allowing this type of imprecision to remain in ethics is not problematic for practical life because it does not lack argument nor does it involve some type of error that could lead us astray in our most important choices and activities. These imprecise claims are not incorrect or unjustified. Instead, they are justified and correct but nonarticulate.

4

The idea that Aristotle's ethics stays as much as possible with claims that are true and justified but not fully articulated needs to be fleshed-out. I suggest we think of Aristotle's ethics as an 'experience-near' account of ethical matters. I borrow this term from contemporary clinical psychology in which a clinician might ask, 'Do you feel invaded by this person?' or 'Do you feel overwhelmed by this person?' rather than, more theoretically, 'Are you finding it difficult to synthesize self and other?' The clinician's question suggests a name that is close to the person's experience not an explanation of it in terms of the developmentally acquired ability to distinguish and connect feelings and perceptions of oneself with feelings and perceptions of an other. What it is to 'feel invaded' or 'feel overwhelmed' is to be unable to distinguish one's own feelings and perceptions from those of another so that one takes the other's feelings or perceptions as one's own without being fully aware that one is doing so. The client is more likely simply to experience himself or herself as invaded or overwhelmed. The clinician's questions are intended to capture the client's experience. They are meant to be experience-near.

Similarly, I suggest that Aristotle's ethics is meant to be an experience-near account of the human good. Perhaps I should say 'experience-near' or 'perception-near', since Aristotle uses these and related terms loosely in the ethics. The reason for experience-near accounts in each case is similar. For the clinician to discuss theory with the client would be digressive. The client need not understand the stages of development of the self (e.g., synthesis of self and other, synthesis of good and bad) to make progress. Similarly, for Aristotle, we need not have theoretical understanding of the human good to become good or to make the citizens good. Neither *phronimoi* nor statesmen need to be metaphysicians.

To see that Aristotle intends the ethics to be an experience-near account not a theoretical account, let us consider again his 1.7 comparison of practical philosophy, including ethics, to carpentry:

> One must recall the things said before and not seek precision similarly in all things, but the precision that accords with the subject matter in each case and the degree that is appropriate to the inquiry. For a carpenter and a geometer seek the right angle differently as well; the carpenter seeks it as far as is useful for his task, while the geometer seeks what and what sort of thing the right angle is, since he is a contemplator of truth. One must act the same way in other cases, then, so that digressions not become more important than the task at hand. Nor must one demand the cause similarly in all cases, but it is sufficient in some cases to exhibit the 'that' beautifully, for example, concerning principles, and the 'that' is a first and a principle. Some principles are seen by induction, some by perception, others by a certain habituation, and others in other ways. (*NE* 1.7 1098a26–1098b4)

As we have seen, one of Aristotle's points in this passage is that there is a type of imprecision in ethics that is due to the type of inquiry ethics is. Ethics is like carpentry in limiting its inquiry to the 'that' not the cause (the 'why') or the 'what is it'. Carpentry is correlated and contrasted with geometry which is a theoretical inquiry into 'why' and 'what is it'. The passage suggests that ethics, too, is correlated with some theoretical inquiry into the 'why' and the 'what is it'.

I have suggested that the more precise account of the human good is found not in one but three sciences, metaphysics, physics, and psychology. As a result, the theoretical correlate of ethics is not one but three as well. An experience-near account of the human good is made more precise, therefore, in three sciences, metaphysics, physics, and psychology.

Aristotle discusses disciplines related to each other in a manner comparable to the relation between carpentry and geometry in *Posterior Analytics* 1.13 (*Post. An.* 1.13 78b34–79a16). There, he refers to the discipline that treats the 'that' as being 'under' the discipline that treats the 'why'. More specifically, he says that when there are pairs of disciplines in which one of each pair is under the other, the first considers the 'that' and the second the 'why'; the practitioner of the first perceives while the practitioner of the second demonstrates causes. As examples of sciences that are under another he mentions the relation of harmonics to arithmetic, stargazing to astronomy, and, notably, optics and mechanics to geometry (plane and solid)—notably since it is reasonable to suppose that the relation of geometry to optics and mechanics is similar to the relation of geometry to carpentry. Extending the 1.7 analogy, then, we can say that ethics is like carpentry, and like optics, mechanics, harmonics, and stargazing: it is a perceptual study of the 'that' not a theoretical study of the 'why'. The stargazer, for example, discovers that the planets are located in a certain place. The astronomer explains why.

To show that this implies that ethics is an experience-near study, we need to see that Aristotle closely connects perception and experience. An earlier passage about astronomy, in the *Prior Analytics*, shows this. About astronomy, he says there:

> Thus it belongs to experience to give the principles of each subject. I mean, for example, that it belongs to astronomical experience to give the principles of astronomical science (for when the phenomena were grasped adequately, the astronomical demonstrations were discovered) and it is the same concerning any other art or science. So, if the properties of each subject are grasped, it will at once belong to us readily to exhibit the demonstrations. (*Pr. An.* 1.30 46a17–24)

Here, stargazing is called 'astronomical experience'. We can see, then, that it and the other disciplines he refers to as being 'under' another are broadly perceptual and experiential disciplines that consider the 'that' and have correlative theoretical disciplines that consider the 'why' and are demonstrative.

Aristotle's discussion of sciences that are under another is part of a general discussion of inquiry into the 'that' and the 'why'. In *Posterior Analytics* 1.13 Aristotle is contrasting cases in which the 'that' and the 'why' are discussed in the same science and cases in which they are discussed in different sciences, one of which is 'under' the other. Aristotle says there that one science is under another when the higher science makes use of forms: "These are those which being something different in substance make use of forms. For mathematics is about forms. For it is not said of something underlying. For even if geometrical objects are said of something underlying it is not *as* said of something underlying" (*Post. An.* 1.13 79a6–9). In the case of geometry and optics or mechanics, then, the science of the 'why' is separate and over the science of the 'that' because it is a science that is solely about geometrical forms and not about anything underlying, such as optical or mechanical phenomena. It can be said of them, but it need not be said of them and, in geometry, is not said of them. That is to say, we can ask about the geometrical properties of optical and mechanical phenomena but in geometry itself, we do not. Aristotle gives another example in what follows, the relation between medicine and geometry: the doctor knows *that* circular wounds heal more slowly; the geometer knows *why*. Presumably he has in mind that the geometer knows the properties of circles themselves, as forms, apart from physical instantiations, that is, he knows what and what sort of thing circles are, and so knows the cause by virtue of which circular wounds heal more slowly.

Similarly we can say, following out our analogy, that ethics is in Aristotle's sense 'under' metaphysics. Metaphysics is first philosophy. It is not said of anything underlying. It is, in that sense, about forms: about quality, quantity, matter, form/the beautiful, end/the good, and so forth. It is about what these are. It can be said of things underlying but need not be said of them and, in the study of metaphysics, is not said of them. We can, for example, discuss the form or end of human beings, animals, or plants. When we do, we may in some cases discover the answer to questions about cause, since, as mentioned in the introduction to this chapter, the universal can make clear the cause. When we know *what* good is, namely, *telos* or *energeia*, we know *why* it is equivocal by analogy.

The movement of the ethics, then, is movement from what is underlying to what is universal—but the study of what is universal is found outside the science of ethics itself. Aristotle echoes his *Nicomachean Ethics* discussion of this type of movement in the analytics. "Prior and more familiar" is said in two ways, he says in *Posterior Analytics* 1.2. There is what is prior and more familiar "by nature" or "simply." This is what is further away (viz., the universal, since the universal is furthest away). Secondly, there is what is prior or more familiar "in relation to us." This is what is nearer to perception (viz., particulars, since particulars are nearest) (*Post. An.* 1.2 71b33–72a5). In ethics, then, we are moving from what is prior for us to what is prior simply—but the study of what is prior simply is an extra-ethical study.

The idea that ethics is one of the sciences that are under another helps to counter a certain objection to my account that could be raised, namely, that by appealing to extra-ethical principles it violates Aristotle's rule that different sciences are autonomous. Roche makes this objection to Irwin's foundationalist interpretation of Aristotle's ethics. Roche maintains that the belief that the ethics has a metaphysical foundation would contradict Aristotle's doctrine of the 'autonomy of the sciences' according to which each science has its own special principles (1988, 53–54).[18] A similar objection could be raised about my interpretation.

It would not be well-founded, however. For Aristotle does not apply his principles of the autonomy of the sciences to those sciences that are under another. In *Posterior Analytics* 1.9 he states that demonstration does not apply to another genus, but then makes exceptions to the claim specifically for the cases of the application of geometry to mechanics and optics and arithmetic to harmonics, cases of sciences that are under another. We can conclude from this that sciences that are under another are not autonomous sciences.

Further support for the idea that ethics is a broadly perception- or experience-near account comes from the numerous passages in which Aristotle states that ethics requires a type of perception or seeing. For example, Aristotle says that "the decision is in the perception" (namely, the decision about how much deviation is required from the mean before a person is blameworthy) (*NE* 2.9 1109b23; cf. 4.5 1226b3–4); that practical insight *(phronēsis)* is concerned with the ultimate which is the object not of science but of perception (*NE* 6.8 1142a26–27); that "we ought to pay attention to the undemonstrated sayings of experienced or older people or of practically insightful people no less than to demonstrations; for due to their having an eye from experience, they see correctly" (*NE* 6.12 1143b11–14); that practical insight includes cleverness which is a certain 'eye of the soul' for what conduces to our aim (*NE* 6.12 1144a28–31). The passages related to perception are not limited to the sense of sight. Aristotle mentions the sense of taste, as well. He says that the many do not even have an insight *(ennoian)* into what is beautiful, that is, truly pleasant, since they have not had a taste of it *(ageustoi)* (*NE* 10.9 1179b15).

The claim that experienced or older people or people with practical insight have an eye from experience and so see correctly, again suggests a close relation between what is called 'perception' or 'seeing' and experience. Of course, the perception Aristotle has in mind regarding ethics must not be the perception of the special senses. Instead, it must be perception by all the senses of the common sense-objects (unity, number, movement, etc.).[19] As a result of their experience, experienced people, older people, and people with practical insight see certain things that are crucial to an understanding of ethics that those who lack such experience do not see. Those things appear to them, due to their experience, and do not appear to others. Of course, on my interpretation, what they see is good things or fine things—they see them as good or fine—though I have yet to argue for this claim. Things appear good or fine to people with experience, age, or practical insight that do not appear so to those who lack experience. For those who lack this experience lack the eye—the developed capacity—to see that things are good or fine since the eye is acquired through experience. The 10.9 passage that mentions taste presumably makes a related point since Aristotle's probable meaning is that since the many have not experienced the beautiful, that is, the truly pleasant, they do not even see it.

More support for this view comes from the passages in which Aristotle asserts that ethics requires experience. For example, Aristotle says that a youth is not an appropriate student of political science since he lacks experience of the actions in life and the arguments in political science are from and about these (*NE* 1.3 1095a2–4); that, since practice is concerned with particulars, "some who do not know, especially those who have experience, are more practical than others who know" (*NE* 6.7 1141b16–18); that the reason youths lack practical insight is that it is concerned with particulars that become familiar from experience and youths lack experience since it is given by time (*NE* 6.8 1142a14–16); that, as mentioned above, "we ought to pay attention to the undemonstrated sayings of experienced or older people or of practically insightful people no less than to demonstrations; for due to their having an eye from experience, they see correctly" (*NE* 6.12 1143b11–14). The 10.9 passage probably belongs on this list as well, if I am right that Aristotle's meaning is that the many, since they have not experienced the beautiful, that is, the truly pleasant, do not even see it.

Ethics, then, is a broadly perceptual or experiential study of the human good. It is perception- or experience-near. It is correlated with theoretical study of topics involved in the study of the human good, study that is found in metaphysics, physics, and psychology. Though such theoretical study is necessary for full understanding and articulation of ethical topics, it is not necessary for the practical goal of ethics. Those who appropriately participate in ethical study and practice need not be metaphysicians. They need only have a certain level of perceptual or experiential knowledge.[20]

Conclusion

In this chapter, I have argued that the argument of Aristotle's ethics requires for its full understanding appeal to extra-ethical principles found in metaphysics, physics, and psychology and that appeal to the relevant principles gives ethics greater articulation or depth. My purpose in doing so is to justify my own procedure in this book, namely, of introducing into my discussion of Aristotle's ethics metaphysical, physical, and psychological principles that he himself shies away from and does not argue for or much discuss in ethics. I introduce these principles because I think they are at the heart of ethics as Aristotle understands it even though they are not fully treated in ethics itself. This essay, then, is in Aristotle's terms an extended theoretical reflection on some topics treated not theoretically but experientially by Aristotle himself in his ethical writings. If the argument of this chapter is sound, the sort of theoretical treatment of ethical matters I propose and engage in does not at all conflict with Aristotle's understanding of proper ethical methodology.

CHAPTER FOUR

The Mean

Having dispensed with some objections to the interpretation I wish to maintain—and, in the process, having given some positive arguments for it as well—it is now time to give a number of freestanding positive arguments for the interpretation. As stated previously, I maintain that the cognitive component of ethical virtue and of emotion in Aristotle's ethical theory is not just knowledge of particulars, but is, in addition, awareness of their value, awareness of them as good or beautiful. An appropriate place to start is with an interpretation of Aristotle's idea that ethical virtue is a mean.

As is well-known, virtue, according to Aristotle, is a mean with respect to passions and actions (*NE* 2.6 1106b16–18, 1106b36). Some recent interpreters, including Bernard Williams and Julia Annas, have argued that the idea of the mean should be rejected because the claim that the virtuous person aims at a mean in passions and actions implies one of two problematic teachings, either the uninspiring teaching that the virtuous person is one whose passions and actions are of a middling amount or the trivial teaching that the virtuous person is one who feels what he or she should feel and does what he or she should do.

Nancy Sherman gives the doctrine of the mean some value but as a heuristic for virtue rather than a component of it. The sense of the doctrine, she says, is that virtue must fit the case, but the doctrine cannot give us sufficient guidance as to what it is to fit the case since the mean is neither a "mathematical algorithm" nor "the principle 'always act moderately'" since many circumstances do not call for moderation

(1989, 34–35). It can, however, give us guidance in devising strategies for discovering what fits the case. For example, if we drag ourselves away from that toward which we are most attracted, we are more likely to hit upon the mean.

I suggest that we look at Aristotle's mean in a different way. I maintain that on Aristotle's view a virtuous person is neither one who is disposed to engage in certain types of action or feel certain types of emotion (excess), nor one who is not disposed to engage in certain types of action or feel certain types of emotion (deficiency), but instead is one who is disposed to engage in types of action or feel types of emotion when they are needed or appropriate. In addition, for Aristotle, as I will argue, 'the needed' and 'the appropriate' mean 'the good'. 'The good', as I have argued in chapter 2, section 3, means 'what is instrumental to or constitutive of development or completion'. The virtuous person, therefore, is one who is disposed to act or feel in certain ways when to do so is or will lead to development or completion and not when it will not. This interpretation solves the interpretive problem addressed by the commentators: it is not a trivializing interpretation since on it the virtuous person aims at emotions and actions that can be independently described; it is not an uninspiring one since on it the virtuous person aims at the valuable not at the middling.

On this interpretation, the point of the discussion of the mean simply is not what critics of it imagine. The point is not to give guidance on what types of acts to perform. Instead, it is to guide us to perform acts not because they are of a certain type but because they are (or lead to) good. Moreover, since the good or value of particulars is determined by deliberation, the goal is to guide us to act deliberately. A virtuous person does not act in a routinized way—the truly courageous person does not always rush ahead; the truly generous person does not always give a lot; the moderate person does not always eat a small amount; the person with the virtue of appropriate anger does not always lack anger. To do so, or tend to do so, would be excess or deficiency, not the mean. To do so (or tend to do so) would be to do too much or too little. Instead, the virtuous person acts flexibly, for he acts deliberately and does actions of a certain type because they are (or lead to) good. The virtuous person's actions are not the routinized performance of actions of a certain type. They are the deliberate performance of actions that are good.

1

One common type of interpretation of the mean is what is sometimes called the 'moderate amount' interpretation. According to it, the claim that virtue is a mean in passions and actions amounts to the claim that virtue is a moderate amount of passions and actions. The term 'moderate' in 'moderate amount' is itself ambiguous. It signifies either, on the one hand, an appropriate or fitting amount or, on the other, a middle amount, that is, an amount neither great nor small. Hence it would be clearer to refer to this type of interpretation as the 'middling amount' interpretation, where a 'middling amount' is a middle amount and 'middling' sometimes also has the pejorative connotation of being ordinary or mediocre. The point of this type of interpretation of the mean is that Aristotle, by saying that virtue is a mean in actions and passions, is, first of all, referring to the amount of the actions and passions of the virtuous person, secondly, claiming that it should always be a middle amount, and (in some cases), third, maintaining that this is an incorrect, uninspired, and depressing view.

Often the middling amount interpretation comes up in discussions of why the claim that virtue is a mean is problematic. It is problematic, some interpreters say, because both of the most plausible interpretations of it are problematic. Either it amounts to the uninspiring teaching that the virtuous person is one whose passions and actions are of a middling amount or it amounts to the trivial teaching that the virtuous person is one who feels and does what he or she should feel and do.

Bernard Williams is one interpreter who criticizes the idea of the mean on these grounds. Calling it "the doctrine of the Mean," he describes it as "one of the most celebrated and least useful parts of his system" because "it oscillates between an unhelpful analytical model" and "a substantively depressing doctrine in favor of moderation." "The doctrine of the Mean," he concludes, "is better forgotten" (1985, 36).

Julia Annas, in her argument that virtue is a skill, concurs in Williams's criticism when she says, "We hardly want to take over Aristotle's unpromising idea that virtue is a 'mean' between extremes, for example" (1991, 2). In her discussion of the relation between emotions and judgments in ancient Greek ethical theories, she spells this out. She sees no way of independently specifying what counts as a mean amount of an action. Bravery, for example, does not correlate with an independently established right number of brave actions performed, nor cowardice with too few brave actions nor rashness with too many. Kant makes a similar criticism using the term 'degree' rather than 'amount' and arguing that since Aristotle's account of the mean "does not specify the *degree*, although it makes the conformity or nonconformity of conduct with duty depend entirely on it, this cannot serve as a definition" (*MM* 6:404). Nor does Annas see a way of giving independent content to the idea of a mean amount of a feeling, for this idea implies either the trivial view that a mean amount of feeling is the due or appropriate amount of feeling or the questionable view that a mean amount of feeling is a middling amount of feeling (1993, 59–61).

Nietzsche precedes Williams and Annas in being dissatisfied with the idea that virtue is a middling amount of passions and actions. He describes Aristotle's view as "that tuning down of the affects to a harmless mean according to which they may be satisfied, the Aristotelianism of morals" and thinks it would be appropriate to discuss in a chapter called "Morality as Timidity" (*BGE* 198).

Though a number of recent commentators have rejected the 'middling amount' interpretation, none of their arguments is entirely satisfying. They have argued in three ways. J. O. Urmson argues that Aristotle does not hold the middling amount interpretation because the view that the virtuous person ought to aim at a middling amount of passion and action is absurd. In any given situation, he argues, one ought to exhibit a zero quantity of most emotions, since only a few and not most emotions are appropriate to any given situation. Moreover, he points out, it would be absurd to claim that he should be middlingly angry with you both when you are trivially rude and when you torture his wife (1973, 160–162). This first argument is inconclusive, of course, since it is possible Aristotle sometimes makes absurd claims.

S. L. R. Clark argues that the middling amount interpretation is false because Aristotle nowhere says it is always wrong to feel a certain emotion to a high degree, despite some passages that may seem to imply this. He points out that Aristotle nowhere says it is always wrong to be extremely angry and that a passage that could be interpreted to say so in fact refers not to acts of extreme anger but the disposition to extreme anger (1975, 84): "For example, with respect to feeling angry, if we feel it vehemently or mildly we are in a bad condition and if we feel it moderately we are in a good condition" (*NE* 2.5 1105b27). This second type of argument, like the first, is not conclusive. It rules out an opposing argument but does not make a positive case.

Third, it is common to point to certain passages in which Aristotle states that a certain type of action should be done to a high degree and that certain other types of action should not be done at all. Clark mentions contemplation as an example of the former because Aristotle says that it should be done with all one's might. In addition, he mentions the emotions of spite, shamelessness, and envy and the actions of adultery, theft, and murder, as examples of the latter, since Aristotle says they should never be done (*NE* 2.6 1107a9) (1975, 84).

This third type of argument needs to be evaluated on an example by example basis. Clark is right to look for an example of a type of action or emotion characteristic of a virtue that Aristotle states should be done or felt either in a high or low degree since, if we found one, we would have a strong argument against the middling amount interpretation. However, are either of the examples Clark mentions actually examples of that type?

Contemplation is not since it is the action of an intellectual virtue not an ethical virtue. There is no ethical virtue that pertains to thinking, as there are virtues that pertain to eating, drinking, and sex; to taking and giving money; to feeling fear on the battlefield; and so forth. We could imagine one, and it would have as its extremes the tendency to contemplate more than is needed and the tendency to contemplate less than is needed. Since Rousseau and Nietzsche, and among some religious people, this sort of topic is a common one.[1] Aristotle, however, does not mention such an ethical virtue.

Nor do the emotions of spite, shamelessness, and envy *(epichairekakia, anaischuntia, phthonos)* provide support for the view that there is a type of emotion that should never be felt. For, strictly speaking, they are not types of emotions. Instead, they are the names of vices: spite and envy are vices related to righteous indignation *(nemesis)*; shamelessness is a vice related to the quasi virtue shame *(aidous)*.[2] Plausibly, the actions of adultery, theft, and murder *(moicheia, klopē, androphonia)*, since Aristotle puts them on the same list, are understood by him in a similar way. Murder, for example, would then not be a type of action but, instead, a type of vicious action (*NE* 4.9 1128b31, 2.7 1107b35–a1).

What we need to refute the middling amount interpretation is an example of a type of action or emotion that Aristotle clearly states is a mean and clearly states involves an action or emotion of a very large or very small amount. There are in fact two clear examples of this: pride and magnificence. Each of these, as their Greek names, *megalopsychia* and *megaloprepeia*, suggest, involves greatness—magnificence involves great expenditure of wealth and pride involves great honor.

Magnificence, like liberality, is a virtue having to do with the giving and taking of wealth, especially with the giving of wealth. Magnificence is distinguished particularly from liberality by the fact that it has to do not with just any scale of wealth, but particularly with large expenditures. "Magnificence, as its name suggests," Aristotle says, "is great expenditure that is fitting in its greatness" *(en megethei prepousa dapanē estin)*[3] (*NE* 4.1 1122a23). It is clear, here, that the actions of the magnificent person are great and at the same time in a mean. They can be great and a mean because what makes the expenditure a mean is not the amount of the expenditure but the appropriateness of the expenditure. "The expenses of the magnificent person are great and fitting," Aristotle says (*NE* 4.2 1122b1–2).

"Pride," Aristotle says, "seems even from the name to be concerned with great things" (*NE* 4.3 1123a34–5). The proud person believes himself worthy of the greatest things and is worthy of them. Since, according to Aristotle, honor is the greatest of the external goods, the proud person is one who believes himself worthy of the greatest honors and is worthy of them. Pride, in other words, is high, merited self-esteem. The proud person, Aristotle says, is a peak with respect to the greatness of his claims but a mean with respect to what is called for *(dei)* in them (*NE* 4.3 1123b13). It is clear, once again, that there is no conflict here between a mean action and a great action: for a person of great virtue, believing yourself deserving of great honor is called for, is the mean.

For Aristotle, then, the mean in passions and actions need not in every case be a middling amount of passion and action. In fact, if we consider the virtue of pride in particular, a more appropriate conclusion is that, for Aristotle, a certain greatness or grandness is central to his understanding of ethical virtue. For, pride—or, more literally, great-souledness—is arguably the highest of the ethical virtues for Aristotle since he says one must have all the others in order to merit it.[4] The height of ethical virtue, then, is to have all the other ethical virtues and a resulting high, merited self-esteem. The person who has it both is great and is aware that he is. In fact, we might better understand Aristotle not as someone who rejects the Greek emphasis on greatness but as one who accepts that idea but radically reinterprets it. Aristotle is not Plato. A sign of a difference between them is that, for Aristotle, irony is a vice, not a virtue. What Aristotle suggests, in his account of the height of ethical virtue, is that greatness and a reflective and flexible sense of what is suitable to each situation can and, in the case of those who have reached such heights, do go hand in hand.

2

Another common type of interpretation of the mean is the type that relates Aristotle's accounts of other types of mean to his account of the ethical mean. It is important to investigate the accounts to see if any or all of them can simply be applied to the ethics. The means that are most relevant for these interpretations are the material or hyletic mean that results in a material mixture, the perceptual or aesthetic mean that makes perception possible and the somatic mean—or, at least, somatic proportion of opposites—that results in health. Some interpretations actually apply accounts of other types of mean to the account of the ethical mean. One example of a type of an interpretation in which this is done has recently been called the 'mixture of opposites' interpretation.

An early twentieth-century interpretation of Aristotle's ethics that includes a mixture of opposites interpretation is John Burnet's in his critical edition of the *Nicomachean Ethics* with notes (1900, 71–73). There, he states that the ethical mean is a mixture of opposites. His interpretation is ably criticized by W. F. R. Hardie in his later work on Aristotle's ethical theory. The most important aspect of Hardie's criticism for present purposes is his assertion that Burnet "fails to produce evidence that the idea on which he lays most stress is, in fact, part of Aristotle's doctrine in the *Ethics*. This is the idea of the combination, or blending, of opposites in determinate ratios. It is not easy to find this in the doctrine of the ethical mean" (1968, 144). Hardie assumes here that the mean can have different senses in different contexts and that, as a result, aspects of the hyletic mean may be different than aspects of the ethical mean.

What we have is a question of methodology. How shall we proceed when faced with different accounts of means that have a number of features in common? The common features are opposites; a mean of some kind between them; sometimes a *logos* of the opposites; sometimes a proportion *(symmetria)* of the opposites; something that results from the mean between opposites, for example, a single entity (hyletic mixture), a capacity (aesthetic capacity), a positive disposition or virtue (somatic virtue, ethical virtue); and sometimes a resulting potential for either of the two opposites. Are we justified in assuming that, given these common features, a feature found in one type of mean is also found in another type of mean?

We could if 'the mean' were univocal for Aristotle. However, it is not. In *On the Heavens*, Aristotle clearly states that "the intermediate *(to metaxu)* and the mean *(to meson)* are said in many ways" (*De Cae.* 4.5 312b2–3). In the *Topics*, Aristotle suggests the same point. Regarding the definition of an odd number as a number that has a middle, Aristotle points out that the middle of an (odd) number, the middle of a line, and the middle of a body are not the same, since a line and a body have a middle but are not odd. As a result, in order to define odd number, one must specify the sense of 'having a middle' that is peculiar to (odd) numbers: "If having a mean *(to meson)* is said in many ways, it is necessary to determine how the mean is said here" (*Top.* 6.12 149a29–37). Since, then, the mean is equivocal, we cannot simply apply central components of, for example, the hyletic mean to the ethical mean. We would need independent grounds for claiming that the ethical mean shares its features. A look at the accounts of the hyletic and aesthetic means will flesh this point out.

The hyletic mean: In *Generation and Corruption* 1.10, Aristotle asks how material mixture *(mixis)* [or blending *(krasis)*] is possible. Some people, he points out, argue that it is not possible for one ingredient to be mixed with another. For (1) if the ingredients still exist and have not been altered, they have not been mixed; (2) if one ingredient is destroyed, the ingredients are not mixed because then one ingredient exists and the other does not; and (3) if both ingredients come together so that each of them is destroyed, then there is no mixture, because neither of the ingredients exists to be mixed with the other.

The first option (which Aristotle rejects), in which the ingredients still exist and have not been altered, is the type of combination Aristotle calls 'composition' *(synthesis)* (*Gen.Corr.* 1.10 328a6). In a composite, the ingredients combine while still retaining their nature. Aristotle's example is a heap of grains of barley and wheat. The grains combine to make a composite of parts each of whose nature is preserved. Another type of composite Aristotle discusses is one whose ingredients appear, on the level of the perceptible whole, to have changed their nature when in fact on a lower, imperceptible level they have retained their nature in small side by side particles.

The second option (which Aristotle rejects), in which one ingredient is destroyed, is the type of combination in which one ingredient changes into another. According to Aristotle, this happens when one of the two is very dominant in number or bulk over the other. When this is the case, the result is an increase in the predominant ingredient as a result of the nondominant ingredient changing into the predominant one. Aristotle's example is a single drop of wine in ten thousand measures of water. The drop of wine does not mix with the water but instead changes form and becomes part of the whole volume of water.

Aristotle rejects the third option, that both the ingredients come together so that each of them is destroyed. Still, he makes use of an aspect of it, as we will see. It must be the case, in a mixture, that ingredients combine to form a combination that is not simply a case of ingredients being collected together and retaining their own natures (as in the case of a heap of grains) or of one ingredient being destroyed (as in the case of the drop of wine in the thousand measures of water), but a combination of elements into (1) a third nature that is different than that of the ingredients that form it, (2) a nature that is the same throughout (both on higher and lower levels), and (3) one in which the ingredients are in some sense still existent (so that they can be said to be mixed).

Aristotle's resolution makes use of the ambiguity of 'to exist'. Things can exist actually or potentially. In a mixture, the ingredients cease to exist actually (and thus Aristotle makes use of an aspect of the third option). However, they continue to exist potentially. Thus, the mixture is a third thing, different in nature from the two ingredients combined in it though those ingredients do still exist in it—potentially and not actually. They exist potentially because (1) they are still capable of being what they were before they were mixed, that is, they can be separated out of the mixture (*Gen.Corr.* 327b26–29)[5] and (2) some of their powers are preserved (*Gen.Corr.* 327b29–31). Aristotle, notably for our purposes, calls that third nature an intermediate *(metaxu)*. An intermediate results when the powers of the ingredients to be combined are fairly equal. One ingredient, though dominant, is not very dominant over the other. When this is the case, the two ingredients change out of their nature and toward the dominant without becoming it. Instead they become a third, intermediate nature with properties common to both of the ingredients (*Gen.Corr.* 328a29–32).

Aristotle fills out his account of mixture by going to the level of elements (earth, air, fire, water) and contraries (hot, cold, wet, dry) in *Generation and Corruption* 2.7. For the purposes of the present discussion of the ethical mean, it is important to note that both elements and contraries are types of opposites. Among the elements, earth (which is cold and dry) is opposite to air (which is hot and wet) and water (which is cold and wet) is opposite to fire (which is hot and dry). Among contraries, hot and cold are opposites, as are wet and dry.

Aristotle's argument about the combination of these opposites is the same in thrust as his argument about mixture on the higher level. How do flesh and bone and similar combinations result from elements? Of course, for Aristotle, elements result from contraries and flesh and bone and their like from the elements. The problem, as he sees it, is how one thing can result from a combination of two of these opposites (whether elements or contraries). The combination is not (1) both of the contraries, (2) neither of the contraries, nor (3) a composite (in which the contraries are preserved and placed alongside one another in small particles). Nor, he adds, is it (4) the underlying matter of the contraries. (Aristotle mentions this possibility since, when a contrary perishes, what is left is either its contrary or the matter.)

Options 1 and 3 are cases in which the ingredients preserve their nature in the combination and hence are not really mixed. Bricks and stones in a wall are Aristotle's example of this type of option. Options 2 and 4 are logical options. Four has just been explained. Two is a case in which the ingredients, when combined, cease to exist at all and so cannot be said to be mixed. The two sets of options suggest what must be true in a mixture: in a mixture, the ingredients must not exist with their nature preserved, for if they do, they have not been mixed; however, it must not be the case that they do not exist at all, for if they do not exist, they cannot be said to be mixed.

Again, Aristotle utilizes the ambiguity of 'to exist'. In addition, he utilizes the fact that there are greater and lesser degrees of hot and cold, wet and dry. In a mixture of opposites, the opposites do not exist actually, but do exist potentially. Mixture is different than cases in which opposites are not equalized, that is, cases in which one opposite is very predominant over the other. In those cases, the nondominant ingredient changes into the dominant. It is destroyed by the dominant. Aristotle's phrasing suggests that a mixture results when the ingredients start out equalized, that is, start out fairly equal in quantity. In these cases, neither opposite changes or destroys the other. Instead, each opposite destroys the excesses of the other: for example, the hot cools down and the cold warms up until each reaches a mean. The opposites reach a mean or intermediate in which neither opposite exists actually but each exists potentially.

The aesthetic mean: In *De Anima* 2.11, Aristotle discusses how sense perception is possible. Change, for Aristotle, must be change between opposites. How can each sense undergo the changes necessary to sense the opposite qualities that determine the field of that sense, for example, hot and cold in the case of touch, dark and light in the case of sight? The answer Aristotle gives is that the faculty is a mean state *(mesotēs)* between opposites, specifically, between the opposite qualities that determine the field of that sense (*De An.* 2.11 424a3). The sense, thus, will be in the middle between the two opposite qualities so that the change required to sense either of them will be a change between opposites.

What Burnet seems to do in his mixture of opposites interpretation is simply to apply his interpretation of the hyletic mean to the ethical mean. The chemical formula H_2O is an example, according to him, for the formula is a *logos* or *mesotēs*. Hydrogen and water in a ratio of two to one forms a third thing—a certain form—called 'water' (1900, 71–72). After quoting a long passage from *Generation and Corruption* on the hyletic mean, Burnet simply concludes, "It is in this sense, then, that goodness is a mean" (where 'goodness' is his older and now nonstandard translation of *'aretē'*). However, since 'the mean' is equivocal, we cannot follow him in this. For, we are not justified in assuming that the relation between mean and the opposites in the case of the hyletic mean is the same as the relation between the mean and the opposites in the case of the ethical mean. We are no more justified in doing that than we are justified in assuming that the fact that a number that has a mean is an odd number implies that a line that has a mean is an odd line or a body that has a mean an odd body.

There would be a certain appeal to applying the hyletic mean to the ethical mean. For, when the opposites are mixed in an organic tissue like flesh or bone, the opposites are, according to Aristotle, still in it potentially and can be separated out from it. If we could simply apply this account to the account in the ethics, we could say that an ethical virtue is a mean between opposed emotions, one of which is a pleasure and the other a pain (e.g., moderation between desire and aversion, courage between confidence and fear), in which neither of the two emotions is actually present but is capable of becoming present. However, one who wants to argue that this is the case will have to find independent grounds.

Moreover, what would it mean for the pleasure and the pain to be mixed in a virtue? Would they be mixed in the disposition to the virtue, in each instance of the virtue, or in a pattern of acts in accord with the virtue? It is just not clear what it would mean to say that the disposition to courage, for example, is a mixture of the disposition to feel fear and of the disposition to feel confidence. How would they be mixed? Doesn't mixture imply contact? If we were talking about instances of courage—that is, actual cases of courageous feeling and action—then the claim that courage is a mixture of confidence and fear seems improbable, since it seems as though some instances of courage are an instance either of confidence or of fear but not of both. If we were talking about a pattern of courageous feelings and actions, then the claim that courage is a mixture of confidence and fear seems false since a series of experiences of confidence and fear is not the same as a mixture of experiences of confidence and fear since a series is not the same as a mixture.

Application of the aesthetic mean to the ethical mean would have its appeal, too. For, the fact that a sense, such as sight, is an aesthetic or sensitive mean makes perception of either of the two opposites that determine the field of that sense possible, as well as all the mixtures in between, for example, light and dark and all the shades in between. Once again, though, since 'the mean' is equivocal, we cannot draw the comparison without independent grounds.

Moreover, each aesthetic mean is a capacity while the ethical mean is not a capacity but a (stable) disposition. An ethical virtue, as Aristotle suggests in his definition of it, is not a mere capacity to experience the opposed pleasures and pains proper to each virtue. Instead, it is a condition of being well-disposed toward feeling those pleasures and pains (*NE* 2.5). The experience of pleasure or pain is, according to Aristotle in *De Anima*, an experience or activity of the aesthetic mean. Pleasure and pain are in fact defined by Aristotle there as the activity of the aesthetic mean on what is good or bad as such: "To be pleased or pained is to activate the perceptual mean toward what is good or bad as such"

(*NE* 2.6 1106b18–21). Since, however, the ethical mean is not simply the capacity to feel pleasure and pain, but is the disposition to feel pleasure and pain when they are needed or appropriate, the ethical mean must have some characteristics that the aesthetic mean lacks—characteristics that make the ethically virtuous person sensitive to the necessity or appropriateness of the experience of the passion in different cases or situations. (That sensitivity, as we know, is a cognitive capacity of some kind and, as I will argue, a rather high-level cognitive capacity, since at least part of what is involved is the capacity to cognize complex value.)

The somatic proportion of opposites: In *Physics* 7.3, Aristotle discusses dispositions (both virtues and vices) of the body and of the soul. The general topic of the chapter is whether dispositions *(hexeis)* are alterations *(alloiōseis)*. His answer is that they are not, since some are virtues, and virtues are not alterations but completions *(teleiōseis)*, and the rest are vices, and vices are not alterations but departures *(ekstaseis)*. As part of this discussion, Aristotle mentions that bodily virtues and vices (health, fitness, beauty, strength, etc.) consist in a blending of hot and cold elements within the body in different proportions in relation either to one another or to the surroundings. The different statements Aristotle makes about bodily virtue and vice in this section can be summarized as follows (*Phys.* 7.3).

Bodily virtue, for example, health, results from a blend of hot and cold, wet and dry in the body in a proportion *(symmetria)* in relation to each other or the surroundings that results in the body being well-disposed toward its proper affections *(pathē)* and toward what naturally alters it. In other words, the blend of contraries found in health results in the body's being unaffected or affected as it should be in order to continue to be generated (in other words, we can suppose, as it should be in order for it to continue to exist and for it to be maintained).

Bodily vice, for example, disease, results from a blend of hot and cold, wet and dry in the body in a proportion in relation to each other or the surroundings that results in the body being badly disposed toward its proper affections *(pathē)* and toward what naturally alters it. In other words, the blend of contraries found in bodily vices such as disease results in the body's being unaffected or affected in the way it should not be if it is to continue to be generated (in other words, we can suppose, as it should not be in order for it to continue to exist and to be maintained, and as it should be in order to be destroyed or harmed).

Though these passages do not make explicit reference to a mean, a number of the common features of accounts of a mean are present. To recall, the common features are opposites; a mean of some kind between them; sometimes a *logos* of the opposites; sometimes a proportion *(symmetria)* of the opposites; something that results from the mean between opposites, for example, a single entity (hyletic mixture), a capacity (aesthetic capacity), a positive disposition or virtue (somatic virtue, ethical virtue); and sometimes a resulting potential for either of the two opposites. In health, there is a proportional blend of opposites that results in a positive disposition or virtue. Not much hangs on whether we do or do not call this passage an account of the 'somatic mean', so we might just as well simply call it an account of the 'somatic proportion of opposites'.

The ethical mean: What Aristotle does next, however, is important for our account. He goes on to discuss virtues and vices of the soul, starting with ethical virtue and ethical vice. Ethical virtue, Aristotle says, makes its possessor well disposed toward its proper affections or passions *(pathē)* and ethical vice makes its possessor badly disposed toward them. Following Aristotle when he says that being well disposed toward one's proper affections or passions means being unaffected or affected by them as one should be, we can interpret him as saying: ethical virtue makes the one who has it unaffected or affected as he or she should be while ethical vice makes the person who possesses it affected or unaffected as he or she should not be. Since in the case of ethical virtue, *pathē* are emotions, we can reparaphrase this as follows: ethical virtue makes the one who has it either feel or not feel the emotions he or she should feel while ethical vice makes the person who possesses it feel or not feel the emotions he or she should not feel. Moreover, Aristotle says, virtue and vice have to do with pleasure and pain.

Only a couple of the features common to accounts of the mean are present here. One cannot help but wonder whether Aristotle planned to sketch the account out further or, alternately, whether the main topic of the passage was such that he did not find it necessary to do so and so did not. Ethical virtue, Aristotle says here, is a positive disposition toward passions, that is, a disposition to feel them when one should. Arguably, these passions are opposites, too, for they all are types of pleasure and pain. But even this claim is not one Aristotle actually makes here.

What is missing from this account is some reference to the term 'proportion'; a clear statement that the passions are types of pleasure and pain and that thus the passions are opposites; and the claim that when we experience those opposite passions in proportion to each other or the surroundings, what results is that the one who has the virtue is well-disposed toward these opposite passions. Though we do not get these claims here, we do get them in the *Nicomachean Ethics*. Since, in this case, both accounts (in the *Physics* and in the *Nicomachean Ethics*) are accounts of the same type of mean, namely, the ethical mean, and since, in addition, there is nothing in either account that casts doubt on the idea that the two accounts are basically the same, it seems reasonable to put the two accounts together.

However, it is important to point out two features that we do not get in the *Physics* account. We do not get the idea that ethical virtue, like somatic virtue, involves a blend or mixture of opposites. Nor do we get the idea that some mean in ethics results only when neither of two opposites is very dominant over the other. The former is a claim Aristotle does make in the *Physics* account of somatic virtue, and it is striking that he does not make it regarding ethical virtue. The latter is a claim that Aristotle makes in his accounts of the hyletic mean, and it does not show up in either of the two accounts in the *Physics* chapter, neither in the account of somatic virtue nor in the account of ethical virtue. I do not think either of these claims shows up in either of Aristotle's ethics, either, which suggests that there is no good reason to apply them to his discussion of ethics.

We are left, then, to look more closely at Aristotle's claims about the ethical mean itself in order to understand the ethical mean—not because there is nothing interesting or heuristically useful about the other accounts and not because there is no relation or analogy between the different accounts, but because each of the accounts is slightly different than the others.

3

Are we left, then, with the trivial or unhelpful idea that the virtuous person is one who is disposed to feel and do what he or she should feel and do—with the "unhelpful analytical model" Williams discerns or the "trivial view" mentioned by Annas? I do not think so. Aristotle's teaching is richer than that. That some have proposed that this trivial idea is what Aristotle's account amounts to is not too surprising, though, because, as is often noted, Aristotle spells the mean out in terms of "what is needed" and some take this to mean "what the agent should." However, such an interpretation leaves us with no understanding of why Aristotle supposes that virtue has two opposites, rather than one. That the virtuous actor is one who is disposed to do what he or she should do is a part of Aristotle's account. However, as I will show, it is only a small part of it.

One way to see this is to look at Aristotle's definition of ethical virtue. In genus, for him, ethical virtue is a disposition *(hexis)*. More specifically, it is a "disposition having to do with choice, consisting in a mean, specifically, in a mean relative to us, determined by a *logos*, specifically, by the *logos* the practically insightful person would use to determine it" *(Estin ara hē aretē hexis prohairetikē en mesotēti ousa tē pros hēmas hōrismenē logē kai hēs an ho phronimos horiseien)* (NE 2.6 1106b36–1107a2).

Recently, commentators have gone back and forth on how to understand and translate '*hexis*'. For some time, the accepted translation was 'state', but now, 'disposition' is coming back in. 'State' suggests a condition. 'Disposition' suggests a condition as a result of which the one who has it tends to act in a certain way. Annas makes this point: "In some ways Aristotle's word *hexis* answers better to our word 'disposition' than to 'state': a virtue like courage is a disposition because it is a condition because of which I am so disposed as to act in brave ways; and this is what a *hexis* is" (1993, 50). This does seem to be true of ethical virtues for Aristotle. They are (in part) conditions as a result of which the one who has them is disposed or tends to act in a certain way: courageous people are those whose souls are in such a condition that they tend to act courageously; magnificent people tend to spend large sums of money in a fitting or tasteful way; just people tend to take neither more nor less than their share; and so forth.

Another reason for thinking that a *hexis* is a disposition for Aristotle is, of course, that he defines it as one. In the *Metaphysics*, Aristotle defines a *hexis* as a type of *diathesis* or disposition (*Met.* 5.20 1022b10–12). What kind of disposition, however, is it? Aristotle distinguishes a *hexis* from a mere *diathesis* in two ways. First, a *hexis* is more stable than a mere *diathesis*. A *hexis*, in other words, is a stable or lasting *diathesis*. Annas makes this point: "Aristotle contrasts it [*hexis*] as being more stable with the less stable 'disposition' or *diathesis*" (1993, 50). The source for this point is the *Categories*: "A *hexis* differs from a *diathesis* by being more stable and more long-lasting. Such are the different types of knowledge and the virtues" (*Cat.* 8 8b27–29).

Secondly, and this is a point Annas does not make, a *hexis* is not just a disposition, that is, not just a condition as a result of which the one who has it is disposed in a certain way, but a good or bad disposition, that is, a condition as a result of which the one who has it is well or badly disposed. Aristotle makes this point in the definition of *hexis* in *Metaphysics* 5.20, mentioned above: "A *hexis* is a disposition according to which that which is disposed is either well or badly disposed, either in itself or in relation to something else, for example, health is a *hexis*, for it is such a disposition" (*Met.* 5.20 1022b10–12). This should remind us of the discussion of health as a somatic *hexis* and virtue in

Physics 7.3. There, as we saw, Aristotle says that a healthy body is well disposed toward what affects it, namely, hot and cold, wet and dry, and he spells out 'well', as opposed to 'badly', disposed to mean that the body is affected or unaffected by hot and cold, wet and dry, in such a way that it continues to exist and be maintained. In other words, the *hexis* of a healthy body is not just its tendency to be affected or unaffected by hot and cold, wet and dry but, instead, is the tendency to be affected or unaffected well by them. Similarly, disease is a tendency to be affected or unaffected by them badly. A healthy body is disposed to take in water, but only the amount of water, and water in the places, which will enable the body to survive and grow. A healthy body can change temperature—from hot to cold—but will do so in such a fashion that the body continues to exist and to maintain itself.

Aristotle makes a similar point in *Metaphysics* 9. There he distinguishes between two kinds of *dynamis*. One kind is the capacity simply to act or be affected. The other kind is the capacity to act or be affected well: "Again what are called 'capacities' are capacities either of simply acting or being affected, or of acting or being affected well" (*Met.* 9.1 1046a16–17). The elaboration of this is similar to the elaboration found in the discussion of a *hexis* in *Physics* 7.3: "one kind is the capacity for being affected;" "another kind is the *hexis* to be unaffected by change for the worse or by destruction" (*Phys.* 7.3 1046a11–12; 13–14).

To the claim that a *hexis* for Aristotle is a disposition, then, two specifications must be added: it is settled and it is evaluatively directed. A virtue, then, is not just a disposition to do a certain type of act. Instead, it is a settled disposition to do a certain type of act well. Similarly, a vice is a settled disposition to do a certain type of act badly. In the case of the body, bodily virtue, for example, health, is not just a settled disposition to change temperature but a settled disposition to change temperature in such a fashion that the body does well.

This understanding of *hexis* derived from Aristotle's discussions of it in the *Categories* and the *Metaphysics* along with the related discussion in *Physics* 7.3 fits well with the discussion of ethical *hexis* in Aristotle's generic definition of ethical virtue in *Nicomachean Ethics* 2.5. There are three conditions of the soul, he there argues, namely, passion, capacity, and *hexis*. Ethical virtue is not a passion or a capacity. Hence, it is a *hexis*. Along the way, he defines each of them:

> Now since there are three [states] arising in the soul—passions, capacities, and *hexeis*—virtue must be one of these. By passions I mean desire, anger, fear, confidence, envy, joy, friendship, hate, longing, emulation, pity, in general the [states of soul] that are accompanied by pleasure and pain. By capacities I mean the [states] by virtue of which we

are said to be capable of experiencing passion, for example, capable of being angry or being pained or of feeling pity. By dispositions I mean the [states] by virtue of which we are well or badly off with respect to the passions. For example, with respect to feeling angry, if we feel it vehemently or mildly we are badly off and if we feel it moderately we are well off, and similarly with the other passions. (*NE* 2.5 1105b27)[6]

The triad is familiar: passions/affections, capacities, and *hexeis*. Ethical virtues are *hexeis*, Aristotle concludes. In other words, ethical virtues are neither particular passions, nor capacities to feel particular passions, but conditions of soul by virtue of which we are well off with respect to particular passions.

An ethical virtue, then, is a settled disposition as a result of which one is well disposed with respect to a certain type of feeling. Later, of course, Aristotle expands the meaning of ethical virtue to indicate that ethical virtue has to do not simply with passions, but also with actions. So, an ethical virtue is, in addition, a settled disposition as a result of which one is well disposed with respect to a certain type of action. How Aristotle spells out 'well disposed' is important to see. For now, we can simply assert that for Aristotle to be well disposed toward a certain type of feeling or action is to be disposed to feel that type of feeling or do that type of action when it is needed or appropriate. Before arguing for that interpretation, let us see that this is not a trivial or unhelpful view but instead one with important consequences, one that helps us resolve a certain interpretive problem, namely, the problem why, for Aristotle, ethical virtue has two opposites rather than only one.

If a virtue were the capacity to feel a certain type of feeling or do a certain type of action, then, it seems, the vice would be the lack of that capacity. Virtue, on that understanding, would have one opposite.[7] Similarly, if a virtue were the disposition or tendency to feel a certain type of feeling or do a certain type of action, the vice would be the lack of that disposition or the counterdisposition. However, since a virtue is a settled disposition to feel a certain type of feeling or do a certain type of action when it is what is appropriate or needed, ethical virtue has two opposites: one is the settled disposition to feel that type of feeling or do that type of action (even when it is not appropriate or needed); the other is the settled disposition not to feel that type of feeling or do that type of action (even when it is appropriate or needed). One of these is what Aristotle calls 'excess'; the other, 'deficiency'.

For example, the courageous person is not a person who is disposed to feel confident, nor, obviously, is the courageous person one who is disposed not to feel confident. Instead, the courageous person is the one who is disposed to feel confident when it is appropriate to do so and to lack confidence when lacking it is appropriate. The person who is disposed to be confident is reckless. The one who is disposed to lack confidence is timid. Moreover, the courageous person is not one who is disposed to rush ahead, nor, obviously, one who is disposed not to rush ahead. Instead, the courageous person is one who is disposed to rush ahead when rushing ahead is appropriate and not to rush ahead when not to rush ahead is appropriate. The person who is disposed to rush ahead is reckless. The one who is disposed not to rush ahead is timid. Courage, then, has two opposites, one of excess (recklessness) and one of deficiency (timidity).

The claim that the virtuous person is one who aims at a mean in passions and actions, then, is not subject to the criticisms raised by Annas. As previously mentioned, regarding actions, Annas claims to see no way of independently specifying what counts as a mean amount of an action. Bravery, for example, she says, does not correlate with an independently established right number of brave actions performed, nor cowardice with too few brave actions nor rashness with too many. As spelled out above, however, Aristotle's view is not that the courageous person does roughly a certain number of courageous actions which number is in between excess and deficiency. Instead, his view is that the courageous person tends to do a certain type of action—rushing ahead—when doing so is appropriate, rather than tending to do that type of act or tending not to do that type of act. A virtue is a stable tendency to do a certain type of action when doing it is appropriate, in contrast with a stable tendency to do that type of action or not to do that type of action.

Regarding passions, Annas claims not to see a way of giving independent content to the idea of a mean amount of a feeling, because that idea implies either the trivial view that a mean amount of feeling is the due or appropriate amount of feeling or the questionable view that a mean amount of feeling is a middling amount of feeling. We have already seen that the 'middling amount' interpretation is faulty. In addition, I have just argued that an interpretation of the mean in passions that involves the appropriateness of the passions is not a trivial interpretation, but is one that has important implications.

What, though, might it mean to say that an emotion is appropriate or good? First, it would not mean some intrinsic appropriateness or goodness. Instead, the emotion would be appropriate or good in the situation at hand. Suppose we paraphrase 'needed' by 'called for' (I shall justify this in what follows). For Aristotle, I maintain, positive emotions (desire, confidence, friendship, joy, etc.) are called for by positive situations, actions, or things, negative emotions (fear, hatred, envy, pity, etc.) by negative situations, actions, or things.

For example, according to Aristotle, the virtuous person enjoys and takes pleasure in virtuous actions, the just person in just actions, the generous person in generous actions, and so on (*NE* 1.8 1099a10–21). Moreover, the virtuous person *desires* what is good, since virtue is a disposition regarding choice and choice is deliberate desire (*NE* 3.4 1113a10–11). Also, pleasure in virtuous acts is a sign of virtue according to Aristotle and pain a sign of vice. For example, the moderate person takes pleasure in appropriate abstinence from bodily pleasures while the immoderate person instead is annoyed by it (*NE* 2.3 1104b3–7).

In addition, what might it mean to say that an emotion might lead to something good? Emotions, according to Aristotle, are types of pleasure and pain. Pleasure and pain lead to desire and aversion. Desire and aversion cause us to act—toward what pleases us and away from what pains us. As a result, if we feel pleasurable emotions (confidence, joy, desire, etc.) toward what is good and painful emotions (anger, fear, hatred, etc.) toward what is bad, then we are likely to do good actions and refrain from bad ones.

At this point in the argument, someone could object that unless 'appropriate' and 'needed' are in fact spelled out, the idea of virtue as a mean still is problematic. Let us backtrack a bit then. I asserted earlier that for Aristotle to be well disposed toward a certain type of feeling or action is to be disposed to feel that type of feeling or do that type of action when it is (or leads to something) needed or appropriate. It is important now both to argue for this claim and to explain what it means.

'The needed': Aristotle routinely states that to aim at the mean is to do an action or feel an emotion 'when it is needed, as it is needed, in the amount which is needed', and so on. For example, in *Nicomachean Ethics* 2.6, he describes virtue as aiming at the mean and then explains what he means in terms of 'the needed' *(dei)*:

> For example, both fear and confidence and desire and anger and pity and wholly pleasure and pain can be felt too much or too little and in either case not well. But to feel them at the needed times and toward the needed objects and toward the needed people and for the sake of what is needed and in the needed manner is both mean and best, and this is appropriate to virtue. Similarly also with actions there is excess and deficiency and the mean. (*NE* 2.6 1106b18–24)

The primary meaning of *'dei'* according to the Greek-English lexicon is 'it is needful' (*LSJ* 372). The person who has courage, for example, feels fear and confidence when it is needful to feel them. Aristotle states this in the *Nicomachean Ethics*: "The one, then, who faces and who fears the needed things, for the sake of what is needed, in the needed manner, and at the needed time, and who feels confident in the same way, is courageous" (*NE* 3.7 1115b17–19). Today, since 'needed' and 'needful' as adjectives are somewhat archaic, we might make the same point by saying that the person who has courage is not a person who rarely feels fear nor, of course, a person who regularly feels fear, but is one who feels fear when the situation calls for fear, toward objects and people that call for fear, and so on. The virtuous person is not someone who is disposed to feel or not feel specific types of emotion or who is disposed to engage or not engage in specific types of actions, but is one who is disposed to feel types of emotion and do types of action that specific situations—in all their particularity—call for.

Nicely, we need not depend only on the lexicon for our view of what Aristotle means by the term '*dei*'. In the *Sophistical Refutations*, he defines it. '*To deon*', he says there, is equivocal. It has two meanings. It denotes something that is inevitable *(t'anankaion)* or, alternately, it denotes things that are good *(t'agatha)* (*Soph. Ref.* 177a24, 165b35).[8] Since Aristotle of course cannot mean that the virtuous person chooses and does what is inevitable, he must instead mean that the virtuous person is one who chooses and does what is good.[9] The meaning of 'the mean', therefore, is, for Aristotle, 'what is needed', and 'what is needed' means 'what is good'. The virtuous person, then, is one who is disposed to feel certain types of emotion or engage in certain types of action when they are good.

'*The Appropriate*': We have already seen in chapter 3, section 1, that, according to Aristotle, good choices about how to act are made not by application of a rule but by perception of what is appropriate to the occasion—*ton kairon:* "And when the general account is this imprecise, the account of particulars is even more imprecise. For they do not fall under any art or rule, but the agents themselves always must consider what is appropriate *(ton kairon)*, as is the case also in medicine and navigation" (*NE* 2.2 1103b34–1104a10).[10] As mentioned in chapter 3, section 1, '*ho kairos*' is the good in the category of time. Good is said in as many ways as being, according to Aristotle, for example, in the category of substance, the god and mind, in quantity, the measured, "in time, *kairos*" (*NE* 1.6 1096a23–27).[11] Aristotle confirms this understanding of '*kairos*' by defining it, in the *Prior Analytics*, as 'needed time' *(chronos deon)* and then associating the needed with the the good, specifically, with the beneficial *(ophelimon)* (*Pr. An.* 1.36 48b35–37).[12] '*Ho kairos*' is a category of 'the needed' or 'the good'. Moreover, it is a term used sometimes simply to stand for the appropriate or good in general.[13] To aim at the mean, then, is to be disposed to feel certain types of emotion or engage in certain types of action when they are appropriate where by 'the appropriate' Aristotle means 'the good'.

If the argument of this book is correct—that the central cognitive component of ethical virtue for Aristotle is not just awareness of particulars but awareness of the value or *energeia* of particulars—and if the argument of this chapter so far is correct—that for Aristotle (1) the mean does not mean an amount of action or emotion (e.g., a middling amount) but (2) appropriate or needed action or emotion and (3) 'appropriate' and 'needed' mean good or *energeia* (or *entelecheia, telos, teleiōsis*, etc.)—then we ought to be able to go through examples of the virtues and show that the central cognitive component in each case is awareness of the value or *energeia* of particulars. For example, in the case of moderation, the central awareness is whether the food, drink, or sex before me will lead to health or fitness or away from them. Health and fitness are, of course, *energeia* of the body (*NE* 3.11 1119a16–17). In the case of magnificence, the central awareness is whether particular large expenditures are fitting or not (*NE* 4.2 1122a22–23). The fitting is, arguably, a case of *energeia*. In the case of pride, the central awareness is of one's own virtue, since pride is believing oneself worthy of the greatest honors when one is worthy of them and the greatest honors belong to those who have the greatest virtue according to Aristotle (*NE* 4.3 1123b1–2, 1123b17–20, 34–36). Virtue is, of course, *energeia* of the soul.[14] In the case of friendship, too, the central awareness is of virtue—specifically, the friend's virtue—since in the best friendships one wishes the other well because he is good or virtuous. Virtue, as just stated, is *energeia* of the soul (*NE* 8.4 1156b6–12).

Some other examples may make reference to particular types of good or *energeia* (*telos, entelecheia*, etc.), but less clearly so. For example, the truthful person is a lover of truth *(philalēthēs)* according to Aristotle. Could truth in this context be understood as a particular type of *energeia*? (*NE* 4.7 1127b3–4) The witty person is one who jokes tastefully, tactfully, or with propriety. Could taste *(emmeleia)*, tact *(epidexiotēs)*, and propriety *(euschēmosynē)* be understood as a particular type of *energeia*? (*NE* 4.8 1128a9–10, 16–19, 24–25) Justice is a tricky case. Justice as the lawful seems to aim not at a particular good but at good as a whole since it aims at the common advantage *(tou koinē sympherontos)* and bids us to do all the virtues (*NE* 5.1 1129b12–25). Justice in distribution has to do not with particular types of good but with proportion between two types of good—merit *(axios)* on the one hand and goods distributed on the other—each of which itself comprises a wide variety of goods—merit includes, for example, wealth, virtue, freedom; distributed goods include honor, money, office (*NE* 5.3 1130b30–32, 1131a20–29).

Still other examples make no reference to particular types of good or *energeia* at all but do mention 'the needed'. This is all I need to at least support my interpretation, however, given that on my interpretation 'the needed' means 'the good' understood as *energeia* (*telos, entelecheia,* etc.). For example, the courageous person faces what is needed as is needed and when needed (*NE* 3.7 1115b17–19). Generous people give and spend needed amounts on needed things (*NE* 3.7 1120a25–26). The angry person gets angry as is needed, when is needed, as long as needed, and so forth (*NE* 4.5 1125b31–32). Using these formulas of Aristotle's to make my point may seem forced until we recall that on my interpretation, to say that, for example, a generous person gives needed amounts on needed things is to say that a generous person is not simply a person who is generally disposed to give but is one who is disposed to give when doing so is called for or good. A generous person is not simply someone who is generally disposed to give anymore than a courageous person is one who is generally disposed to rush ahead, a moderate person one who is generally disposed to refrain from eating. Such dispositions are vices of excess. They are not virtues.

We see again, then, that Aristotle's teaching about the mean is not a trivial one. Instead, it has important implications. It implies that the virtuous person is not disposed to act or feel in a routinized manner, but is flexible. A virtuous person is not one who is generally disposed to do acts or experience feelings of a certain type. He is one who is disposed to do acts of a certain type when they are or lead to some good. Aristotle's goal in discussing the mean is not to tell us what types of actions to do or feelings to have. It is to guide us to avoid the routinization of action and feeling that is a counterfeit of true virtue, such as the counterfeit courageous person who is disposed simply to rush ahead, the counterfeit good-tempered person who is disposed simply to lack anger. The truly virtuous person is flexibly disposed toward types of action and feeling, engages in them when they are called for by or good for the situation at hand, refrains from them when they are not.

Another way to support this interpretation is to look at the cognitive component of ethical virtue itself and see if it makes reference to awareness of the good (or *energeia, entelecheia, telos,* etc.) of particulars.

The cognitive component of ethical virtue is variously understood to be deliberation *(bouleusis)* or practical insight *(phronēsis)*. As we have seen, ethical virtue is a disposition having to do with choice and consisting in a mean determined by a *logos*, specifically, by a *logos* the practically insightful person would use to determine it (*NE* 2.6 1107b36–a2). Choice is "deliberate desire of things that are up to us" (*NE* 3.3 1113a10–12). The progression of practical decision making is:

deliberation, decision, choice. For "the object of choice is that which has been decided upon as a result of deliberation" (*NE* 3.3 1113a4–5). Or, more precisely, the progression is: deliberation, decision, desire/choice. For, "when we have come to a decision as a result of deliberation, we desire in accordance with our deliberation" (*NE* 3.3 1113a11–12). What is deliberation like? We deliberate, according to Aristotle, about practicable things that are up to us (*NE* 3.3 1112a30–31). In addition, we do not deliberate about ends themselves but about what conduces to ends *(tōn pros ta telē)* (*NE* 3.3 1112b11–12). As has come to be accepted by commentators, 'what conduces to ends' includes both means to ends and also constituents of ends.

The practical progression just described is not quite complete, however. For good deliberation about what conduces to ends that are up to us involves correct or true cognition of those ends. An incontinent or bad person who is clever can attain specified goals as a result of deliberation and, as a result, achieve a great evil for himself. Such a person may be said to have deliberated correctly, but not well. The practically insightful person, to the contrary, deliberates both correctly and well since the practically insightful person attains specified goals as a result of deliberation and, in addition, achieves what is good. This is a broader type of correctness, one that includes correctness both about what conduces to ends and about ends themselves. Excellence in deliberation, then, is "correctness regarding what conduces to the end of which practical insight is a true apprehension" (*NE* 6.9 1142b32–33).

Here, Aristotle describes practical insight *(phronēsis)* as a true apprehension *(hypolēpsis)* of the end. Presumably 'apprehension' indicates an unmediated type of cognition, a taking in or taking as—as in the Greek-English lexicon definition of *'Hypolambanō'* as 'to suppose' or 'conceive', or 'to conceive something to be so and so' (*LSJ* 3.1); for, in another context, Aristotle uses it regarding practical insight and says that we believe Pericles and others like him to have practical insight because they can theorize (contemplate, see) what is good for themselves and others and, immediately after that, refers to this theorizing what is good as a *hypolēpsis* (*NE* 6.5 114068–13).[15] The *hypolēpsis* involved in practical insight, then, would be a correct and unmediated cognition of something as good. It is also, as Aristotle indicates in another context, a correct and unmediated cognition of something as end (excellence in deliberation is "correctness regarding what conduces to the end of which practical insight is a true apprehension") (*NE* 6.9 1142b32–33). The fact that Aristotle uses good and end interchangeably here provides more support for my claim that good means end for Aristotle.

Perception *(aisthēsis)*, Aristotle's more common description of practical insight (e.g., practical insight concerns the ultimate of which there is not knowledge but perception [NE 6.8 1142a26–27]), is an unmediated type of awareness as well, as are the other terms he uses to describe practical insight, such as *theōrein* (NE 6.5 1140b8–10, mentioned above; it is to that which theorizes well things concerning itself that we ascribe practical insight, NE 6.7 1141a25–26); *phainetai* (to someone who has been ruined by pleasure or pain, the principle or end does not appear); *gnōrizein* (practical insight must be acquainted with particulars).[16] Possibly, Aristotle uses the term '*hypolēpsis*' here in order to indicate that correct cognition of the end is an intellectual accomplishment, one that the bad but clever person does not attain, while the practically insightful person does attain it. According to the Greek-English lexicon, '*hypolambanō*' generally refers to false conceptions or suppositions and, when intended to indicate accurate ones, appropriate adverbs are added (*LSJ* 3.1). In this case, since a noun is used rather than a verb, what is added is an adjective. To call practical insight a true apprehension of the end is to say that it is an apprehension of something as the end that really is the end and to suggest that incorrect apprehension is possible.

The progression of practical decision making must then be expanded to include practical insight—or, better put, to include the part of practical insight that has to do with unmediated awareness of something as end or as good, namely, perception (or apprehension, theory, appearance, acquaintance). Where shall we put it, though? Presumably, perception of the end precedes deliberation about the means to or constituents of it, and the progression would be: perception, deliberation, decision, choice. Aristotle's well-known claim that "the decision is in the perception" supports this conclusion (NE 2.9 1109b23). Presumably also we must include in deliberation the comparative aspect of deliberation, namely, deliberative imagination, the type of imagination that imaginatively combines different ends into combined ends and compares the combined ends and their value (*De An.* 3.11 434a5–10).[17]

Does the cognitive component of ethical virtue, as thus described, then, make reference to end or the good? The answer clearly is 'yes'. Deliberation, though not directly about ends, is about what conduces to them—that is, about the means to or constituents of them. Practical insight is required for ethical virtue as we have seen both from the definition of ethical virtue (as a mean determined by a *logos* utilized by the practically insightful person) and from the discussion of the distinction between cleverness and practical insight (practical insight, and not just cleverness, is required for good deliberation; good deliberation is required for ethical virtue, as the definition of ethical virtue indicates) and is a true or correct and unmediated apprehension of the end or the good (where the interchangability of end and good provides support for my claim that good means end according to Aristotle). Decision, which follows, is in or dependent on the perception, which is (in part) of ends. Choice adds nothing cognitive, but only the desire that is consequent upon deliberation and decision.

Finally, then, relating perception, deliberation, decision, and choice back to the topic of this chapter, namely, the mean, we can recall that, according to the definition of ethical virtue, the mean is determined by a *logos*, specifically, by a *logos* used by the practically insightful person, and that practical insight involves both unmediated apprehension of an end or a good and deliberation on what conduces to an end or a good, where the terms 'end' and 'good' are used interchangeably. Cognition of the mean is, then, for Aristotle, cognition of a good understood as an end. This conclusion provides additional support for the general claim made in this chapter that the mean, according to Aristotle, denotes a good understood as end (*telos, entelecheia, energeia*, etc.).

Moreover, since the goal of Aristotle's discussion of the mean is not to give guidance on what types of acts to perform but instead to guide us to perform acts because they are (or lead to some) good, and since the goodness of particulars is determined by deliberation and practical insight, the goal of the discussion is, also, to guide us to act deliberately and with insight.

Conclusion

Aristotle's well-known claim that virtue is a mean with regard to passions and actions, then, does not imply that the virtuous person is disposed to do a certain amount—a middling amount—of specified actions nor that he or she is disposed to feel a certain amount—a middling amount—of specified emotions. Nor does it imply that the ethical mean is a mixture of opposites or that the ethically virtuous person's disposition results from a blend of opposites. Instead, it implies that the virtuous person does not act in a routinized way—does not tend to do actions of a certain type or tend not to do them and does not tend to feel emotions of a certain type or tend not to feel them. Instead, the virtuous person acts flexibly since he or she is disposed to engage in specified actions or feel specified emotions when to do so is appropriate, that is, when to do so will lead to or constitute some good.

What would this mean in practice? Would it mean that the virtuous person concludes that a certain emotion is good and so he or she feels it? No. Instead, the virtuous person would look at the situation he or she is in, in all its complex particularity and, through perception, deliberation, deliberative imagination, and practical insight, determine what is good and then, as a result, desire it, and, as a result of the desire, do it. Nor would it mean that the virtuous person does an act because it is, for example, the courageous thing to do. That is to say, it does not mean that he or she does the act in order to manifest the virtue. Instead, it means that he or she does the act because it is or leads to some good and that, as a result of doing the act, he or she manifests courage. That is, he or she does the act because it is good and, as a result, manifests the virtue. Central to the virtuous person's cognition, then, is cognition of the value of particulars.

CHAPTER FIVE

Analogy, Habit, Beauty, Unexpectedness

1
Analogy

The idea of the mean, as just interpreted, suggests that the virtuous person possesses both flexibility and insight *(phronēsis)*—flexibility in that he or she does and feels what each situation calls for rather than acting and feeling in certain routinized ways; insight in that he or she sees in each situation what the situation calls for.

A brief detour through ancient ethical theories will give us a sense of what a great accomplishment this view of Aristotle's is. Socrates is known as the one who brought philosophy down from the heavens, that is, from discussions of cosmology, to discussions of ethics. We are too narrow in our understanding, however, if we do not include Homer and the lyric poets as ethical thinkers, as well.[1]

Achilles, in the *Iliad*, is portrayed as a man at one with himself. He is also portrayed as a man identified with his anger. Those two qualities are manifest in Achilles' Book 9 refusal to reenter the battle even after Agamemnon makes a strong plea replete with apologies, and offers of honors and gifts, including the return of his concubine. Achilles is still so angry that he refuses. He states, "For as I detest the doorways of death, I detest that man, who hides one thing in the depths of his heart, and speaks forth another" (*Il.* 9.312) and then he goes on to elaborate his refusal. By his remark, Achilles indicates that he will not hold down his anger and his offended honor in order to reenter the battle. He has no way of managing his rage. He feels one way and will not act or speak another.

The *Odyssey* gives us a hero of a different type. Known not as 'swift-footed', but as 'crafty' and 'enduring' *(polymētis, talasiphronos)*, Odysseus is a person who has learned to manage his feelings, who has learned to do the very thing that Achilles despises, to say one thing when he feels another, to act on what he believes, in his craftiness, to be best, even when his feelings would lead him in another direction. He does not cry out, in the cave of Polyphemous, the cyclops, even though he wishes to, because he keeps his mind on his aim of getting out of the cave; he even calls himself, ingloriously, 'nobody'. He goes in his own house, disguised as a beggar, and allows people to strike and humiliate him, since he believes such disguise will better enable him to retake power. He restrains himself, the night before the final battle, from killing the servant women right there and then, servant women who have slept with the men who are terrorizing his wife and eating up his substance.

That night, struggling with himself over whether to kill the servant women right then and there as he very much desires to do, Odysseus makes an important remark indicating how virtue—in this case endurance or moderation (*saophrosynē*, or, literally, 'saving your mind')—is learned:

But the spirit deep in the heart of Odysseus was stirred by this,
and much he pondered in the division of mind and spirit,
whether to spring on them and kill each one, or rather
to let them lie this one more time with the insolent suitors
for the last and latest time; but the heart was growling within him.
And as a bitch, facing an unknown man, stands over
her callow puppies, and growls and rages to fight, so Odysseus'
heart was growling inside him as he looked on these wicked actions.
He struck himself on the chest and spoke to his heart and scolded it:
'Bear up, my heart. You had worse to endure before this
on that day when the irresistible Cyclops ate up
my strong companions, but you endured it until intelligence *(mētis)*
got you out of the cave, though you expected to perish.'

(*Od.* 20.9–21)

Odysseus, unlike Achilles, acts and speaks differently than he feels. He learned this in the cave of the cyclops. Lying in bed, with his spirit pulling him to kill those servant women then and there, Odysseus says to himself, 'No, this situation is like that other one I was in, the situation I was in in the cyclops' cave, where I endured pain in my heart and used a disgraceful and deceitful name in order to keep my mind and get out of the cave.'

'This situation is like that one.' Odysseus sees that it is. He perceives an analogy. Later, Archilochus will generalize the analogy by saying not just that the situation I am currently in is like situations I have been in previously, but that a certain aspect of life is like this in general:

> Heart, heart, battered by helpless cares,
> get up! Bare your chest and defend yourself
> against those who hate you. Stand firm against
> the onslaught of the enemy. And neither boast openly
> in victory, nor cry at home on your bed in defeat.
> But rejoice over joyful things and over evils do not mourn
> too much. Know the rhythm that controls human beings.
> (West, 1971, 128)

"Know the rhythm that holds human beings." Some translators go so far as not only to interpret, but to translate, this phrase to show that the point of the poem is that one must stand fast not just through the pleasant, but also the painful, aspects of life. Richmond Lattimore, for example, translates it: "All our life is up-and-down like this" (1960, 3). In Archilochus, we see the birth (or, a birth) of the generalized idea of moderation, the genesis of which we see in Homer's *Odyssey*.

In Plato's dialogues, we see this idea of keeping your mind or intelligence *(mētis)* developed even further. For Plato's Socrates, virtue is intelligence and the victory of intelligence over feeling, as it is in the *Odyssey* and in Archilochus' poem. In the *Phaedrus*, for example, it is intelligence *(nous)* that rules our passions (*Phdr.* 246b1–3, 247c6–8). However, for Socrates, the kind of intelligence involved has changed. No longer is it, simply, craftiness, or the ability to choose appropriate means to an end. Instead, now it becomes wisdom, where wisdom is knowledge not simply of how to be victorious, but of how to be victorious in a just or moderate or pious fashion. In the *Meno*, for example, in which Socrates appears to be arguing that virtue is wisdom *(phronēsis)*, he regularly refutes Meno's attempted definitions of virtue because they leave out justice, moderation, and piety (*Meno* 73a7–b2, d7–8, 78d3–6). Wisdom involves knowledge of ends as well as means. In the *Republic*, Socrates appears to claim that the just is the good as the appropriate (*Rep.* 1.342e9–11).[2]

Aristotle takes over Socrates' idea that virtue requires wisdom and not just craft and that wisdom—at least, practical wisdom or insight—

is knowledge of what is appropriate. He rejects, however, the idea that virtue is the control of wisdom over our emotions, or, as Plato's Socrates likes to put it some of the time, that virtue simply *is* wisdom. For Aristotle, as stated previously, virtue requires wisdom, but also requires suitable emotional development. A person who has both of these will not be controlling his emotions or acting against them, but will be acting on emotions that have been suitably developed so that they are in accord with reason. In this idea of accordant or unified development, Aristotle goes back to the ideal announced so angrily by Achilles, that one should not speak, and presumably act, differently than one feels. He does so, however, in a fashion that allows him to keep the sort of flexibility Odysseus is portrayed as possessing: the flexibility to act in the way that the situation calls for, not in a routinized way that one has decided is suitable to one's character or status as a warrior in every time and in every place. Odysseus acts differently in different situations, sometimes violently and other times peacefully, sometimes like a king and other times like a beggar. The virtuous person, for Aristotle, is the one who sees, in different situations, what the situation calls for, and who both feels and acts in accord with what he or she has seen.

I have stated that the virtuous person's practical perception is perception of an analogy. By looking at the example of Odysseus, we can see what this might mean. In the cave of the cyclops, Odysseus learned to endure the pain of silence and of a dishonorable name in order to attain his goal. The night before the battle with the suitors, faced with the evident pleasure he would take in killing the traitorous servant women right then and there, he refrains because he sees that the situation he is in is like the one he was in with Polyphemous. We could articulate the analogy in this way: just as in the cave of the cyclops, enduring pain and shame was necessary as a means to the eventual aim of defeating the cyclops and saving his life and the life of his companions, so now, enduring pain and shame is necessary as a means to the aim of defeating the suitors and saving his life and the life and substance of his family.

I maintain that, for Aristotle, the practically insightful person's perception is of this sort. It is seeing that this is like that—that this action or complex of actions is like a complex of actions seen or taken previously.[3] Specifically, it is seeing them as constitutive of—or, secondarily, instrumental to—some end, development, or completion.[4] Since the types of actions that lead to development vary from one complex practical situation to the next, the virtuous person must be flexible and must have practical insight, that is, must be able to perceive in each situation what the situation calls for.

This interpretation of Aristotle's idea of practical reasoning is appealing not only on intrinsic grounds but also on interpretive grounds. It makes it possible for us to solve a puzzling interpretive problem. As we have seen previously, Aristotle maintains that the person of practical insight does not utilize art or a rule in determining how to act but instead looks to or perceives what is appropriate to the situation at hand: "And when the general account is this imprecise, the account of particulars is even more imprecise. For they do not fall under any art or rule, but the agents themselves always must consider what is appropriate *(ton kairon)*, as is the case also in medicine and navigation" (*NE* 2.2 1103b34–1104a10).[5] He also states, in his definition of virtue as a disposition that has to do with choice and consists in a mean, that the mean is "determined by a *logos*, specifically by the *logos* the practically insightful person would use to determine it" (*NE* 2.6 1107a1–2). How can Aristotle both say that the practically insightful person utilizes a *logos* and that he does not utilize a rule in determining how to act?

Nussbaum deals with this interpretive problem by assuming that, in the definition of virtue, *logos* means rule or account ("the person whose choices are paradigms for ours is depicted as using a rule or account" she says, referring to the definition) and then arguing that though sensitivity to concrete, particular situations is of course central for Aristotle, rules can be second-best—useful guides for us when we have not yet acquired practical insight, useful tentative aides for virtuous adults when they are picking out the salient features of particulars, and useful as well in cases in which we do not have time "to formulate a fully concrete decision" (1986, 299, 304).

Nussbaum is right to point out that Aristotle does not wholly reject the use of rules (as his discussion of the role of law indicates). However, supposing that Aristotle conflates rule and account in the definition of virtue itself is a mistake. For it is there that Aristotle must be concerned most with the agent's attention to particulars and not with second-best scenarios. He cannot there be concerned with those who need a useful guide since they have not yet acquired practical insight, since the person with virtue has practical insight. He cannot be thinking of cases in which we do not have time for a fully concrete decision, since virtue involves choice and choice involves deliberation. And he cannot be thinking of the *logos* as a tentative aide for virtuous adults when they are picking out the salient features of particulars, for the *logos* is not a tentative aide to be used as a first step to be supplemented by a second and more particular sensitive determination of the mean. Instead, according to the definition, the mean is actually determined by a *logos*. Moreover, as Aristotle says in the definition, virtue has to do with choice and, as we know, unimpeded choice leads to action. Hence the passage in which Aristotle says the person of practical insight utilizes a *logos* in making choices and the one in which he states that in action we must not follow a rule but instead consider what is appropriate must be seen to refer to the same subject matter, namely, what we consult when we engage in good choice and action.

Utilizing the interpretation of Aristotle's practical reasoning developed in this essay, the claims in the two passages need not be seen as contradictory. The *logos* the practically insightful person uses to determine the mean is not an art or some kind of rule. Instead, it is perception of an analogy or proportion. It is perception of a similarity between certain aspects of the situation at hand and certain aspects of previous situations. The analogy or proportion I have in mind is, of course, the imprecise analogy or proportion Aristotle says holds between examples of different kinds of *entelecheia* or *energeia*, that is, between different types of development or completion. As noted previously, in *Metaphysics* 9.7, Aristotle states that *energeia* cannot be defined but must be seen *(synhoran)* in different cases by analogy. This, as I have maintained previously, is the same analogy Aristotle alludes to in *Nicomachean Ethics* 1.6 when he suggests that the equivocity of the good is not focal but analogical, mentioning the analogy that sight has to the body and mind to the soul. The fact that this interpretation of Aristotle's ethics makes it possible to square two seemingly incompatible statements that he makes is a positive reason for believing that the interpretation is an adequate one.

2
Habit

Several years ago, Myles F. Burnyeat argued successfully that the reason why young people are not appropriate listeners to lectures on ethics is that, lacking experience in action, they lack a certain kind of knowledge that comes from action (1980, 69–92). "Practice has cognitive power," Burnyeat states, thus summarizing his view of why, for Aristotle, practice or habituation is necessary for ethical virtue (1980, 73). Through practical activity, according to Burnyeat, the person of experience learns what things are enjoyable. Learning to enjoy certain types of actions is also, according to Burnyeat, learning that they are enjoyable (1980, 76).

Burnyeat's argument is an important one, but needs to be taken one step further. What a person learns through action is not simply that certain activities are enjoyable but that they are valuable. The two cognitions are not separate, since, for Aristotle, as I will argue in chapter 6, pleasure *is* the perception of something as valuable. Still, the two cognitions are different and we must give the perception of value priority for Aristotle if we are not to make him into a type of relativist or emotivist.

The passages Burnyeat refers to in giving his interpretation are found in Book 1 and Book 10. In Book 1, Aristotle states that students of ethics must have a fine upbringing, must have experience in action, and must not simply follow their passions if they are to gain any benefit from listening to lectures on ethics:

> Hence a youth is not an appropriate listener to [lectures on] political science. For he is inexperienced in the actions in life and the arguments of political science are from and concerning these. Further, since he tends to follow his passions, he will listen in vain and without profit, since the end is not cognition but action. It makes no difference whether he is young in age or youthful in character. For the deficiency is not due to time but to living and pursuing each thing in accordance with passion. For to such people, just as to incontinent people, cognition brings no benefit, while to those who form their desires and act in accordance with *logos*, knowledge concerning such things will be of much benefit. (*NE* 1.3 1095a2–11)

> Hence, the one who is to listen sufficiently to speeches concerning the beautiful and just and in general concerning political subjects must have been brought up in beautiful habits. For the 'that' is the principle and if it should appear sufficiently, there will be no additional need for the 'why'. Such a person either has such principles or can easily get them. (*NE* 1.4 1095b4–8)

In Book 10, Aristotle says that arguments can only aid someone in acquiring virtue if they are already lovers of what is beautiful:

> Argument and teaching surely are not strong with all people [viz., strong to make them good], but the soul of the student must have been prepared by habits for rejoicing and hating beautifully, just like earth that is to nourish seed. For one who lives in accordance with passion would not hear an argument that discouraged him nor would he understand it [if he did hear it], and how could someone who is in such a condition be persuaded? In general, it seems that passion does not yield to argument but to force. It is necessary, then, that the character already be somehow akin to virtue, loving *(stergon)* what is beautiful and hating *(dyscherainon)* what is ugly. (*NE* 10.9 1179b23–31)

Arguments will have no effect on most people, Aristotle also says, since most people do not abstain from bad acts because such acts are ugly but because they fear the pain of punishment. They pursue pleasure and flee pain. They lack even an insight *(ennoian)* into what is beautiful and truly pleasant since they have not had a taste of it:

> For the many do not naturally obey shame but fear, and do not refrain from base actions because they are ugly but because of the punishment. For living by passion they pursue their own pleasures and the means to them and flee the opposed pains and do not even have an insight into what is beautiful and truly pleasant since they have not had a taste of it. What argument could reshape such people? (*NE* 10.9 1179b11–16)

In these passages, Aristotle makes a distinction between people whose actions are motivated by undeveloped pleasure and pain on the one hand and those whose activities are motivated by the beautiful and the ugly on the other. Putting the two sets of passages together, we can put Aristotle's point this way: through a fine upbringing, one begins to become the sort of person who is motivated not by an undeveloped tendency to feel pleasure and pain, but by developed tendencies to feel pleasure and pain, tendencies developed in such a way that what one takes pleasure in are activities that are beautiful (i.e., fully or truly pleasant); someone who has not received a fine upbringing and therefore had little experience in or taste of actions of this richer, more beautiful kind will take pleasure in activities that are ready to hand for anyone and will be motivated to pursue those simple pleasures and to avoid the corresponding simple pains, pleasures and pains that are available to any child.

Burnyeat's interpretation can be pushed further by noting that Aristotle discusses two progressions in these passages: a progression in motivation or enjoyment and, in addition, a cognitive progression. The motivational progression is from simple to complex pleasures. The cognitive progression is a progression in awareness of the beautiful. In order to move from enjoyment of simple or mere pleasure to enjoyment of the complex or true pleasure one takes in what is beautiful, awareness of what is beautiful is required. Such awareness is not by nature, but comes from experience or habituation. Those who simply follow their passions do not even have a rudimentary awareness of it. They "do not even have an insight into what is beautiful and truly pleasant since they have not had a taste of it."

The cognitive progression suggested, then, is something like this: first, a taste of what is beautiful (where by 'a taste' Aristotle presumably means a single perception); then, from one or a few tastes, a resulting insight into what is beautiful. The progression is the progressive acquisition of 'thats'. For we can conclude that according to Aristotle what those who have not received adequate habituation have not experienced is, on the one hand, virtuous actions (since that is what adequate habituation involves) and, on the other, the beautiful (since according to him they have not had a taste of it and as a result lack an insight into it). In sum, what they lack is awareness *that* some actions in accordance with virtue are beautiful.

I say 'some' rather than 'a few' because Aristotle says the appropriate student must *love* what is beautiful, not just that he must have tasted it or have an insight into it. Plausibly, love of what is beautiful would result from a somewhat broader experience of beautiful actions than is required for a first insight. For Aristotle says that one becomes a lover of what is beautiful as a result of habituation and that a lover of what is beautiful has a character already "somehow akin to virtue." The cognitive progression, then, would be: first, a taste of what is beautiful; then, from one or a few tastes, a resulting insight into what is beautiful; then, a broad enough taste of what is beautiful that one becomes a lover of what is beautiful and, as a result, an appropriate listener to lectures on ethics. Put less metaphorically, the progression is: first, experience doing and perception of a beautiful action; then, from one or a few experiences doing such actions, a resulting insight into their beauty; then, a broad enough experience of and insight into beautiful actions that one comes to be motivated by their beauty to engage in them and, as a result, becomes an appropriate listener to lectures on ethics.

The cognitive progression does not stop at this third level, however, though it is all that is needed by one who is to listen profitably to lectures on ethics. For as argued in chapter 3, though ethics for Aristotle moves in the direction of the 'why' (i.e., of causal premises and arguments), it stays on the level of the 'that' and not the 'why' as much as possible; and, at the same time, the student of ethics must actually learn something from the lectures he attends. Hence, lectures on ethics must convey to him knowledge of a broader range of 'thats' than he brings with him when he comes to the lectures.

This suggests a plausible interpretation of Aristotle's claim in the last sentence of the 1.4 passage quoted above. Regarding the one who is beautifully habituated and who as a result has the 'that' and does not need the 'why' in addition, Aristotle claims that "Such a person either has such principles or can get them." Plausibly he means that such a person has a small range of 'thats', and can expand the range. That is, he perceives the beauty of a small range of virtuous actions and can extend his awareness. For example, perhaps he has, through habituation, come to see certain types of frightening and difficult actions that call for courage as beautiful and, as a result, can extend that knowledge further by coming to see that certain just acts are beautiful. And, from there, perhaps he can come to see that certain types of jokes are tasteful and beautiful while other types buffoonish and gross. Having some awareness of some actions as beautiful—having some 'thats' or principles—makes it possible or easier for the student to acquire more. As Odysseus sees that his situation in relation to the suitors is good by analogy to the way his situation in relation to Polyphemous was good, so the one who is beautifully habituated can extend the range of his or her awareness of beautiful actions. Aristotle immediately goes on:

> Best of all is one who understands everything himself.
> Noble, too, is the one who listens to someone who speaks well.
> But one who neither himself understands nor takes to heart
> What he hears from another is a worthless human being.
> (NE 1.4 1095b10–13)

This poem from Hesiod suggests that (at least some of) the additional knowledge will come from listening to another. But, to whom exactly? The context of the cited poem, a discussion *in* a lecture on ethics of what an appropriate listener *to* lectures on ethics ought to be like, suggests that such a person ought to listen to the lecturer. In fact, the poem functions as an exhortation to those in the audience to take to heart, to open themselves up to, what is said in the lectures if they are to show themselves as persons of character, which presumably the members of an Athenian audience at this time would want to do. The claim is not limited in extension only to the lecturer, however. In the 6.11 discussion of knowledge of ultimates, Aristotle says, "one ought to pay attention to the undemonstrated assertions and opinions of experienced people, old people, or practically insightful people no less than to demonstrations. For, because they have an eye from experience, they see correctly" (NE 6.11 1143b11–14). They see correctly, though they cannot demonstrate. In other words, they have the 'that' and not the 'why'. And, as a result of their experience, they have more 'thats' than other people do. The beautifully habituated person, then, ought to listen also to those who, from their experience, have a broader range of 'thats' or principles, namely, to experienced people, old people, and people of practical insight. Such people are those who are on the fourth level of our cognitive progression. They not only love the beautiful but have a broad experience of it, broad enough that less experienced lovers-of-the-beautiful can learn from them and ought to listen to them. Since ethics is part of political science and political science is an exercise of practical insight, the lecturer would be one of them (NE 6.8 1141b23–24).

3

If our beautifully habituated student continues on in his studies, moving from his study of ethics into physics, metaphysics, and psychology, he will move from the now very broad range of 'thats' he possesses into the 'why'. That is, the student will now move to an understanding of the causes of the truths discovered in ethics. The movement of cognition from the 'that' to the 'why', from perception and insight *(ennoia)* to theoretical insight and knowledge, is a familiar one. It is not limited to, or primarily associated with, cognition of the beautiful, but is associated with cognition in general. It is the cognitive progression described by Aristotle in *Metaphysics* 1.1 and *Posterior Analytics* 2.19. In other words, the progression of cognition of the beautiful indicated in the *Ethics*—from a single perception of it to an insight into it to a broader range of experience of it to causal knowledge of it—is simply one example of the progression of cognition in general that is, according to Aristotle, from perception and insight into particulars to theoretical insight into and knowledge of universals.

The use of the term 'insight' *(ennoian)* in *Nicomachean Ethics* 10.9 is no accident (they "do not even have an insight into what is beautiful and truly pleasant since they have not had a taste of it"). It suggests theoretical insight *(nous)* into *(en)* particulars. That is, it suggests the first and unarticulated awareness of particulars as instances of a universal. It suggests, in other words, the unarticulated initial operation of theoretical insight *(nous)* on particulars that is what makes Aristotelian induction, the derivation of universals from particulars, possible. For Aristotle, induction is the articulation of universal claims implicit in particular perceptions. The first awareness of particulars as instances of a universal is called by Aristotle *'ennoia'* (*NE* 10.9) and its intentional objects are called *'ennoēmata'* (*Met.* 1.1).

We are so used to the (correct) idea that for Aristotle *nous* is knowledge of universal first principles or premises that we tend to overlook the fact that *nous* is also, according to him, unmediated and unarticulated knowledge of particulars as instances of universals. Practical *nous (nous praktikē)* is probably the most commonly discussed example of *nous*'s operation on particulars (*NE* 6.11). But *Metaphysics* 1.1, where Aristotle discusses the cognitive progression from perception of particulars to knowledge of universals, provides another example, namely, the many insights *(ennoēmatōn)* that are gained in experience from which a universal apprehension of similars is produced (*Met.* 1.1 981a5–7).

Our progression in cognition, as described there, is: perception/percepts, memory/memories, experience/insights, art and knowledge/universal apprehensions about similars, and *logos*. The intentional object of perception is a percept, of memory is a memory, of experience is an insight, that is, an unarticulated awareness of a universal, of art and knowledge is universal apprehensions about similars and *logos*. It is from insights that articulated universal apprehensions are derived. It is important, too, that the example Aristotle uses in this passage to discuss the difference between *ennoēmata* in experience and universal apprehensions in art is an example of practical reasoning about an evaluative premise, namely, 'this benefited him'. We can conclude, then, that the *Metaphysics* claim that *ennoēsis* is unarticulated awareness of particulars as instances of a universal could be applied to 'insight into the beautiful' in *Nicomachean Ethics* 10.9 since the *Metaphysics* claim is not limited to nonevaluative claims.

Additional support for the idea that according to Aristotle there is a fairly broad operation of theoretical insight on particulars comes from the fact that Aristotle refers to 'contemplation' *(theōria)* of particulars and contemplation is the activity of theoretical insight. For example, Pericles and men like him have practical insight according to Aristotle specifically because they can see *(theōrein)* what is good for themselves and what is good for human beings in general *(NE* 6.5 1140b8–10). For another example, according to Aristotle it is to that which theorizes well things concerning itself that we ascribe practical insight *(NE* 6.7 1141a25–26). Additionally, in the discussion of why the happy person needs friends, Aristotle discusses contemplation of a good friend's good actions and states that such contemplation is a constituent of blessedness *(NE* 9.9 1169b30–70a4).[6] In each example, *theōria* is said to operate on particulars, thus strengthening the case for the claim that, for Aristotle, *nous* operates on particulars as well as on universals. In addition, two of the examples are evaluative *(theōria* of what is good for himself and for people in general, *theōria* of one's good friend's good actions) thus broadening the range of examples of *nous*'s operation on particulars that are instances of evaluative universals.

With these four passages in mind, Aristotle's *Nicomachean Ethics* 6.11 discussion of practical *nous (nous praktikē)* seems like a familiar discussion rather than an unusual and divergent one. The passages suggest that *nous*'s theoretical insight into unchanging universals is preceded by and results from *ennoēsis*, that is, by and from *nous*'s theoretical insight into particulars. In addition, three of the illustrative examples in each passage are examples of *nous*'s operation on particulars that are instances of evaluative universals (with the fourth left unspecified). The 6.11 discussion of two operations of *nous* is a fifth discussion of the same sort:

> Theoretical insight, too, is concerned with ultimates and in both directions. For both the first terms and the ultimates are objects of theoretical insight *(nous)* and not of reasoning *(logos)*; in demonstrations, theoretical insight is of the unchangeable terms and firsts; while in practical matters, theoretical insight is of the ultimate and changeable and the other premise. For these latter are the principles of the 'for the sake of which', since the universal is reached from particulars. Of these particulars, therefore, we must have perception, and this perception is theoretical insight. (*NE* 6.11 1143a35–b5)

Nous, according to this passage, is unmediated knowing of what we might call 'primitives'. It is contrasted with *logos* by which, in the context, Aristotle means mediated knowing, that is, reasoning or argument. In demonstrations, *nous* is of primitive terms that are unchangeable. Aristotle calls these primitives 'firsts'. In practical matters, by which presumably Aristotle means practical reasonings, *nous* is of primitives that are changeable. Aristotle calls these primitives 'ultimates'.

The language Aristotle uses is confusing, because he begins by calling both types of primitives 'ultimates' and then shifts to calling those in demonstrations 'firsts' and those in practical reasoning 'ultimates'. This type of confusion is familiar to us, however, from the similar confusion in Aristotle's *Nicomachean Ethics* 1.4 discussion of the proper student of ethics. There, as we have seen, he uses the term 'principle' equivocally, initially using it for primitives in demonstrations and then for primitives in dialectic (which Ross, to undo the equivocation, calls 'starting points', 1980, 33–35), initially for what is first in itself and then for what is first for us. The student, Aristotle suggests there, will have dialectical principles or will be able to get them and so he will not need demonstrative principles in addition; he will, Aristotle says, have the 'that' and so will not need in addition the 'why'.

Following Burnyeat, I have connected the 1.4 discussion of the beautifully reared student's knowledge of the 'that' that precedes and puts off the necessity of the 'why' to the 10.9 discussion of the insight *(ennoia)* into the beautiful that results from fine habituation. In 6.11, Aristotle makes a similar connection when he says that practical *nous*'s insight into changeable primitives is insight into principles of the 'for the sake of which'. In each case, what we have is *nous*'s unmediated knowledge of particulars as instances of evaluative universals.

Norman O. Dahl has argued successfully that what practical *nous* knows according to Aristotle in the 6.11 passage is principles or premises for an inductive inference to a universal end (1984, 227–236, 277–282). All induction moves from particulars to universals, Dahl points out, and Aristotle supports his view that ultimates are principles of the 'for the sake of which' by maintaining that universals are reached from particulars. In addition, Dahl points out, for Aristotle in general, perception provides the starting point for induction and practical *nous* is here described as a type of perception (1984, 230). Dahl is correct, then, in concluding that what is at issue are principles from which a universal can be induced. From that we can conclude that the ultimates that are known by practical *nous* are inductive principles for a universal. When we add the fact that, for Aristotle, the 'for the sake of which' is a close equivalent of 'end', Dahl's full conclusion is merited. What practical *nous* knows are inductive principles for a universal that is an end. The 6.11 passage, then, makes the same basic point as the 1.4–10.9 combination with the latter referring to inductive principles for the beautiful and the former to inductive principles for the good.

Dahl's explication of his claim is important. Practical *nous*, according to him, is an implicit grasp of a general principle. One who has it has a capacity, acquired through experience, to see in a particular situation that a particular action is to be done (1984, 278–279). Dahl draws this conclusion from the next passage in 6.11:

> This is why these [dispositions, viz., judgment, understanding, practical insight, and theoretical insight] seem to be by nature, and why on the one hand no one is thought to be wise by nature, but by nature to have judgment and understanding and theoretical insight. A sign of this is that these [dispositions] are thought to go with times of life, for example, that a particular age has theoretical insight and judgment, as if nature were the cause. [Hence, theoretical insight is both beginning and end; for demonstrations are both from and about these.] So it is necessary to attend to experienced people and old people or those with practical insight no less than to demonstrations. For because they have an eye from experience, they see correctly. (*NE* 6.11 1143b6–14)

Aristotle's point in this passage is that since these intellectual dispositions are types of unmediated knowledge of primitives, they incorrectly seem to be by nature, in contrast to wisdom *(sophia)* which is mediated knowledge since it involves demonstration; while instead these dispositions (Dahl calls them 'capacities') come through experience. People with experience, though they cannot demonstrate, nonetheless see correctly. They see correctly, though they cannot articulate or make explicit what it is that they see.

Dahl goes further in his explication of this passage. According to him, what they see is what is to be done: they have "the capacity to pick out the right thing to do in specific circumstances" and that capacity is "an implicit grasp of a general principle" (1984, 230); they have "the capacity to see in a particular situation that a particular action is to be done" (1984, 230; 278). Since the capacity is acquired through experience, it is not confined to one situation. Instead, it is a capacity to pick out actions like this one in situations like this one. In sum, people who have this capacity have an implicit grasp of the general principle that in situations like this one, actions like this one are to be done. They have this capacity even though they may not be able to articulate what it is for a situation or action actually to be like this one (1984, 278).

Dahl's point is a nicely nuanced one. Experienced people's unmediated knowledge is not awareness of brute particularity; it is not knowledge simply that 'This is to be done.' For their awareness is experiential; that is, they pick out actions of this sort more than once. That they do so indicates some awareness of a universal. They are aware that actions *like this* are to be done. Dahl's point is that implicit awareness of a universal precedes the ability to explicate or articulate that universal. So, their awareness is not awareness of brute particularity. Nor is it full awareness of a universal. It is the implicit grasp of a universal principle.

For expository purposes, I have simplified Dahl's point somewhat. For he shifts back and forth between 'is to be done' and 'is good'. In my view, Dahl is justified in claiming that what practical *nous* is aware of is that actions like this are *good* but not that they are *to be done*. Presumably, Dahl gets the phrase 'to be done' from the preceding passage (*NE* 6.11 1143a33–35): "And all things to be done are included among particulars and ultimates. For the person of practical insight also must cognize these [viz. things to be done], and understanding and judgment concern things to be done, and these are ultimates." However, though Aristotle says in this passage that all things to be done are included among particulars and ultimates, of course not all particulars and ultimates are things to be done. In addition, the passage does not say that practical *nous* concerns what is to be done, and, importantly, a central point of the immediately following passage (*NE* 6.11 1143a35–b5, quoted above) is that practical *nous* cognizes a different type of ultimate, namely, those that are the principles of the end (or the 'for the sake of which'): "in practical matters, theoretical insight is of the ultimate and changeable and the other premise. For these latter are the principles of the 'for the sake of which', since the universal is reached from particulars." Since, according to the argument of this essay, good *means* end for Aristotle, we can translate this point as Dahl does and say that practical *nous* cognizes or perceives that 'Actions like this are good.'

However, not every act that is good is an act that is to be done. To conclude that an act is to be done, deliberation is required. This, of course, is one of the central points of *De Anima* 3.11, previously discussed (chapter 2, section 1), namely, that practical *nous* sees particulars as good while deliberative imagination takes the various perceptions or images of different particulars as good and combines them into one unified image not simply of what is good but, instead, of what is best.

To complete our interpretation of *Nicomachean Ethics* 6.11 on practical *nous* we must respond to an objection that could be made to the interpretation, namely, that what practical *nous* understands is not an evaluative proposition at all but a descriptive one. Why not simply say that *nous*'s awareness of the principles of an end is awareness of descriptive propositions that are relevant to drawing evaluative conclusions (i.e., conclusions about ends)? We can respond to this objection in two ways. First, we can respond by again maintaining that according to *De Anima*, practical *nous* sees particulars as good.

Secondly, we can recount Dahl's answer to this imagined objection (1984, 278–279). Dahl responds by pointing to Aristotle's 6.7 comments on why experience is better than knowledge for practical purposes:

> Nor is practical insight concerned only with universals, but it must also discern particulars. For it is practical and practice concerns particulars. On account of this, some who do not know, especially those who have experience, are more practical than others who know; for one who knew that light meats are digestible and healthy, but did not know which sorts of meat are light, would not produce health, but one who knows that chicken is light and healthy is more likely to produce health. (*NE* 6.7 1141b14–21)

What practical insight knows from experience, Dahl points out, is that chicken is healthy, a particular evaluative proposition; implicit in it, Dahl says, is the general principle that light meats are healthy.

The person with knowledge knows the universal proposition 'Light meats are digestible and healthy.' He does not know which meats are light. Hence, he is not able to produce health. The syllogism suggested by Aristotle is:

> Light meats are digestible and healthy.
> Chicken is light meat.
> Therefore, chicken is digestible and healthy

The person who has knowledge has the first premise (a universal premise), but not the second premise (a particular premise) or the conclusion (a particular proposition). As a result, though he knows, he is not able to heal. The person of experience has the conclusion—'Chicken is healthy.'—without either of the premises and as a result is able to heal. What he knows is a particular evaluative proposition, not a simply descriptive one.

Dahl's use of this passage to support the claim that *nous* is awareness of evaluative not descriptive propositions rests on the assumption that it is *nous* that is operative in practical insight's achievement of particular evaluative knowledge from experience. The passage does not actually say this, however, so Dahl's point needs support. Let us step back, then, and ask a background question. Supposing it is correct that practical *nous* knows particular evaluative premises (implicit in which are universal evaluative claims), what is the relation between practical *nous* and practical insight *(phronēsis)*? The most plausible conclusion is that practical *nous* is a component of practical insight, specifically, that it is the component of practical insight that knows particular evaluative propositions—or, to put it more precisely, that sees particulars as good. For practical insight does involve seeing particulars as good, and that is what practical *nous* does as well. Dahl makes a similar point by describing practical insight as '*nous*-like'.

> That practical insight is not knowledge is evident. For practical insight concerns the ultimate, as has been said, since what is to be done is of this sort. Hence, it is opposed to theoretical insight. For theoretical insight is of terms of which there is no argument *(logos)*, while practical insight is of the ultimate of which there is not knowledge but perception. This is not the perception of the special senses but the sort by which we perceive that the ultimate among mathematicals is a triangle. For in that way, too, there will be a stop. But this is perception rather than practical insight, though it is another type of perception. (*NE* 6.8 1142a23–29)

Practical insight, as here described, is awareness of particulars ('ultimates') through perception. Practical insight is, then, Dahl is right to conclude, like *nous* in its operation on particulars.

How to take the example of the triangle as the ultimate among mathematicals is disputed. As Dahl points out, two interpretations are commonly given. One interpretation is that the perception discussed is the perception of a particular as an instance of a universal: 'this is a triangle'. The other interpretation is that what one perceives is that a specific triangle is the last mathematical figure into which a given geometrical figure can be divided and thus is the first step in the construction of that figure. The example is brief enough that there is no completely conclusive way to determine how Aristotle means it. The very brevity of the example, however, suggests that he has the 'this is a triangle' interpretation in mind since it is the simpler of the two, the one that would require the least supplementary explanation. Moreover, the passage suggests that the perception involved is not perception by the special senses (sight, hearing, smell, etc.) but presumably perception by all the senses of the common sense-objects (unity, movement, number, etc.) which involves perceiving a sensible object as something (a human being as one, e.g., which is parallel to the case of perceiving the figure in front of us as a triangle or, similarly, perceiving a certain action as good), once again favoring the 'this is a triangle' interpretation.

It is enough for purposes of the argument to find an interpretation of the passage that is compatible with one's interpretation of Aristotle's related views. Dahl maintains that either interpretation is compatible with his view that in perception of particular actions to be done there is implicit grasp of a general principle. I would maintain that the 'this is a triangle' interpretation is compatible with the general idea that practical *nous* is awareness of particulars as good: 'this is good'.

At this point in his argument, Dahl argues that it is only in ethics that the perception of particulars contains within it an implicit grasp of a universal principle. Perception of the practical matters involved in ethics is different than perception in general in this way, Dahl maintains, because ethics is imprecise, being concerned with what is true for the most part. Following John McDowell, Dahl states that there is for Aristotle an essential indeterminateness in the ends involved in moral behavior so that the best one can do in problematic cases is to say, for example, just actions are ones that are like those in the unproblematic cases. "Exactly how they are alike, though, one cannot say. Whether an action is like such actions is something that has to be discovered by *perception*, but a perception based on *experience*" (1984, 233–234). Just as Wittgenstein pointed out that we learn how a number series goes on only by saying that the rest of the series will be *like* what has gone on before, that is, by learning from experience what our practice of counting such a series is, so we must learn from experience what our moral practice is (1984, 234).

In ethics, according to Dahl, universal principles cannot be given content independently of experience of a wide variety of particulars, whereas in a precise subject such as mathematics "basic concepts and principles can be given precise content after contact with only a few instances that fall under them" (1984, 235). In ethics,

> Content cannot be given to basic principles without a wide experience of particulars, and one cannot perceive particulars as falling under these principles without a wide variety of experience. It is only in the latter sorts of cases that the perception of particulars will involve an implicit grasp of general principles. As a result, it will only be in the latter sorts of cases that one will have reason to say that *nous* is involved in the perception of particulars. (1984, 235)

Dahl is right in claiming that, since ethics is imprecise in a certain way, the process of grasping a universal principle in the ethical domain is different than the process of grasping a universal in a more precise domain such as mathematics. Nothing justifies him, however, in concluding from this that it is only in the ethical domain that *nous* is involved in the perception of particulars, or that there is an implicit grasp of a universal principle, and for several reasons. First, *Metaphysics* 1.1 suggests the contrary. There, as we have seen, Aristotle says that a universal judgment about similars is produced from "many insights" *(ennoēmatōn)* gained in experience. An insight *(ennoēma)* is an implicit grasp of a universal principle. Moreover, a universal judgment about similars is produced not from one or a few but from many insights, according to Aristotle.

In addition, as pointed out previously, in that passage Aristotle moves from talking about the general derivation of universals from particulars to an evaluative example. This movement suggests that he himself sees both descriptive and evaluative cases as examples of the same general process of deriving knowledge of universals from the inarticulate or implicit awareness of particulars as instances of universals.

Next, mathematical examples seem to follow the same general pattern that Dahl describes. As I have suggested in the introduction to chapter 3, a person may see various items as circles without being articulately aware of the criterion on the basis of which he or she does so. When a person sees them as circles, we can say that he or she has an insight *(ennoēma)* into them. From many such insights, he or she can derive the universal that is the definition of circle.

Finally, Dahl's McDowell-inspired conclusion is based on a vague understanding of what Aristotle means by imprecision in ethics. As I have argued, there are two types of imprecision in ethics according to Aristotle, inquiry imprecision and subject matter imprecision. Inquiry imprecision can be, and is to an extent, overcome in physics, metaphysics, and psychology. Subject matter imprecision results from the fact that ethics is about ends and ends are imprecise in a certain specifiable way. End means completion for Aristotle and completions of different things are themselves different, as we have seen. We do not need to assume a vague or indefinitely specifiable universal involved in the ethical domain to account for the imprecision in ethics. Instead, the universal is specifiable even though its instantiations are quite different one from another. Hence, the issue is not how to give content to the universal. Instead, the issue is what particulars (or complexes of particulars) are instances of the universal. It is the identification of instantiations that is most difficult and not the specification of the universal.

Thus it is reasonable to conclude that for Aristotle all perception of particulars contains within it an implicit grasp of a universal principle. Or, to be more precise, it is reasonable to conclude that there is an operation of *nous* on all types of particulars that is the initial and unarticulated awareness of those particulars as instances of universals. That operation is called by Aristotle '*ennoēsis*' or, specifically in cases of the initial and unarticulated awareness of ends, 'practical *nous*', and it is also sometimes called 'contemplation' or 'perception' (or, as we have seen in previous chapters, 'appearance', 'acquaintance', or 'true apprehension'). With regard to ethics, that implicit grasp is referred to as practical *nous* that grasps the principles for an inductive inference to universal ends (*NE* 6.11) or, alternately, it is referred to as an insight *(ennoēsis)* into the beautiful that comes from habituation (*NE* 10.9)

We are justified now in drawing the conclusion suggested at the beginning of this section that the progression of cognition of the beautiful indicated in the *Ethics*—from a single perception of it to an insight into it to a broader range of experience of it to causal knowledge of it—is simply one example of the progression of cognition in general that is, according to Aristotle, from perception and insight into particulars to theoretical insight into and knowledge of universals.

4
Beauty

What, though, is the beautiful according to Aristotle? I have argued previously in this essay that good for Aristotle means end or final cause. Beauty, for him, is identified with form. One of Aristotle's main objections to the metaphysical views of his philosophical predecessors is that they do not introduce principles that can account for things being or becoming good or beautiful. Specifically, they introduce material cause and efficient cause, but do not, or do not in an adequate way, introduce final cause (end) and formal cause (form). The predecessors introduce material cause because the generation and destruction of beings proceed out of and into one or more elements. The predecessors are then compelled by "the things themselves" to introduce efficient cause, that is, the beginning of movement, because "the substratum itself does not make itself change" (*Met.* 1.3 984a21–22).

Inclusion of these two causes—material cause and efficient cause—is inadequate in an account of the nature of beings, however. Nature appears to include more than simply a plurality of elements set in motion by an external push or pull. In addition to elements, there appear to be wholes. Moreover, in addition to movement, there appear to be constitutive ends of movement. Aristotle indicates this phenomenal inadequacy of metaphysical accounts that include only material and efficient cause by saying that such accounts do not state the cause of what is beautiful or good. The predecessors, he says, are compelled by "the truth itself" to introduce formal cause; and, after that, final cause: "after these people and principles of this sort, since the latter are not adequate to generate the nature of beings, people were again compelled by the truth itself, as we said, to seek the next principle. For it is not likely that fire or earth or any other such [principle] is the cause of things being or becoming good or beautiful . . ." (*Met*. 1.3 984b8–13). We have seen that the good is identified with final cause or end for Aristotle. We can conclude, then, that the beautiful is identified with form. Further support for this conclusion comes from the fact that good is found only among beings that move while the beautiful is found also among beings not susceptible of movement: "the good and the beautiful are different, for the good is always in action while the beautiful is also among immovables" (*Met*. 13.3 1078a31–32). Material cause is incomplete without formal cause (since matter forms wholes), and efficient cause incomplete without final cause (since movement is not chaotic but orderly). I have discussed final cause in chapter 2, section 3, and will now discuss formal cause.[7]

An account of wholes requires the introduction of a third cause. For material and efficient cause cannot account for them and, in addition, "all things which have a plurality of parts in which the all is not like a heap but is a certain whole beyond the parts have a cause" (*Met*. 8.6 1045a8–10). As is well-known, the cause according to Aristotle, is substance understood as form understood as the 'what was being'.

Substance, for Aristotle, is primary—in *logos*, knowledge, and time—and being in all the other categories is secondary and dependent according to him. For example, being is said in many ways, according to Aristotle, but all with reference to *(pros)* substance. More specifically, substance is what beings in all the other categories are said of while it is never said of anything else. Substance cannot be reduced to or derived from being in the other categories—quantity, quality, relation, time, space, action, passion—while they are dependent upon substance for their very being (*Met*. 4.2 1003a33–b10, 7.1 1028a10–20). These very general statements about substance are almost enough on their own to support the idea that substance is the cause of wholes. Still, we need a more precise statement to that effect.

First, though, why does Aristotle identify substance with form? As is well-known, Aristotle answers the question, what is substance, by considering the conditions substance must meet. It must, according to him, be a substratum, that is, what is underlying *(hypokeimenon)*, and it must be a 'this-what' *(tode ti)* (*Met.* 5.8 1017b23–25). It must be a substratum because as we have seen it must be what others are said of while it is not said of anything else (*Met.* 7.3 1028b35–37). It must be a 'this-what' since it alone of beings must be separable (*Met.* 7.3 1029a27–28).

There are three candidates for what is substance—matter, form, or the compound of the two (*Met.* 7.3 1029a2–3). It cannot be the compound, for the compound is "posterior and obvious" (i.e., of compounds, we must still ask what is underlying) (*Met.* 7.3 1029a30–32). It would seem instead to be matter, since matter is prior to all that is composed out of it, and all things are said of matter, not matter of all things (*Met.* 7.3 1029a10–19). Matter, however, does not meet one of Aristotle's conditions, namely, separability, or independence. For matter is not a 'this-what' (by which Aristotle presumably means to include both that matter is neither an independent 'this' nor a 'what') (*Met.* 7.3 1029a26–28). Substance must, therefore, be form.

Aristotle must, still, decide how best to understand form since there is more than one candidate for how to understand it. Plato, for example, understands form as the universal according to Aristotle. Aristotle, however, concludes that substance cannot be the universal since the universal does not meet the conditions he has laid down. The universal is not underlying but is said of what is underlying (*Met.* 7.13 1038b15–16). Nor is the universal a 'this-what' but instead a mere 'such' *(toionde)* (i.e., a universal is a 'what' but not a 'this') (*Met.* 7.13 1038b34–1039a2).

Aristotle asserts instead that form must be understood as the 'what was being' (*Met.* 7.6, 7.17). The relationship between the 'what was being' and that to which it belongs is not a mere accidental unity according to him but a more intimate one. A being and its 'what was being' according to Aristotle are necessarily one and the same (*Met.* 7.6 1031a15–1031b22). The 'what was being' is primary not accidental. The account *(logos)* of a being in terms of its 'what was being' is not a mere accidental attribution but instead is a definition *(horismos)* (*Met.* 7.5 1031a11–14). For a definition is an account of something primary, namely, of what something is.

As a result of these characteristics, the 'what was being' does meet Aristotle's conditions for substance. Since it is primary, it is underlying. It is also a 'this-what'. For as its very name implies, it is a 'what'. The 'what was being' is what something is. It is also a 'this'. For, a being and its 'what was being' are one and the same. Therefore, substance for Aristotle is form understood as the 'what was being'.

My interpretation of Aristotle's account of substance relies on an interpretation of his term *'tode ti'* as 'this-what'. I am justified in that interpretation by Aristotle's comments about substance in 7.17. There Aristotle understands substance, that is, the form or 'what was being', as the answer to the question,

> why the matter is a 'what'. For example, why is one 'this' *(tadi)* a house? Because 'what house was being' belongs to it. And why is another 'this' *(todi)* (or a 'this' *(todi)* having this form) a human being? So what is sought is the cause of the matter [namely, the form], the cause by virtue of which the matter is a 'what'; and this is substance. (*Met.* 7.17 1041b5–9)

In 1921, J. A. Smith draws the same conclusion regarding *'tode ti'*. He rejects interpretations according to which either *'tode'* or *'ti'* is a general term restricting the other term to a single, random instance. He rejects the idea that the general class is *ti* (i.e., the class of 'whats') with *'tode'* singling out a particular *'ti'* (this 'what', any 'what') on the grounds that the Greek for such a term would be *'to ti tode'*. He rejects the idea that the general class is *'tode'* (i.e., the class of 'thises') and *'ti'* the indefinite article 'a' or 'any' (a 'this', any 'this') on two grounds. First, it would imply that Aristotle holds the doctrine that there is a class of 'thises' with the general characteristic of 'thisness'. Second, the meaning *'tode ti'* would carry on such an interpretation is not the meaning it carries in Aristotle's work. Smith argues instead that both words are general terms. *'Tode'* in Greek means a 'this'. *'Ti'* in Greek means a 'what'. *'Tode ti'* means anything that is both a 'this' and a 'what', that is, it is "both (a) singular and so signifiable by 'this' and (b) possessed of a universal nature, the name of which is an answer to the question *ti esti* in the category of *ousia* . . ." (1921, 19).

The passage from 7.17 supports this interpretation. There the question is why some particular 'this' is a particular 'what'. 'This' (*tode* or *tade*) and 'what' *(ti)* are general terms delimited in this case. Aristotle asks why one 'this' is a particular 'what', namely, house, and why another 'this' is a different 'what', namely, human being. Substance, for Aristotle, is the cause by virtue of which a 'this' is a 'what'.

Aristotle goes on and draws the further conclusion that substance as form or the 'what was being' is the cause by virtue of which beings are wholes (syllables) and not heaps. For composed beings, he says, substance is the cause by virtue of which "the all is one, not like a heap but like a syllable" (*Met.* 7.17 1041b11–12). Using the example of a syllable composed out of elements or letters (the two words are the same for

Aristotle), the elements are the matter and what is responsible for the elements composing the syllable is the substance. The whole or syllable, is something other *(heteron ti)* than the elements:

> The syllable is not the elements, nor is 'ba' the same as 'b' and 'a', nor is flesh fire and earth. For when decomposed, they, namely, the flesh and the syllable, no longer exist but the elements exist and so do fire and earth. Therefore, the syllable is something—not merely the elements sounded and unsounded—but also something other, and flesh is not merely fire and earth or hot and cold, but also something other. (*Met.* 7.17 1041b14–33)

Substance, then, is the cause of the whole being something other than its elements. Substance is responsible for the unity of the elements being the unity of a whole and not the unity of a heap or what we might call a 'collection' (for 'b' and 'a' composing 'ba' and not {'b', 'a'}.

According to Aristotle, the question, 'What is substance?' is permanently puzzling: "a question that was asked of old, is asked now, and will always be asked and will always be a subject of puzzlement" (*Met.* 7.1 1028b2–3). Though he gives answers to the question, he does not believe his answers resolve all that is puzzling about substance. For there is a difficulty that remains. Aristotle wants to give account of the whole, for example, the syllable or flesh. He cannot account for the unity of the whole simply by listing its elements, so he introduces the notion of substance. Substance is what the elements are being: 'ba' is what 'b' and 'a' are being; flesh is what fire and earth are being. Doesn't that leave him now simply with a greater plurality? He began with 'ba' and has now reduced it to {'b', 'a', substance}; and he began with flesh but has now reduced it to {fire, earth, substance}. Hasn't he begun with a whole in each case, and reduced it to a heap or a collection?

Aristotle's response is that a whole is not an element. An element, according to Aristotle, is that into which a thing is divided and that is present in it as matter. The whole, he says, in this case the syllable or flesh, is something other than the elements that compose it. In addition, it is not just some other element, nor is it composed of elements. For

> if (1) it is an element, the same argument applies. For flesh will be of fire and earth and something else, so it will go on indefinitely. But if (2) it is out of elements, it is clear that it will not be out of one but out of many (or it itself would be the element). Thus we will use the same argument about this as about the flesh or the syllable. (*Met.* 7.17 1141b20–25)

A substance is not an element, the passage argues, for if it were, wholes would be indefinite pluralities. Substance, is, however, a cause or principle. Hence, it must be a nonelemental cause or principle.

Moreover, since substance is the cause or principle by virtue of which a 'this' is a 'what', or the elements are a whole, or the elements actually are something, it is in fact not just any cause or principle but the primary cause or principle of being. Aristotle's predecessors cannot generate the nature of the beings, then, we could say in summary, because they leave out the primary cause of being—substance as the 'what was being'. Substance is the primary cause, and prior even to the matter since without substance matter would not be something but would instead simply be prime matter or 'pure stuff'.

Aristotle understands 'principle' in two ways: that from which, by being present in it, a being comes to be; and that from which, although not present in it, a being comes to be. The former is an element of a certain type, specifically, it is the first element, for example, the keel of a ship or the foundation of a house. As we have seen, however, substance must be a nonelemental principle. Substance, then, must be that from which, although not present in the element, the element comes to be. The elements, in other words, would not be what they are without the existence of the substance. This shows another aspect of the meaning of Aristotle's coined term, the 'what was being'. What the elements are (imperfectly or incompletely) being is the whole. But how can that be? Don't 'b' and 'a' have their own being independently of the syllable 'ba'?

We are compelled by the phenomena, as Aristotle might say, to answer 'no'. 'B' is a consonant and cannot be what it is by itself. By themselves, consonants are incomplete. They require for their completion—for their very existence, that is, for their very being what they are—that they be elements of a syllable composed of consonant and vowel. So also with 'a'. 'A' is a vowel and is not complete by itself. It requires for its completion—for its very existence or being what it is—that it be part of a syllable composed of consonant and vowel. Vowels are incomplete by themselves and cannot be what they are—cannot be a 'what'—without a syllable. In general, for Aristotle, elements are incomplete by themselves.

Despite the advances Aristotle believes he has made in understanding substance, he still believes that substance remains puzzling in a certain way. Though substance is a principle and not an element, it still is "something other." As a result, we still have the problem of the unity of substance with the elements. Aristotle treats this difficulty by turning to *logos*. What is the difference, he asks, between the *logos* of substance, which is a definition, and the *logos* of accidental attribution? What is the difference, for example, between saying that a human being is rational and that a human being is white? In each case, we have substance and another item—"something other." If we proceed in our usual way of definition and *logos*, Aristotle says, we cannot resolve the difficulty. "But if, as we say, a human being is on the one hand matter and on the other hand form *(morphē)*, the one potentially and the other actually, what is sought will no longer seem a puzzle" (*Met.* 8.6 1045a23–25). The solution, then, is that the proximate matter is only potentially *(dynamei)* what the form is actually *(energeiai)*, namely, the substance. The puzzle results from looking for a unifying *logos* as well as a difference between potentiality and actuality *(dynameōs kai entelecheias)*:

> But as has been said, the proximate matter and the form *(morphē)* are the same and one, on the one hand potentially and on the other hand actually *(energeiai)*. So it is like seeking what is the cause of the one and of being one, for each something is one, and potentiality *(to dynamei)* and actuality *(to energeiai)* are somehow one. (*Met.* 8.6 1045b18–21)[8]

Form is "something other." Nonetheless, form and matter are potentiality and actuality, and potentiality and actuality are somehow one. The 'somehow unity' of potentiality and actuality is as far as we can go in resolving our difficulty. We have a difficulty when we try, in *logos*, to separate them and then unify them. For once we have separated them we cannot unify them again since to separate them is to treat them as if they could be analyzed into elements. It is not surprising, then, that the attempt to unify what has been separated results in a heap and not a whole. Potentiality and actuality are somehow one. To ask for the cause of that unity is to ask for the cause of unity in general ("the cause of the one and of being one")—not the cause of the unity of any particular whole whose unity is in question. Our accounting can go no further. In every case of the unity of a whole not a heap the cause is the 'somehow unity'—the not fully comprehensible unity—of potentiality and actuality.

That unity is a hierarchical, not an egalitarian, unity, since actuality is prior to potentiality in *logos*, time, and substance. This hierarchy extends through all of being as we can conclude from a passage in the *Politics*:

> For in all compounds, that is, things which come to be one common something out of many, whether out of the continuous or the discrete, the ruler and the ruled show up. And this, out of all of nature, belongs to the animate *(empsychois)*, for there also is some rule in those that do not participate in life, for example, in a musical mode. (*Pol.* 1.2 1254a28–33)

We must not, then, separate matter and substance and then seek a unifying *logos* to reunite them. Instead, we should suppose from the beginning that, as is phenomenally evident, matter and substance are somehow one. Aristotle's use of the term 'somehow' *(pōs)* indicates that he believes that though they are so to speak one, they are also so to speak two. Hence, despite all the difficulties regarding substance that have been resolved, substance still remains puzzling. Aristotle, however, does not assume that the fact that a puzzle remains in an account means that the account is incomplete or inaccurate. Instead, what is hard to grasp may be capable of existing, as he says in the passages on motion (*Met.* 11.9 1066a26; *Phys.* 3.2 202a1–2). Moreover, sometimes the knot is in the things not in our reasoning about and reflection on the things (*Met.* 3.1 995a30–31).

5

The beautiful, then, is formal cause. It is substance understood as form understood as the 'what was being'. It is the cause or principle by virtue of which beings are wholes rather than heaps, by virtue of which a 'this' is a 'what', by virtue of which matter is something. It is, as a result, the primary cause of being.

The fourth cause Aristotle must introduce, in order to account for things becoming or being good, is final cause. As we have seen, Aristotle identifies final cause with the good as end. Aristotle introduces final cause as the cause of motion in a way that parallels his introduction of formal cause as the cause of substance.[9] For Aristotle, end is the primary cause of motion. We might think, instead, that the mover (efficient cause) is the primary cause of movement. We know, however, that the same movement on a mover's part may cause different movements in different cases: if, using a certain arm movement, I throw a piece of chalk on a table, the chalk will roll across the table and fall off and on to the floor, while if I use the same arm movement to throw some water on a table, it will splatter and sink in. The mover, then, appears to be a cause but not the primary cause of movement. The material of that which I throw is different in the two cases. Perhaps, then, the matter is the cause of the movement? It is, but only insofar as it has a certain potential for movement of a certain type. Potential is of course relative to actuality as we have seen: "potentiality and actuality are somehow one" and actuality is prior to potentiality in *logos*, time, and substance. For example, chalk has the potential to roll, water to seek its level. So the actuality, or end, is the prior, and primary, cause. The change is named by the 'into which', Aristotle says (Phys. 5.1 224b7–8). End or actuality is the cause of the movement being the sort of movement that it is. Form or the beautiful is the primary cause of being, as we have seen, and end or the good, as this example shows, is the primary cause of movement.

Sometimes, however, Aristotle appears to confuse these claims. He sometimes says that not form but end is the cause of being: "But while the latter cause [the first mover] is sought of generation and destruction, the former [the 'for the sake of which'] also of being" (*Met.* 7.17 1041a31–32). He sometimes suggests that end is the primary cause since he says that it is most of all a principle: "Yet in all things the good most of all is a principle" (*Met.* 12.10 1075a37). He sometimes says that end is the cause of the matter: "for the 'for the sake of which' is the cause of the matter, not the matter of the end; and the end is the 'for the sake of which'" (*Phys.* 2.9 200a33–34).

It is not a confusion, however, but an intentional identification. Sometimes Aristotle identifies form and end:

> What is form? The 'what was being'. What is the 'for the sake of which'? The end. But perhaps these both are the same. (*Met.* 8.4 1044a36–b1)

> For the 'what' and the 'for the sake of which' are one. (*Phys.* 2.7 198a25–26)

> And since nature is said in two ways, on the one hand as matter and on the other hand as shape, and the latter is the end, and the others are for the sake of the end, the shape must be a cause, namely, the 'for the sake of which'. (*Phys.* 2.8 199a30–32)

> For the necessary is in the matter and the 'for the sake of which' is in the *logos*. (*Phys.* 2.9 200a14–15)

How, though, can formal cause and final cause be the same for Aristotle? For, according to him, formal cause is the beautiful and final cause is the good and the good is not found among immovables, although the beautiful is?

> For how can a principle of motion or the nature of the good be among immovables? If indeed everything which is good by itself and due to its own nature is an end and thus a cause because for the sake of it the other things both come to be and are? And the end, that is, the 'for the sake of which', is the end of some action, and all actions are together with motion? So that it would be impossible for this principle to be among immovables and for there to be a good-itself. This is why also in mathematics nothing is demonstrated by this cause. (*Met.* 3.2 996a22–30)

> Nor does it [the science we are seeking] concern the 'for the sake of which'. For this is the good, and this belongs among actions and beings in motion; and it is the first mover—for this is the end—but there is no first mover among immovables. (*Met.* 11.1 1059a35–38)

the good and the beautiful are different, for the good is always in action while the beautiful is also among immovables. (*Met.* 13.3 1078a31–32)

The answer is that sometimes, but not always, formal cause and final cause are the same. There is no final cause among immovables—mathematicals, for example—and so there the two are not the same. Final cause is not always a substance—for example, the final cause of a human action or artifact—and so there the two are not the same. Whenever formal cause is the cause of something that moves then it also is final cause—for example, the form of a living being that grows and maintains itself as what it is over time. Whenever final cause is a substance—and not merely a human aim or goal—then it also is formal cause. Substance as the 'for the sake of which' of a motion is a final cause; end as the 'what was being' is a formal cause.

This explains why end sometimes is the cause of being since it sometimes is the cause, over time and through motion, of a 'this' being a 'what'. It is the cause of being because it constitutively limits beings that persist over time. That toward which a temporal being tends, and by which the temporal being is constitutively limited, is the end or final cause. Since temporal beings only acquire their being over time, the cause of their being over time is their most primary cause: "yet in all things the good most of all is a principle" (*Met.* 12.10 1075a37).

6

What would it mean, then, with all this in mind, for the finely reared young person to achieve, through habituation, an insight into the beautiful? Or, to be more precise, to achieve an insight into the beauty of virtuous activities?

I have characterized Aristotle's understanding of the beautiful in a number of ways. The different characterizations are in interesting and important contrast. On the one hand, the beautiful, for him, is the cause or principle by virtue of which a 'this' is a 'what'; the cause or principle by virtue of which matter is something; the cause or principle by virtue of which an all is a whole and not a heap (sometimes through time and change). In general, it is the primary cause or principle of being.

Similarly, the beautiful is the 'what was being' of a being; it is what a being is (imperfectly) being; it is one and the same as the being whose 'what was being' it is; it is what the elements of a whole are (imperfectly) being.

On the other hand, and by contrast, the beautiful, for Aristotle, is the cause by virtue of which a whole is something other than its elements.

And, more generally, the beauty of a whole is something other than the elements of which the whole is composed.

What is striking about these different characterizations is that the first characterizations suggest that the beautiful is what something is, and the second characterizations suggest that the beautiful is what something is not. The contrast should not be surprising for us now, however. We can simply invoke the 'somehow' *(pōs)*. A beautiful being and its beauty are *somehow* one, we could say—by which I mean to imply that, for Aristotle, they are also somehow two. A being and its beauty for Aristotle are as one as any two beings can be. Their unity is the paradigm unity of composed beings, namely, the somehow unity of potentiality and actuality.

At the same time, we can say that, for Aristotle, beauty raises matter or elements to a higher level. Beauty is a principle of increase: by virtue of beauty, matter is something, and not pure stuff; by virtue of beauty, elements are parts, not just elements; by virtue of beauty, nature contains wholes, not just heaps.

What the finely reared young person sees when he or she sees certain actions as beautiful, then, is those actions being raised to a higher level. He or she sees an increase in their being. He or she sees those actions achieve their own being in such a way that they are utterly changed or new. The insight is a striking one, and reflecting on it helps us to see why Dahl is right to want to distinguish insight into evaluative terms from insight into ordinary categorical universals (though, as I have argued, wrong to reserve the term 'insight' only for the former). To see something as beautiful is not to see it as of a certain type or category.

We can now go back to Burnyeat's discussion of what the finely reared young person learns through experience or practice. Burnyeat is right to maintain that what such a person learns is that certain actions (to be called 'actions in accordance with virtue') are enjoyable or pleasurable. We can fill that claim out now, however. What the person who has been beautifully reared discovers is that activities that in themselves are unpleasant or even painful can be part of a larger whole and, as a result, be pleasurable. For, to perceive them as part of a larger whole is to perceive them as beautiful; and to see them as beautiful is, according to Aristotle, to take pleasure in them. (As I will argue in chapter 6, pleasure, for Aristotle, is the perception of particulars as valuable.) When Aristotle says that most people lack even an insight into the beautiful and truly pleasant he means 'the beautiful, that is, the truly pleasant'.

Burnyeat uses skiing as an example of such learning through practice (1980, 76). Through actually skiing, he says, we learn that skiing is pleasurable. Let me extend his example. Through skiing we come to see actions which, in themselves, would be dangerous as part of a larger complex action within which they are not dangerous at all but flow smoothly into the next, creating a beautiful, whole, complete action. For example, leaning backward to an extreme degree ordinarily is dangerous and thus unpleasant. While moving along on skis over terrain that involves a sudden dip, however, leaning backward can make for skiing with some finesse rather than falling with indignity. So also with leaning forward. Lean forward when you are walking, and you may fall. Lean forward when you are skiing and you will glide smoothly along. Leaning forward is part of a complete, integrated, successful activity. The successful skier is one who sees actions which, in themselves, would be dangerous and nonfunctional as part of a larger action in which they are not dangerous but functional and safe. Moreover, the successful skier is one who is flexible, who does not utilize the same movements over and over but sees in each situation what sort of movement is appropriate and uses the sort that is. The person who sees and does all of this will, generally, take pleasure in what he is doing rather than being frightened of it. Actions that at first are frightening become pleasurable, once one sees the whole of which they are a part.

I have discussed the example of skiing previously, in chapter 2, section 3. As I say there, in skiing, sometimes leaning forward is a constituent of skiing while other times it is destructive of skiing since it causes you to fall. Sometimes speeding up is a constituent of skiing and other times it is destructive of it. Leaning forward, leaning back, speeding up, slowing down—each can be either cause and constituent of skiing or, alternately, destructive of skiing, depending on the whole action of which it is a part. When leaning back (or leaning forward, speeding up, slowing down) is the cause of continued skiing, it is not just cause, but also constituent of skiing. It is a component of what it is to be skiing. Sometimes you intend for leaning back to be a constituent of skiing and, comically or painfully, it is not. When, to the contrary, you leaned back and skied, your intention was fulfilled. Your leaning back was skiing all along. It was a constituent of skiing. Skiing was what leaning back, along with the other movements made, was being.

We can now fill this out in terms of Aristotle's understanding of the beautiful. When leaning back is part of a complex whole action known as skiing, leaning back *is* skiing. The whole action, then, is cause of a 'this' (leaning back) being a 'what' (skiing). The elements of the action compose not a series of actions but one whole action (skiing). Skiing is the 'what was being' of leaning back; that is, skiing is what leaning back is being. Also, when leaning back is part of the complete, whole action called 'skiing', leaning back becomes something different and new. Ordinarily, it is dangerous. Now, to the contrary, it is functional and safe.

Skiing is an example of a bodily virtue, not an ethical virtue. Nonetheless, reflection on the example is useful for thinking about Aristotle's views on ethical virtue. Through actually skiing one has new insight into various actions (leaning forward, leaning back, speeding up, slowing down). One sees them as part of larger wholes in which they have new and increased value. One sees them, in other words, as beautiful. As a result of seeing them in this way, one comes to enjoy them.

In addition, one comes to realize that a variety of actions may change their value in the new and varied contexts of skiing. As a result, one begins to look at them in that light. One selects actions in terms of the larger wholes they could compose. One's perception of the actions changes. One's feelings about them change as well.

The connection to ethical virtue is easy to make. Ethical virtue is a developed disposition to experience appropriate emotions and engage in appropriate actions. Specific ethical virtues are developed dispositions to experience specific emotions not routinely but when they are appropriate, to engage in specific types of action not routinely but when they are appropriate. Specific vices are developed dispositions routinely to experience specific emotions (excess) or routinely to refrain from those emotions (deficiency), routinely to engage in specific types of action (excess), or routinely to refrain from those types of actions (deficiency). Courage, for example, is not a disposition routinely to rush ahead (excess) or routinely to refrain from rushing ahead (deficiency) but, instead, is a disposition to rush ahead when doing so is appropriate and to retreat when to do so is appropriate. Nor is courage a disposition routinely to feel confidence (excess) or routinely to lack confidence (deficiency) but, instead, to feel confidence or lack confidence when doing so is appropriate.

When, however, is it appropriate for one to rush ahead? Moreover, when is it appropriate to feel confidence? It is appropriate to rush ahead when one accurately sees rushing ahead in one's context as a constituent of a larger complete whole action. It is appropriate to feel confidence when one accurately sees the action one is about to perform as a constituent of a larger complete whole action. In other words, it is appropriate to engage in an action when it is constitutive of a beautiful action (or, alternately, instrumental to one) and it is appropriate to feel positive feelings about one's actions when they are constitutive of (or instrumental to) a beautiful action. Ethical virtue, then, requires for its development insight into the beauty of one's actions.

Someone could object and say that acts of vice, too, sometimes fit into larger complete wholes, for example, the immoderate act of eating a tasty but excessive meal. The objector would be right that an act of vice in itself can be complete. However, what makes the act vicious is that the act is part of a larger whole in such a way that it detracts from that whole's completeness. To use the example of the immoderate meal again, the larger whole is one's body over time, the excessive meal leads to deterioration of the heart and, as a result, also of other parts of the body.

The cognitive capacity that must be somewhat developed before a student is ready to benefit from lectures on ethics, then, is the capacity to perceive beauty. That is, it is the capacity to see actions as part of larger wholes or contexts within which they change. As a result of the change, one's perception of and feelings about them change as well. Specifically, while engaging in appropriate practices, one begins to perceive aspects of those practices as constituents of or means to development or fulfillment and, thus, as beautiful or good. Just as the skier sees leaning backward as a component of skiing, so Odysseus sees going as a beggar as a means to defeating the suitors and so, for example, a moderate person sees refraining from a certain type of food as a means to bodily fitness.

We can now see how progression of insight into the beauty of virtuous actions might occur according to Aristotle. For a boy, courage might be the first example. He comes to see, through training, how actions that seemed dangerous and, therefore, unappealing can come to seem fine and those that originally seemed appealing and desirable come to seem shameful and base. Once the boy has had this experience, he can, over time, extend it. He can come to see just actions as being like courageous ones. That is, he can come to see actions that in themselves are aversive become desirable when part of a larger whole—refraining from taking something that does not belong to him as part of each one achieving his due. The action, as part of proportionate distribution, is a beautiful one. He can come to see that moderation is like courage. Free consumption of food seems in itself pleasant and desirable. When seen to lead away from fitness and health, it comes to seem harmful and therefore unappealing. All these insights are insights into the beautiful. In each case, as well, they are analogical insights. Once certain actions are seen to be raised to a higher level in the realm of courage, one becomes aware of the possibility that this may be true in other spheres of action. Then one can be receptive to such possibilities even when one has not yet come to see them for oneself.

Once one has had this type of experience a few times, one becomes aware of the fact that the context or whole of which an action is a part can change its value. Going as a beggar in itself is shameful, but doing it to defeat the suitors is crafty; refraining from some perfectly enjoyable food in itself is frustrating, but doing it in order to be able to fight a battle or compete in a footrace is useful. Once one is aware that the context of an action can change its value, one will be more ready to listen to lectures on ethics, for one will be ready to listen to others—old people, for example, or practically insightful people—who have experienced wholes or contexts that one has not experienced oneself in order to learn about the value they found there. One will be ready to at least listen to the views of old people or practically insightful people because one will realize that they may have seen actions in a context or as part of a whole in which their value is increased. This helps to explain Aristotle's selection of the poem from Hesiod (cited already in section 2 of this chapter) to support his views about who is an appropriate student of ethics:

> Best of all is one who understands everything himself.
> Noble, too, is the one who listens to someone who speaks well.
> But one who neither himself understands nor takes to heart
> What he hears from another is a worthless human being.
> (NE 1.4 1095b10–13)

The best situation would be to know, from your own experience, how you should act and, in general, what is beautiful or good. Next best would be to have learned enough from your own experience and upbringing to know that when you lack experience you can be mistaken about what is beautiful or good and ought therefore to at least listen to others who do have experience. The worst situation of all is to be one who neither knows from their own experience nor knows enough to listen to the experience of others. Such a person is an inappropriate listener to lectures on ethics, for he or she will not benefit from them.

7
Unexpectedness

Ethical virtue is, then, the disposition to choose value, specifically, to choose what is good or what is beautiful. 'Good' and 'beautiful' are understood (though differently) as what is developed, enriched, complete, or whole. Ethical virtue requires that one see aspects of the present situation as means to or components of value. That is, it requires that one see them as means to or components of some kind of development, enrichment, completeness, or wholeness. It requires, in addition, flexibility and insight as well as the developed capacity to see the present situation as analogous to previous ones—and analogous in sometimes new and unexpected ways. The analogy, as previously mentioned, is an imprecise one. What accounts for the element of newness or unexpectedness in the making of choices?

It would strengthen my view that the cognitive component of ethical virtue and of emotion is not just perception of particulars but also perception of their value if the element of unexpectedness involved in insight and choice were to result from an element of unexpectedness found in the concept of value itself, that is, in the concept of the good or the beautiful. This is exactly what we find. According to Aristotle, as I have argued, 'good' means 'end' and 'beautiful' means 'form'. Form, for Aristotle, is substance *(ousia)* understood as the principle by virtue of which something is a whole and not a heap or arbitrary collection of parts (*Met.* 7.17 1041b11–27). End, for him, is the principle by virtue of which something is a whole and not a heap or arbitrary collection of parts through time and change. The whole is not the same as its parts, Aristotle argues, because when we dissolve the whole, the parts still exist: "The syllable is not the elements, nor is 'ba' the same as 'b' and 'a', nor is flesh fire and earth. For when decomposed, they, namely, the flesh and the syllable, no longer exist but the elements exist and so do fire and earth" (*Met.* 7.17 1041b14–16). The whole, as Salkever has put it in his interpretation of Aristotle, is not reducible to its parts, nor are the properties of the whole reducible to the properties of the parts. A syllable is not the same as the letters that compose it, Aristotle points out, and flesh is not the same as fire and earth or hot and cold: "Therefore, the syllable is something—not merely the elements sounded and unsounded—but also something other, and flesh is not merely fire and earth or hot and cold, but also something other" (1990, 16–17). The properties of polity *(politeia)* are not the same as the properties of the forms of government that compose it, democracy and oligarchy, since democracy and oligarchy are unjust and polity is just. Parts form wholes in unexpected ways. Hence, our awareness of wholes is not derived simply from awareness of their parts, nor can we perceive parts *as* parts without perceiving the whole of which they are parts. In wholes, parts are something other than they were prior to being parts. In skiing, leaning back is part of skiing, not part of falling; in Polyphemous' cave, enduring pain and shame is part of being a hero, not part of being a coward. All kinds of activities change their value as a result of the whole of which they are a part: refraining from and indulging in eating certain kinds or amounts of food, giving and taking certain amounts of money, rushing ahead and retreating in battle, feeling and not feeling anger, and so forth. To perceive value is, thus, to perceive a certain analogy, since in each case value is wholeness, enrichment, or development, but is also to be flexible enough to see how that analogy shows up in new and unexpected ways in different complex concrete situations, since wholes are not reducible to their parts.

CHAPTER SIX

Emotions as Perceptions of Value

I have now given several positive arguments which, cumulatively, make a case for the claim that, according to Aristotle, the cognitive component of ethical virtue is the cognition of value where value can be understood as 'enriching relatedness' and shows up in analogous but unexpectedly different ways in different situations. What about the cognitive component of emotion for Aristotle? Is it cognition of value as well? It would be helpful to an interpretation of Aristotle's ethical theory if it were, since it would go some distance in explaining what it means to say that emotions are shaped or developed, according to Aristotle, rather than simply suppressed or channeled. Emotions would be shaped, on this account, when our perception of the value of particulars changes. When our perception of value becomes richer our emotions become richer; when our perception of value changes, our emotions change. Could this be Aristotle's view?

1

In "Changing Aristotle's Mind," Martha Nussbaum and Hilary Putnam argue that, according to Aristotle, emotions are species of perception. The argument is a textual one. When Aristotle uses phrases of the form "X, Y, Z, and in general *(holōs)* A," what he means is that A is a genus of which X, Y, and Z are species. In *De Anima*, Aristotle says, "getting angry, being confident, desiring appetitively, in general perceiving" (*De An.* 1.1 403a5ff.). Hence, emotions are forms of perception (1992, 44).[1]

The argument is persuasive, but puzzling. If emotions are species of perception, why doesn't Aristotle say so in his definitions of emotion? Instead, he defines emotions as states (of the soul) accompanied by pleasure and pain. For example, in the *Eudemian Ethics* he says, "By emotions I mean such [states of soul] as spirit, fear, shame, desire, in general those [states] that are in themselves usually accompanied by perceptual pleasure and pain" (*EE* 2.2 1220b12–14). Similarly, in the *Rhetoric* he says, "Emotions are [states of soul] due to changes in which our decisions come to differ and which are accompanied by pleasure and pain, for example, anger, pity, fear, and all other such [states] and their opposites" (*Rhet.* 2.1 1378a19–22). In the *Nicomachean Ethics* he says, "By emotions I mean desire, anger, fear, confidence, envy, joy, friendship, hatred, longing, emulation, pity, in general the [states of soul] that are accompanied by pleasure and pain" (*NE* 2.5 1105b21–23).

A page later in the *Nicomachean Ethics*, Aristotle goes even further and indicates that it is not simply that emotions are accompanied by pleasure and pain but that pleasure and pain are the genus of which emotions are the species: "For example, both fear and confidence and desire and anger and pity and in general pleasure and pain can be felt too much or too little and in either case not well" (*NE* 2.6 1106b18–21).

A number of Aristotle's definitions of specific emotions in the *Rhetoric* conform to this third understanding of emotion, namely, that specific emotions are types of pleasure or pain. Pity, for example, is defined not as a state accompanied by a type of pain, but simply as a type of pain. Pity is "a certain pain at an apparent destructive or painful evil happening to someone who does not deserve it and which one might expect oneself or one of one's own to suffer..." (*Rhet.* 2.8 1385b13–14). Fear, too, is a type of pain. Fear is "a certain pain or disturbance [resulting] from the appearance of a future destructive or painful evil" (*Rhet.* 2.5 1382a21–22). Four other emotions are defined as types of pain: shame is a certain pain and disturbance regarding the type of evils that appear to bring one into disrepute (*Rhet.* 2.6 1383b12–14); indignation is pain at undeserved good fortune (*Rhet.* 2.9 1386b8–11); envy and emulation are a certain pain and disturbance at the success of one's peers, the former at the fact of the other's success, the latter at the fact that one does not share that success) (*Rhet.* 2.9 1386b18–20, 2.10 1387b22–25, 2.11 1388a32–35). A fifth comes close to being defined as a type of pleasure: a friend shares pleasure in good things and pain in painful things due to the friend (*Rhet.* 2.4 1381a3–5). Only one emotion, anger, is said to be *accompanied* by pleasure or pain. Anger is "desire, accompanied by pain, for evident revenge due to an evident slight directed inappropriately at oneself or those close to one" (*Rhet.* 2.2 1378a30–32).

With these definitions in mind, how can it be that Aristotle thinks emotions are species of perception? Moreover, if emotions are species of perception, of what are they the perception? To put the question more broadly, if we are to speak of emotions as types of awareness, openness, or rational orientation to the world, of what part of the world are they an awareness, openness, or rational orientation?

For Aristotle, there would be a limited number of candidate answers, limited by the number of types of beings there are, that is, by the number of categories and transcategories. Emotions would be perceptions of certain qualities, quantities, times, places, substances, and so forth. We do not, however, want to say that emotion is a perception of white, or of fifty feet, or of five o'clock or of Athens or of a human being. A perception of something as white is just a perception of it as white. A perception of something as fifty feet long is just that, a perception of it as fifty feet long. Neither of these perceptions is even necessarily accompanied by an emotion, much less is it a species of one.

There is a transcategorial, however, the perception of which Aristotle could, plausibly, believe emotion to be, namely, *telos* or the good. In other words, Aristotle might believe that emotion is the perception of value. More precisely, we can hypothesize, the perception of value is positive emotion and the perception of disvalue is negative emotion. Since perception is of particulars, we can amend this to say: the perception of particulars as good is positive emotion and the perception of particulars as bad is negative emotion. On this view, the emotivists got things backward: evaluations are not disguised emotions; instead, emotions are types of evaluation. Positive emotion is perception of (something as) good; negative emotion is perception of (something as) bad.

Our interpretive puzzle remains, however. For unless Aristotle has a way of connecting perception of particulars as good with pleasure and perception of particulars as bad with pain, we have conflicting definitions and categorizations of emotion: as perception of particulars as good or bad; as pleasure or pain. Nicely, he does have a way of making a connection between them. He simply defines pleasure as perception of particulars as good and pain as perception of particulars as bad: "To be pleased or pained," Aristotle says in *De Anima*, "is to activate the perceptual mean toward what is good or bad as such" (*De An.* 3.7 431a10–11). The most plausible interpretation of "as such" in the statement "To be pleased or pained is to activate the perceptual mean toward what is good or bad as such," is that pleasure is perception of something good as good (not as white, or a triangle, or large, etc.) and that pain is perception of something bad *as* bad since perception is of particulars, according to Aristotle, not of universals. Hence, by "good as such" or "bad as such," Aristotle cannot mean something like 'the good' or 'the bad'.

Taking all the definitions and categorizations together, we can say that, for Aristotle, emotion is both perception (of particulars as good or bad) and pleasure or pain since, according to him, pleasure and pain are themselves a type of perception (of particulars as good or bad). Perception of particulars as good is positive emotion, or pleasure, and perception of particulars as bad is negative emotion, or pain. When we perceive something as developed, enriched, or fulfilled, we are pleased. When we perceive something as stunted, harmed, or deprived, we are pained.

Actually, Aristotle's definition of pleasure is broader than I have indicated; pleasure is not just a type of perception, but is a type of perception *or* appearance *(phantasma)*. To see that it is, it is helpful to consider his claim that to be pleased or pained is to activate the perceptual mean toward what is good or bad as such in its textual context.

> Now perceiving is like mere saying *(phanai)* and intuiting *(noein)*; but whenever [a perceptual object is] pleasant or painful, [which is] like assertion *(kataphasa)* or negation *(apophasa)*, [the soul] pursues or avoids it. To be pleased or pained is to activate the perceptual mean toward what is good or bad as such. And avoidance and desire, when at work, are this. And the faculty of desire and of avoidance are not different, either from one another or from the faculty of perception; but their being is different. To the thinking soul appearances are like perceptions; and when it asserts or denies [that they are] good or bad it flees or pursues [them]. (*De An.* 3.7 431a8–16)

Aristotle begins the passage by drawing an analogy. Perceiving, he says, is like mere saying (or intuiting); being pleased or pained, he goes on, is like asserting or denying: "Now perceiving is like mere saying *(phanai)* and intuiting *(noein)*; and when something is pleasant or painful, [which is] as it were assertion *(kataphasa)* or negation *(apophasa)*, the soul pursues or avoids it" (*De An.* 3.7 431a8–11). The point of the analogy is not that pleasure or pain is a type of assertion or denial, but that pleasure or pain is a type of perception, specifically, a type of perception that has the same relation to mere perception that assertion or denial does to mere saying (or mere intuiting).[2] Assertion and denial are second-order saying, parasitic on first-order or mere saying; similarly, the experience of pleasure or pain is second-order perception, parasitic on first-order or mere perception. To assert or deny is to say something about something that has been said or thought; similarly, to experience pleasure is to have a perception of something that has already been perceived.

It is after drawing this analogy that Aristotle says that to be pleased or pained is to activate the perceptual mean toward what is good or bad as such. Now we can understand this claim further to mean that being pleased or pained is a type of perception—not the initial kind of perception, mere perception of something (of yellow, e.g., or of sweet), but perception of something as something, namely, as good or bad. Being pleased or pained is a secondary kind of perception, parasitic on the primary kind, just as asserting and denying are secondary to naming or intuiting. You have to take something in, we could say, if you are to be pleased or pained by it.

Aristotle then says that avoidance (and presumably pursuit) and desire, too, when at work, are activation of the perceptual mean toward what is good or bad as such. He is pointing out an orderly progression: mere perception of an object; pleasure in the object (i.e., perception of the object as good); desire and pursuit (further activated perception of the object as good).

At this point, Aristotle says that appearances *(phantasmata)* can take the place of perceptions. "To the thinking soul," he says, "appearances are like perceptions; and when it asserts or denies [that they are] good or bad it avoids or pursues [them]"[3] (*De An.* 3.7 431a14–15). This suggests that to the definition of pleasure as perception of particulars as good or bad we can add the disjunct 'or appearance': pleasure, then, would be perception or appearance of particulars as good or bad. In the case of pleasure as appearance, we would have an orderly progression similar to the one we have in the case of pleasure as perception: appearance of an object; pleasure in the object (i.e., appearance of the object as good); avoidance or pursuit (further activated appearance of the object as good). Appearing is parallel to mere perception and is like naming or intuiting; appearing as good or bad is pleasure or pain and is like asserting or denying; from pleasure and pain, pursuit or avoidance results. It is in this way that appearances are like perceptions to the thinking soul. We are justified, then, from this analysis of the cited passage to conclude that, for Aristotle, pleasure or pain is not just perception of particulars as good or bad but is perception or appearance of particulars as good or bad.

The definitions of emotions in the *Rhetoric* bear this interpretation out since several of them are defined as pain at (or from or due to) a *phainomenon*—that is, an appearance. Anger, for example, is "desire, accompanied by pain, for apparent *(phainomenēs)* revenge due to an apparent *(phainomenēn)* slight directed inappropriately at oneself or those close to one" (*Rhet.* 2.2 1378a30–32). Pity is "a certain pain at an apparently *(phainomenōi)* destructive or painful evil happening to someone who does not deserve it . . ." (*Rhet.* 2.8 1385b13–14). Fear is "a certain pain or disturbance [resulting] from the appearance *(phantasias)* of a future destructive or painful evil" (*Rhet.* 2.5 1382a21–22). Confidence involves "hope of safety with appearance *(phantasias)* that it is near" (*Rhet.* 3.5 1383a17–18). Shame is "a certain pain or disturbance regarding the sort of evils that appear *(phainomena)* to bring one into disrepute" (*Rhet.* 2.6 1383b12–14). Both envy and emulation are a certain pain at the apparent *(phainomenōi)* presence of success among one's peers (*Rhet.* 2.10 1387b22–25, 2.11 1388a32–35). Being indignant is "being pained at the appearance *(phainomenōi)* of undeserved success" (*Rhet.* 2.9 1387a8–9).

By 'appearance' in these examples, Aristotle means neither image nor judgment. Sometimes, as Nussbaum points out, by 'apparent X', Aristotle means to convey how X appears to us, as in the phrase 'apparent good' meaning what appears good to us (*NE* 3.4; 1978, 233). Sometimes, to the contrary, he means the image of X when X itself no longer is present, for example, the image of something previously perceived or the image of a person in a dream (1978, 249). In Aristotle's definitions of emotions just listed, 'appearance' or 'apparent' does not carry the latter meaning since the question whether the appearance corresponds to what is is irrelevant. I feel angry at someone when they appear to have slighted me. In some cases, the appearance corresponds to reality; in some cases it does not. I am angry in either case. I feel pity when it appears that someone is suffering destructive or painful evil undeservedly. I will feel pain both in cases in which the appearance corresponds to reality and in cases in which it does not. I am afraid if my circumstances suggest the imminence of destructive or painful evil. When it sounds as though a burglar is outside my window, I become afraid as a result of that appearance, both in cases in which there is a burglar there and in cases in which what I hear is just the sound of the branches of the tree scraping against the window.

Something interesting results from this understanding of emotions. The fact that they result from appearances whether those appearances correspond to reality or not leaves room for the idea that emotions, for Aristotle, can be more or less appropriate. My fear is appropriate if destructive or painful evil in fact is imminent. My pity is misplaced if directed to someone whose suffering was merited. Anger at someone who in fact has slighted me is a suitable or appropriate response.

Room is left as well for the need for deliberation. There is no suggestion in Aristotle's definitions and characterizations of emotions that they result from or are constituted by a type of deliberation. We know from *De Anima* that some but not all appearances result from deliberation (*De An.* 3.11 434a5–7). Therefore, we cannot conclude from the fact that emotions involve appearances of particulars as good or bad that they involve deliberation that reaches the conclusion that particulars are good or bad. We also know from various remarks Aristotle makes that appearance does not imply belief since appearance and belief can be at odds: the sun can appear to me to be a foot wide though I do not believe that it is (*Insomn.* 460b19; *De An.* 3.3 428b3–4); something pleasant can appear good to me even though I do not believe that it is (*EE* 4.2 1235b25–29) (Nussbaum, 1978, 245). Hence, we cannot conclude from the fact that emotions involve appearances of particulars as good or bad that they even involve the belief that those particulars are good or bad. None of the *Rhetoric* or *De Anima* passages about emotion cited above mention deliberation or judgment. It is plausible that they would if Aristotle meant to suggest that judgment is required for emotion.

It is reasonable to conclude, then, that emotions need not result from deliberation. Presumably, however, they can result from deliberation since, as mentioned above, appearances can result from deliberation. Add to that the idea that at least in one sense of the term 'appropriate', emotions can be more or less appropriate. All this leaves room for a theory of ethical virtue—that is, for a theory of the good development of our capacities to experience emotion. It would be a theory that includes discussion of the development of those capacities in such a way that we tend to experience emotions appropriately and to experience them on the basis of deliberation.

In sum, then, emotions, for Aristotle, are perceptions *or appearances* of particulars as good or bad—positive emotions are perceptions or appearances of them as good, negative emotions are perceptions or appearances of them as bad. When we perceive particulars as good or they appear to us as good, we are pleased; when we perceive particulars as bad or they appear to us as bad, we are pained.

2

I have drawn this conclusion in part from the assertions Aristotle makes that imply that emotions are types of pleasure and pain. As we have seen, however, Aristotle vacillates between definitions of emotions as states accompanied by pleasure or pain and assertions that imply that emotions are types of pleasure and pain. Which is his final view?

Perhaps, however, this is not the most appropriate question to ask about the two formulations. Perhaps, instead, we can conclude from

Aristotle's rapid vacillation in usage that he does not intend the two different formulations to denote two different relationships. Consider, for example, the fact that in the *Rhetoric*, Aristotle defines emotions as states (usually) accompanied by (perceptual) pleasure and pain, but then goes on to define seven emotions as types of pleasure or pain and only one as a state accompanied by pleasure or pain. Consider also that in the *Nicomachean Ethics*, Aristotle shifts within a page from 'are accompanied by' to a statement that implies 'are a type of'.

With this in mind, it seems likely that both 'emotions are states accompanied by pleasure or pain' and 'emotions are types of pleasure or pain' are Aristotle's final view and that he uses two formulations because the relationship denoted is an intimate (close, internal) relationship but not a complete identity.[4] In general, how do we convey intimate or close relations? The difficulty in conveying them is that, when A and B are intimately related, we want to convey the *intimacy* of the connection between the two, but we also want to convey that the intimate connection is between *two*.

For example, if A is fundamentally or essentially B, we convey the intimacy by saying 'A *is* B'. We convey the fact that the intimate connection is between two and that there are other aspects of A besides what A is fundamentally or essentially (i.e., that there are aspects of A other than the fact that it is B) by saying 'A involves B' or 'A is in part B'. Consider the following examples:

Human being *is* rational animal.
Human being *is in part* rational—but also emotional, bodily, and
 so forth.

To be human *is* to be rational.
To be human *involves* being rational—but also being emotional, bodily, and so forth.

Emotion *is* perception.
Emotion *involves* perception—but also certain bodily changes, and
 so forth.

In ordinary discourse, we shift from formulation to formulation without thinking much of it and without intending the two formulations to refer to two different relationships. Instead, we make the shift in order to convey two different aspects of one and the same relationship. We do the same in philosophical discourse.

For example, Aristotle himself is notorious for using external relations as examples of internal relations. He uses the relation between the form and matter of artifacts to illustrate the relation between form and matter of natural substances even though he makes a point of the fact that artifacts do not have a nature.[5] Perhaps he does this because the form and matter of artifacts are more separate (first the form is in the mind of the maker, then it is put into the matter in order to achieve a certain end, also in the mind of the maker). As a result of the greater separateness, discussions of artifactual form and matter are in a way clearer than discussions of the form and matter of natural substances (the form is present in the matter from the beginning but only as potential). In any case, whether or not that is Aristotle's reason for using the external relation to exemplify the intimate relation, he does use it to exemplify in that fashion. As Sarah Broadie says, "it is from artifacts that Aristotle draws his favourite illustrations of the form-matter distinction—a distinction primarily devised to make sense of the substances which artifacts are not" (1991, 182).

Similarly, it seems likely that though Aristotle in some cases makes assertions that imply that pleasure and pain are the genus of which emotions are species and in other places says that emotions are accompanied by pleasure and pain, he does not mean the use of the more external term 'accompanies' to indicate any relation other than the genus-species relation. It makes his point clear enough for works of practical philosophy—the *Nicomachean* and *Eudemian Ethics* and the *Rhetoric*—since, after all, great precision is not required for the goal of practical philosophy, namely, the goal of becoming good.

In what I have said so far, have I given sufficient evidence for the claim that emotions are perceptions/appearances of *particulars*? I have argued that the 'as such' in Aristotle's claim that to be pleased or pained is to activate the perceptual mean toward what is good or bad as such must mean 'as good' or 'as bad', since perception according to Aristotle is of particulars and so Aristotle cannot mean by 'the good' or 'the bad' the universal (or, more accurately, transcategorial) that goes by that name. Nor can Aristotle mean 'the good' in the sense of the highest good or the best life. Perhaps the emotions of a virtuous person often are informed by an appearance of an overall developed and flourishing life but the emotions of others often are not. Moreover, Aristotle's definitions of specific emotions confirm the view that emotions are directed to particulars. For many emotions are defined as pleasure or pain at a particular person appearing to be good or bad.

For example, Aristotle defines anger, as we have seen, as "desire, accompanied by pain, for apparent *(phainomenēs)* revenge due to an apparent *(phainomenēn)* slight directed inappropriately at oneself or those close to one" (*Rhet.* 2.2 1378a30–32). He goes on to say that the pleasure and pain are directed to a particular person and because of a slight to a particular person. "If this is the definition of anger," he says, "then it is necessary that the one who is angry is angry always at some particular person, for example at Kleon not at human being, and because that person has done or is going to do something to him or one of those close to him" (*Rhet.* 2.2 1378a32–35). The pain results from the appearance of a slight directed by a particular person (unspecified) to a particular person (either oneself or someone close to one). The person directing the slight is doing something bad; the person receiving the slight is receiving something bad.

The example helps to clarify my account. I have said that for Aristotle emotions are perceptions or appearances of particulars as good or bad. In the case of anger, the particulars involved are particular persons. One is bad in the sense that he or she is doing something bad (inappropriately directing a slight) while the other is bad in the sense that he or she is experiencing something bad (experiencing a slight). We will find, as we consider more examples of emotions, that it is reasonable to suppose that in every case the particulars involved are particular persons. We will also find, as we just found in the case of anger, that to say that someone appears as good or bad can have more than one meaning: in some cases, it can mean that they appear to be *doing* good or bad; in other cases, it can mean that they appear to be *suffering* something bad.

For example, in the case of friendship, one wishes good things, and whatever is productive of good things, for one's friend (*Rhet.* 2.4 1380b36–37). In addition, one shares in pleasure at good things and in pain at bad things experienced by one's friend.[6] The emotion, friendship, is directed at a particular person, one's friend, and at their *experiencing* something good. Fear is pain or disturbance from the appearance *(phantasias)* of an imminent destructive or painful evil (*Rhet.* 2.5 1382a21–22). The pain is directed toward someone *experiencing* evil (of a destructive or painful sort). The particular person involved is the one who fears, as Aristotle says a bit later: "It is necessary then that those who believe they might suffer something experience fear" (*Rhet.* 2.5 1382b33). Confidence is hope of safety with appearance *(phantasias)* that it is near (*Rhet.* 2.5 1383a17–18). The feeling is directed at experiencing something good, safety, and, as in the case of fear, the particular person involved is the person experiencing the emotion, as evidenced by a number of Aristotle's general remarks about confidence such as, "And [people are confident] when, endeavoring to do something, they believe they are not likely to suffer or will succeed" (*Rhet.* 2.5 1383b8–10).

Pity is, as we have seen, "a certain pain at an apparent *(phainomenōi)* destructive or painful evil happening to someone who does not deserve it . . ." (*Rhet.* 2.8 1385b13–14). In the case of pity, we experience pain at a person apparently experiencing something bad, namely, destruction or pain, undeservedly. Once again, then, the particular involved is a particular person and, in this case, the person is experiencing something bad. Shame is "a certain pain or disturbance regarding the sort of evils that appear *(phainomena)* to bring one into disrepute (*Rhet.* 2.6 1383b12–14). The pain is at evils experienced by oneself, specifically, at those appearing to bring one into disrepute.

Envy and emulation are directed to particular persons (one's peers) but at first these emotions appear to be contradictions to the general pattern of pain at apparent bad, pleasure at apparent good. For both envy and emulation are a certain pain at the apparent *(phainomenoi)* success of one's peers, envy at the fact of the other's success, emulation at the fact that one does not share that success (*Rhet.* 2.9 1386b18–20, 2.10 1387b22–25, 2.11 1388a32–35). In each case, however, it is reasonable to suppose that the emotion has to do with one's awareness of one's own relative lack of success (hence the term 'peers') and the difference between them being that in the case of emulation, one perceives a remedy, namely, that one comes to be successful as well, while in the case of envy, one simply focuses on one's relative lack of success.

Indignation is pain at undeserved good fortune (*Rhet.* 2.9 1386b9–11). As with the examples of envy and emulation, this emotion may seem to be a counterexample to the pain at bad, pleasure at good pattern since it is pain at someone's good fortune. However, the pain is not simply at the fact that someone experiences good fortune, but at the fact that someone who does not deserve good fortune experiences it. For "what takes place contrary to desert is unjust" (*Rhet.* 2.9 1386b13–14).

Emotions, then, are perceptions or appearances of particular persons doing or experiencing something good or bad. Perceptions or appearances of them doing or experiencing something good are types of pleasure. Perceptions or appearances of them doing or experiencing something bad are types of pain. This narrowing down—from 'emotions are perceptions or appearances of particulars as good or bad' to 'emotions are perceptions or appearances of particular persons doing or experiencing good or bad'—suggests a refinement of our account. Pleasure and pain are perceptions or appearances of particulars as good or bad. Those that are perceptions of a certain type of particular would be a particular type of pleasure and pain. Emotions, for example, are perceptions of a certain type of particulars, namely, particular persons. Emotions, as a result, are a particular type of pleasure and pain. Another type of pleasure and pain is bodily pleasure and pain, distinguished from emotion by the particulars perceived in it. Bodily pleasure and pain are perceptions of one's body or its parts experiencing something good or bad. We take pleasure in the smooth functioning of the body, for example—in healthy digestion, easy walking, sexual activity, and so forth. We are pained by the body's poor functioning—by disease, injury, weakness, and hunger.

Once pleasure and pain are divided into types, they are then divided into subtypes. Emotions are distinguished into subtypes by who the persons are and what sort of good or evil they experience or do. There is one type of emotion, pity, distinguished by the fact that the pain is at suffering experienced by someone who does not deserve it; there is another type, friendship, distinguished by one's friends experiencing good things; another type, fear, distinguished by future destructive or painful evil to oneself; and so on. Emotion, then, is a type of pleasure or pain—specifically, the type that is directed toward particular persons—and specific emotion types such as fear, anger, friendship, and so on are subtypes—distinguished by the type of good or evil done or experienced and by whom.

To flesh out our interpretation, we need to consider what Aristotle might mean by the claim that pleasure is perception of particulars as good and pain the perception of particulars as bad. Deborah K. W. Modrak appropriately glosses Aristotle's statement that "To be pleased or pained is to activate the perceptual mean toward what is good or bad as such," to mean that pleasure and pain are forms of perception: "To feel pleasures and pains . . . is just another way of relating to objects in the world and thus is a form of perception" (1987, 141). Elsewhere, however, she expresses puzzlement about Aristotle's meaning: "The difference between perceiving a white shape as a cookie and perceiving it as a source of pleasure is not obvious" (1987, 210, note 60). The resolution, as I have been arguing, is that one perceives the white shape—if that is the relevant particular—as good and then one takes pleasure in it—even more strongly, that one perceives the relevant particular as good and doing so is to take pleasure in it. The puzzle is not resolved that simply, however, but requires longer consideration.

Regarding the cookie, Modrak is pursuing the following chain of reasoning. According to her, there is for Aristotle a two-stage cognitive process that results in desire and emotion: first, perception *(aisthēsis)* or intuition *(noēsis)* presents an object; then, appearance *(phantasia)* elaborates on the object, reinterpreting it in the light of anticipated pleasures and pains (1987, 97). Suppose the object is a white cookie. I perceive the white shape as a cookie. That, presumably, is her stage 1. Then, I perceive it as a source of pleasure (stage 2) as a result of which I come to desire it and have an emotional response to it. What, however, is that second stage? What is it to perceive that white cookie as a source of pleasure?

The resolution of the puzzle she raises comes in two parts: (1) We can be moved to desire and have feelings about a cookie as a result of construing it to be a source of pleasure. If we do, however, this is a second-level movement to desire, caused by my memory or decayed sense image of cookies I have found pleasurable in the past. (2) We can be moved to a first-level desire of a cookie based not on memories of cookies past but simply on the pleasure I take in this cookie that is before me. There is a two-stage cognitive process, as Modrak points out, but it is not quite the one that she delineates: Stage 1: I perceive the cookie—specifically, I taste it—the semisweet flavor of the chocolate bits, the sweetness of the sugar, and so forth. Stage 2: I perceive the cookie as good—that is, it tastes good to me. The second stage is not identical to the first, but is parasitic on it. I must taste the cookie, we could say, if it is to taste good to me. This fits with Aristotle's analogy, mentioned above, according to which perceiving something is to perceiving it as good/taking pleasure in it as *phasis* is to *kataphasis*. I maintain that the two cognitive stages are not the two mentioned by Modrak, namely, first, perceiving the white shape as a cookie and, second, perceiving it as a source of pleasure, but, first, tasting the cookie and, second, it tasting good to me.

Still, what is it for the cookie to taste good to me? Aristotle says that pleasure is the perception of particulars as good (in this case, their tasting good). Alexander Grant, in 1874, is not puzzled by Aristotle's claim that pleasure and pain are perception of particulars as good and bad. He makes clear in his translation of that claim from *De Anima* that he thinks what Aristotle gives there is, first of all, a *definition* of pleasure and pain, secondly, that Aristotle there defines pleasure and pain as types of perception ('sense'), third, that good or bad ('good or evil') are the object of the perception and, fourth, that, more specifically, the object of the perception is good or bad particulars ('coming in contact with'): "Again, [Aristotle] defines pleasure and pain to consist in 'the consciousness, by means of the discriminating faculty *(tē aisthētikē mesotēti)* of the senses, of coming in contact with good or evil'" (1874, vol. 1, 256).

In addition, Grant then supports his interpretation of the passage by adducing two other passages in which Aristotle assumes that human beings perceive good or bad. The first is a *Politics* passage according to which human being has a perception of good and bad, just and unjust: "For this is peculiar to human beings in relation to the other animals, that human being alone has perception of good and bad, just and unjust, and the rest" (*Pol.* 1.2 1253a15–18). The second is a *Nicomachean Ethics* passage according to which the good man takes pleasure in good actions and pain in bad ones: "For the serious person, just as serious, enjoys virtuous actions and is displeased by bad actions, just as a musical person takes pleasure in beautiful melodies and is pained by base ones" (*NE* 9.9 1170a8–11).

We might add to that Aristotle's claim, in the same chapter, that "to perceive that something good is present in us is pleasant" (*NE* 9.9 1170b2–3) where the thing that is good that is present in us is life and that "one's own existence is pleasant because one perceives that one is good, and this sort of perception is pleasant in itself" (*NE* 9.9 1170b8–10). Reference to perception of good and bad, then, is not unique to the passage under question, but occurs also in important passages in the *Politics* and the *Nicomachean Ethics*.

We can complete our exploration of what Aristotle might mean by the claim that pleasure is perception of particulars as good and pain perception of particulars as bad by adding a comment on where perception of particulars as good or bad fits in Aristotle's classification of perception into three types, special, common, and incidental. Perception of good or bad particulars must be common perception. It is not special perception since it is not perception of any of the five special sense-objects (color, sound, smell, flavor, or the tangible) each of which is sensed by a separate sense-organ. It is not incidental perception similar to perceiving that the white thing is the son of Diares or that the white thing is a human being since in these cases the second term ('son of Diares', 'human being') is not really but only incidentally perceived. Instead, to perceive a particular as good or bad must be similar to perceiving a human being as one or as moving. It must, in other words, be common perception.

Still, though, going back to Modrak's example of the pleasure I take in a cookie, which I interpreted to be a two-part process of, one, tasting the cookie and, two, it tasting good to me, why does the cookie taste good to me? According to Aristotle, pleasure is the perception of particulars as good (in this case, their tasting good). Why, for Aristotle, is the perception of something as good pleasure? It is unlikely that we will find a conclusive answer to these questions, but some speculations are instructive.

In *Nicomachean Ethics* 7.12, Aristotle defines pleasure as unimpeded activity of a natural *(kata physin)* disposition (*NE* 7.12 1153a14–15). If pleasure is the perception of particulars as good, then perception of particulars as good is a type of unimpeded activity, namely, unimpeded activity of our perceptual faculty. If something is good because it is complete, developed, or fulfilled, our perception of it as complete, developed, or fulfilled then would be unimpeded perception. Perceiving something's completeness—its stretching out for and attaining its end—would be pleasurable on this account. Perceiving something that stretches out for and misses its end would be painful—because it would be impeded activity of a natural disposition.

It is no objection to this (speculative) claim that I can have impeded perception of something complete—for example, if my eyesight is poor. For Aristotle, pleasure requires both a good object and a well-disposed perceptual or intellectual faculty (*NE* 10.4 1174b18–20). If the object is complete but my eyesight poor, the perceptual activity will not be at its best and my pleasure will be lessened. Similarly, it is no objection to point out that I can have unimpeded perception of something incomplete. If my perceptual faculty—my eyesight—is well disposed, I will be able without impediment to perceive something incomplete. I will not, however, be able to perceive its incompleteness (or its being incomplete). To perceive something's incompleteness is to begin the process of perceiving its completeness and be impeded or thwarted.

For example, when we read a philosophical argument in which claims are made and carried through, we enjoy it. When we read one in which lines of thought are sketched but not carried through, or in which they become diffuse or disorganized, we are frustrated, and do not enjoy it. When we watch a tragedy in which the beginning, some choice on the part of the tragic character, leads into the middle, the results of that choice, which leads to the end, the resulting misfortune suffered by the tragic character, we follow and enjoy the development of the plot. When we watch one in which the end does not clearly result from the initial choice, our expectations are thwarted, and we are dissatisfied.

Aristotle may believe that something like this is true of pleasure in general—both of those pleasures that are perceptions and of those that are appearances. When I see someone good not leading a flourishing life of virtuous activity together with others but, instead, suffering misfortune, my imaginative intentions regarding him are thwarted in a certain way that is a particular type of pain that we call 'pity'. When I see a vicious person winning a political battle, my imaginative intentions regarding her are thwarted and I feel another type of pain, the one we call 'indignation'. When I taste a cookie in which the flavors complement each other, my ability to take in each taste is activated. When I taste a cookie in which the flavors do not complement each other, my tasting of each flavor is inhibited.

According to Aristotle, actual perception and its object are the same—the same in form (*De An.* 3.8 431b20–432a1). Perception of (something as) good must, then, itself be good. I have argued that good for Aristotle means *entelecheia* or *energeia* and their variants in all their varied meanings: complete, completeness, activity, and so forth. It would follow then that when I perceive something as good, my perceiving is itself complete or active. This is just what I have suggested in these remarks. When I perceive something as good—that is, when I perceive something as complete—my perceiving itself is unimpeded in its activity. Hence, when I perceive something as good, my perceiving is itself pleasure, since pleasure is unimpeded activity.

3

Supposing that emotions are pleasure or pain at particular persons doing or experiencing good or bad, why is Aristotle's definition of emotions in the *Eudemian Ethics* narrower than his others? In the *Eudemian Ethics*, rather than defining emotions as states of soul accompanied by pleasure or pain, he defines them more narrowly as [states] of soul *usually* accompanied by *perceptual* pleasure or pain (*EE* 2.2 1220b12–14).

It is unclear that we can answer this question conclusively. One possibility is that the qualification 'usually' is used in order to accommodate the example of hate since hate is on Aristotle's list of emotions but is not, according to him, accompanied by pain. Stephen R. Leighton claims that 'usually' indicates that many but not all species of emotion involve pleasure or pain (with hate as a counterexample) (1984, 135–138). He argues against Michael Woods (1982, 109–110) who claims that Aristotle's point is that each species of emotion is usually but not always accompanied by pleasure or pain. As Leighton points out, it is unlikely that Aristotle means to say that each emotion type is usually but not always accompanied by pleasure or pain since he does not in his detailed discussions of particular emotions ever say about them that they are usually pleasant or painful.

Hate, for Aristotle, is a borderline case, most likely put on the list because it shares enough qualities with nonborderline case emotions to be relevantly similar. The main differences between hate and the other emotions are that hate does not involve pain and is directed at universals as well as particulars. Regarding the latter, Aristotle says, "And anger always concerns particulars, such as Callias or Socrates, while hate is also directed to types. For, everyone hates the thief and the sycophant" (*Rhet.* 2.4 1382a5–7). Hate is similar to other emotions in that it is a negative feeling directed toward an evil and in that it is sometimes directed to particulars. Understanding hate is important for a rhetorician since persuasively assigning a person to a hated class could change a jury or assembly's judgment of him or her.

What about another possible interpretation of the passage, namely, that Aristotle's point is that emotions are usually accompanied by *perceptual* pleasure and pain but some of them are accompanied by nonperceptual pleasure or pain? Leighton rules this interpetation out for two reasons. He begins by interpreting 'perceptual' to mean 'bodily' and interpreting Aristotle's claim to be that usually emotions stir our body but sometimes they stir our mind and not our body. Then he points out that Aristotle claims that emotions are bodily in *De Anima* (*De An.* 403a16–19) and that the claim that emotions usually stir our body but sometimes stir our mind and not our body implies a Cartesian distinction between mind and body, a distinction that Aristotle does not draw (1984, 137–138).

It is more likely, however, that by 'perceptual pleasure' here Aristotle means the type of pleasure that is attained through our perceptual faculties, that is, pleasure attained through the senses—sight, hearing, smell, and so forth. The difference between perceptual pleasure, so understood, and bodily pleasure would be the difference between faculty and object. A pleasure is perceptual because the perceptual faculties are at work in it. A pleasure is bodily because the body or its parts are the object of the pleasure. Aristotle uses 'perceptual pleasure' to mean pleasure in which the perceptual faculties are at work in the *Nicomachean Ethics*. In 10.3, he distinguishes pleasures that result from a replenishment of a lack in the body with those that do not involve such replenishment, including the pleasures of learning and some of the perceptual pleasures, such as smell (*NE* 10.3 1173b7–19). In 10.4 and 10.5, he contrasts perceptual pleasure with pleasures of thought *(dianoia)* and contemplation *(theōria)* (*NE* 10.4 1174b20–21, *NE* 10.5 1175a27, 1175b36–76a3). Moreover, as we have already seen, in *De Anima* Aristotle divides pleasures into those that are the perception of particulars as good or bad and those that are the appearance of particulars as good or bad.

It is just not clear where to go with this, however. If Aristotle were going to categorize emotions by whether or not they are perceptual, it seems more likely that he would say that emotions usually are appearances and sometimes but less often are perceptions. As we have seen, many of the emotions on his list of emotions in the *Rhetoric* are examples of appearances. For similar reasons, if he were going to say that emotions sometimes are from learning and sometimes perceptions, once again it seems likely that the balance would tip against perceptions.

Given the close connection between perception and appearance for Aristotle—so close that plausibly they are activities of the same faculty, the faculty of perception—it is possible that Aristotle has a different contrast in mind. For by the 'perceptual' in 'perceptual pleasure' he may mean to denote the whole range from perception to appearance and to contrast the perceptual/apparent and the bodily. He could mean that emotions are usually pleasures and pains that result from perception/appearance, but sometimes also are pleasures and pains we experience in our bodies. If that is his point in the *Eudemian Ethics*, by 'bodily' emotions, he could intend to denote desire, which he refers to as an emotion in the *Eudemian Ethics* but not in the *Rhetoric*. If so, then his point would be that most but not all species of emotion are perceptual/apparent with desire as the one species that is not.

There is ground for arguing that Aristotle does use perceptual in this broader way, namely, to mean either perceptual or apparent. The first passage that indicated to us that emotions are species of perception is the passage from *De Anima* cited by Nussbaum and Putnam. In it, Aristotle uses anger, confidence, and desire all as species of perception. Anger and confidence do not seem to come simply from how we perceive certain persons if we use 'perceive' in its narrow meaning of perception of the special sensibles. We do not narrowly perceive something to be a slight, for example. We imaginatively construe it to be a slight. Desire, on the other hand, at least in great part involves our perceptual or sensual faculties. This insight could help us explain Aristotle's use of the term 'perceptual' in his *Eudemian Ethics* definition.

Still, the interpretation does not help us answer our question about 'usually'. Two candidates are strong: that 'usually' means that most but not all species of emotion involve pleasure and pain (since hate does not); that 'usually' means that most but not all species of emotion involve imaginative construal (with desire as the exception). The argument does, however, suggest that Aristotle's *Eudemian Ethics* definition of emotion is not likely to cause any serious problems for our interpretation of his account of emotion. Both of the strong candidates fit well with the claim that emotions, for Aristotle, are pleasures or pains at particular persons doing or experiencing good or bad.

Finally, what about Aristotle's inclusion of hate on his list of emotions in the *Rhetoric*? Does it cause a problem for our general interpretation of emotion as perception of particular persons doing or experiencing good or bad? There are two reasons one might think that it does. First, though hate clearly is directed at evil, it is not a type of pain according to Aristotle. Second, hate is directed at universals as well as at particulars, as we have seen: "And anger always concerns particulars, such as Callias or Socrates, while hate is also directed to types. For, everyone hates the thief and the sycophant" (*Rhet.* 2.4 1382a5–7). These two points about hate in fact provide support for our general interpretation of emotion, however, for it is likely that it is because hate is more universal that it is not a type of pain. In addition, it is likely that hate is a borderline case. (1) According to our interpretation, negative emotions are perceptions of particular persons as doing or suffering something bad. Such negative emotions are types of pain. Hate is not a pain; and it is not directed to particulars. This correlation fits with our definition. (2) Hate, then, would be a borderline case. The inclusion of borderline cases in a list of examples of specific cases of a definition does not, in itself, invalidate the definition. For example, Aristotle includes shame on his list of ethical virtues, though it is a borderline case, and we do not as a result alter our understanding of his definition of ethical virtue. It is reasonable to suppose that hate plays a similar role here on Aristotle's list of emotions.

Conclusion

The central cognitive component of emotion *is*, then, cognition of value. For, emotions are perceptions of the value of particulars. More specifically, they are perceptions or appearances of particular persons doing or suffering good or bad. As a result, when our perceptions of value change, our emotions change; when our perceptions of value become richer, our emotions become richer. This explains why it is that emotions, according to Aristotle, can be shaped or developed and not just suppressed or channeled. I need not in every case suppress or channel an unwanted emotion. Instead, since emotions are perceptions of value, if I change my perception in a certain way, there will be no need to suppress, channel, or control the emotion. For example, if I cease to perceive other people as fundamentally threatening and come to see some of them as mutual participants with me in a flourishing life, then I need not suppress or channel my fear of them, but can instead act on my emotional response to them since it will be in accord with my perception.

By now, I hope to have shown through both negative and positive arguments involving extensive interpretation of numerous texts that, according to Aristotle, the cognitive component of ethical virtue and of emotion is not just the perception of particulars but also perception of their value, that is, perception of them as good or beautiful, bad or ugly. Moreover, I have argued for a certain interpretation of Aristotle's notion of value according to which value is a kind of enriching relatedness that cannot be defined but can be perceived by induction and that shows up analogously but differently in different cases. What does my interpretation add to recent interpretations of the cognitive component of ethical virtue and of emotion in Aristotle's theory, interpretations that quite rightly point to the importance, for ethical virtue, of perception of one's concrete, particular situation rather than knowledge of universal rules? Just this. It points out that, in addition to the importance of detailed knowledge of particulars, our perception of a certain kind of relatedness among particulars is important as well: our perception of particulars as constitutive of or instrumental to development, along with our perception of larger and larger contexts and wholes within which particulars become constitutive of or instrumental to development; our perception of particulars as destructive or harmful to development, along with our awareness of larger contexts and wholes within which particulars become destructive or harmful to such development. For Aristotle, ethical virtue requires from us more than the detailed and sensitive knowledge of particulars. It requires that we see whole things whole and partial things partial.

CONCLUSION

Imaginative Construction

In this concluding chapter, I will begin a process of assessing Aristotle's account of the cognitive component of ethical virtue by giving a new characterization of cognition of value in Aristotle's ethics, by pointing to some of the strengths of Aristotle's account, and by pointing to some of the weaknesses of his account.

1

As we have now seen, the central kind of cognition in Aristotle's ethics is unmediated awareness of the value of particulars. This awareness has different names and types.

Aristotle often calls it 'perception'. By this he means, as we have seen in chapter 2, section 1, awareness of particulars as instances of ends or goods (*De Motu* 6 700b19–22). Perception of particulars as end or good, as we saw in chapter 6, section 2, is not perception by the special senses (sight, hearing, smell, etc.) but is perception by all the senses of the common sense-objects (unity, number, movement, etc.). Parallel to the common perception of, say, a human being as one or moving is the common perception of a thing, person, or state of affairs of some particular sort as good (or beautiful).

When the unmediated awareness of particulars as instances of evaluative universals is least articulate (since such awareness differs in degree of articulation), Aristotle will sometimes call it 'insight' *(ennoia)* as we have seen in chapter 5, sections 2 and 3: [the many] "do not even have an insight into what is beautiful and truly pleasant since they have not had a taste of it" (*NE* 10.9 1179b15–16). Insight *(ennoia)* is the unarticulated initial operation of theoretical insight *(nous)* on particulars that makes Aristotelian induction, the derivation of universals from particulars, possible.

At his most technical, Aristotle of course calls unmediated awareness of particulars as instances of ends or goods 'practical insight' *(phronēsis)*. More precisely, unmediated awareness of particulars as instances of ends or goods is a component of practical insight (though Aristotle often speaks imprecisely). Practical insight, he says, is a "true apprehension *(hypolēpsis)* of the end" (*NE* 6.9 1142b32–33) as we saw in chapter 4, section 3. He also describes it as contemplation *(theōrein)*, appearance *(phainetai)*, and acquaintance *(gnōrizein)*—and, of course, as perception *(aisthēsis)*: "practical insight is of the ultimate of which there is not knowledge but perception" (*NE* 6.9 1142a26–27).

Finally, sometimes Aristotle mentions not perception or insight but our capacity to receive appearances, namely, imagination *(phantasia)*. In some cases our actions are motivated not by a particular perceived as good or beautiful (common perception) but, instead, by a particular that appears to us as good or beautiful. In those cases, appearances take the place of percepts as we saw in chapter 2, section 1, and chapter 6, section 1 (*De An.* 3.7 431a9–14).

In cases of practical insight, of course, one sees a particular as good or beautiful when it is good or beautiful. To be good or beautiful is, as I have argued, to be complete or developed or constitutive of completion or development. Hence, the person with practical insight sees a particular as good or beautiful when it is complete or developed or constitutive of completion or development, and not when it is not. For example, he or she would see food as good that leads to health or fitness—that is, to the development of my body—or at least is not destructive of it. He or she would value people who possess intelligence and character and not just wealth or good birth. I propose that we call this kind of perception an example of 'imaginative construction'.

As we have seen, to see an action as part of a larger whole *is* to see it as good or beautiful according to Aristotle (chapter 5, section 7). For, as I have argued, for Aristotle, 'good' means 'end' and 'beautiful' means 'form', where form is substance *(ousia)* understood as the principle by virtue of which something is a whole and not a heap or arbitrary collection of parts and end is the principle by virtue of which something is a whole and not a heap or arbitrary collection of parts through time and change (*Met.* 7.17 1041b11–27). For example, to see rushing forward in battle as a constituent in the larger, complete action of a successful strategy of winning a war is to see it as beautiful. To see giving each person involved in a common enterprise an equal share of resources attained in that enterprise as proportional distribution is to see it as beautiful. Similarly, to see another as a constiutuent of mutual virtuous activities—intellectual activities, for example—is to see the other as good. To see a law that limits citizens' activities—a law that mandates just distribution or school attendance—not as a constraint on them but as a constituent of their flourishing lives is to see it as good. In each of these cases, to see particulars as beautiful or good is to see them as part of a larger whole. It is a type of imaginative construction.

'Imaginative construction' is best understood by its contrast with what I will call 'imaginative deconstruction'. A kind of imaginative deconstruction is recommended by, for example, Marcus Aurelius. As mentioned in the introduction to this essay, Marcus believes that virtue requires extinction rather than development of emotions and recommends a type of imaginative deconstruction as the method for achieving virtue understood in this way: think on the fact that you will die (not on what you could accomplish but on the fact that, no matter how much you accomplish, you, too, will die) (*Med.* 6.24); think of the meat you long to eat *as* nothing but the dead carcass of an animal; break the melody you wish to hear down into the notes that compose it; think of the purple robe as sheep's wool dyed with the blood of a shellfish; of sexual intercourse as internal rubbing accompanied by a spasmodic ejection of mucus (*Med.* 6.13). In general, analyze things into their component parts and despise them: break a pleasant melody into its individual notes; analyze a dance into individual movements and postures; apply this method to the whole of life (*Med.* 11.2).

Marcus and Aristotle would have us think on different types of 'ends', we could say: Marcus would have us think of the end or cessation or dissolution of different activities; Aristotle would have us think of the end or goal of those same activities. Marcus would have us imagine the inevitable dissolution of things we care about; Aristotle would have us construct in our imaginations the larger wholes of which they could be a part. All perception of value is a type of imaginative construction for Aristotle, since all of it involves seeing particulars as constituents of larger wholes. The cognition of value involved in ethical virtue is even more highly constructive, however, since it requires that we compare the value of different valuable particulars and combine the images of different valuable particulars into one unified image of them all. One must, as we saw in chapter 2, section 1, "make one image out of many" (*De An.* 3.11 434a5–10).

For Aristotle, then, virtue results from the imaginative construction of wholes. That is, it results from seeing particulars in the light of the wholes they could compose: my current activities in terms of the life goals I wish to attain; the food before me in terms of my overall bodily health; other people in terms of the joint activities we could engage in; and, in general, every event, situation, and thing in terms of an overall flourishing life. For Marcus, by contrast, virtue results from the imaginative deconstruction of such wholes: all lives in terms of their inevitable death; meat in terms of the dead animal that it comes from; music as nothing but notes; a robe as mere wool dyed with blood; sex as rubbing followed by ejection of mucus; and so forth.

2

The strength of Aristotle's 'imaginative construction' is that it provides an explanation of the fact that ethical virtue results from shaping and developing our emotions rather than from simply suppressing, controlling, or eliminating them. Emotions, for Aristotle, are perceptions of ourselves and others doing or suffering good or bad. Consequently, as we come to have richer and richer perceptions of how our concrete situation fits into one or another realizable picture of an overall developed and flourishing life, our emotional dispositions change as well. We come to desire, pursue, and take pleasure in those activities, institutions, and people who we see as part of that life. According to Aristotle, we need not simply channel our fear of others, as recommended by Hobbes, but can come to see at least some others as important constituents of our own developed and flourishing life, either as fellow citizens or as good friends, and thus cease to fear them. We need not simply channel our desire for unlimited property, as recommended by Locke, but can develop a richer picture of how property does and does not enable us to develop and flourish so that we come to desire property more as a means to the good and less as a good in itself. We need not simply extinguish our desires, as recommended by Marcus, but can shape our desires by shaping and developing our picture of a realizable developed and flourishing life. We can shape our desires, emotions, and pleasures so that what we want and what we think is best for us are in harmony.

3

The weakness of Aristotle's account is that it is not clear that everything that is appropriate for us to do is something that we can or ought to come to desire. In a politically repressive society, for example, we may have to do many things that we appropriately find undesirable. In such a situation, ethical virtue would require of us that we use some psychological mechanism to manage our distaste or aversion rather than that we shape or develop it. For example, we could channel our distaste into some other activity—covert political activity, for example—or we could simply learn to distance ourselves from the aversion or lessen its impact on us.

Nor is it clear that everything that we ought to refrain from doing is something that we ought to cease to desire. Sexual desire provides an example. Though, as previously stated, Freud is wrong in supposing that all ethical development results from sexual repression—since the pre-oedipal stages of development of the self already involve learning to accept limitations on fulfillment of desire—he is right that some of it does. Moreover, sexual repression provides us with vivid examples. It is reasonable to assume that the opposite sex parent (for heterosexuals) and a variety of other people, simply *are* both desirable and off-limits. In such cases, proper emotional development would not be to develop or shape our emotions so that we no longer find such a person desirable but, instead, would be to somehow put aside, repress, or channel our desires.

Another way to approach this criticism is to reflect on Aristotle's views on pleasure. Aristotle's ethical teaching is a subtle type of antihedonism. He rejects the view that pleasure is the human good but wants to stay close to—or, as he would say, preserve—the common intuition that pleasure is the good (*NE* 1.8 1098b9–12, 25, 99a7–31; 7.14 1154a22–26). He has rhetorical and dialectical reasons for doing so. Rhetorically, if he can show why a false view appears true, he is more likely to engender belief in the true view (*NE* 7.14 1154a22–25). Dialectically—or as we would say today, methodologically—what is commonly believed is likely to be true in some way or to an extent (*NE* 1.8 1098b27–29). Aristotle stays close to common intuitions by arguing that the best life for a human being (viz., a life of activities in accord with virtue) is also the most pleasant life for a human being: "Happiness, then, is the best, most beautiful, and most pleasant" (*NE* 1.8 1099a24–25). He beats the hedonist at his or her own game, for though he does not believe that pleasure is the good, he believes the good is what is most pleasant.

In 1.8, for example, Aristotle distinguishes between a life that has its pleasure in itself and a life that lacks intrinsic pleasure and as a result requires some extrinsic pleasure as an attachment or ornament. A life of actions in accord with virtue is pleasant in itself since actions in accord with virtue are pleasant in themselves. Those whose lives do not consist in virtuous activities need some type of surface pleasure that can compensate for the lack of pleasure in their daily lives. Regarding those who lead a life of actions in accord with virtue, the 'lovers-of-the-beautiful', Aristotle says, "Their life has no need in addition of pleasure as a superficial ornament, but has pleasure in itself" (NE 1.8 1099a15–16).[1]

Aristotle's point is that if our life has the pleasures intrinsic to the activities that compose it, namely, the pleasures intrinsic to those activities when virtuously done, then we will not need to pursue other pleasures as compensation for the painful quality of our experiences. An example of what he has in mind occurs in his discussion of friendship. The decent or virtuous person wishes to live with himself, Aristotle says, because he finds it pleasant. He takes pleasure both in his memories of past acts and, as a result, in his hopes for the future. In addition, his intellect is well-stocked with subjects of contemplation (NE 9.4 1166a23–27). Bad people, to the contrary, find being with themselves to be difficult and seek others with whom to spend their time as a result. When they are by themselves, they remember many regrettable deeds and, as a result, their hopes are for others like them. When they are with others, they forget (NE 9.4 1166b13–17). An ethically virtuous person's deeds, past and future, are pleasant to contemplate. A person with intellectual virtue has a developed mind and so always has highly pleasurable subjects to contemplate. This person can spend time alone with pleasure and need not run to others in the hope that they will drive the painful feelings away. In this example, the pleasures of friendship are a superficial ornament or attachment, a compensation for the unpleasant quality of a life that is not a life of virtue. In addition, the friendship is a low-quality one since it is used, in utilitarian fashion, to drive out pain.

Aristotle's understanding of the role of superficial pleasure in making up for an otherwise unpleasant life is an appealing one, and contains some truth. When we do not enjoy what we do, we seek other pleasures to compensate. Then there is a superficial quality to our pleasures, since they cover over, rather than eliminating, pain. Moreover, our pleasures are unstable (Aristotle says they "conflict"—*machetai*). A neo-Aristotelian discussing the problems of addiction might utilize Aristotle's insight and suggest that, at least in some cases, a tendency to excessive drinking or obsessive television watching be overcome by developing the qualities required to do one's ordinary activities well—that it be overcome, in other words, by developing one's virtue. Then one would not need easy pleasures as compensation, but would have pleasure in the day-to-day. One who lacks courage, for example, will be continually uncomfortable in office interactions (or, for Aristotle, on the battlefield) and may drink or watch television to forget about life at the office. Aristotle's examples are not drink and television, but horses and spectacles (*NE* 1.8 1099a9–10). His point, however, is the same. One whose virtues are not developed experiences pain in the day-to-day, and so turns to the easy pleasures of horses or spectacles as compensation.[2]

A neo-Marxist might retort, however, that it is not lack of virtue but lack of meaningful work that leads to such compensatory activities—and to others, such as wife-beating and barroom brawls. The neo-Marxist and at least a certain type of neo-Aristotelian could agree about this, however. Aristotle's theory of pleasure includes the idea that the best pleasures are activities not just of the best-developed faculty but also in relation to the best objects. The most pleasant activity, he says, is that of "the best conditioned faculty in relation to the best of its objects" (*NE* 10.4 1174b18–19). Hence, worthy objects, as Aristotle would say, or meaningful work, as Marxists and liberals would say, is necessary for pleasant lives.

The question we would want to ask Aristotle and the neo-Aristotelian, though, is, To what extent can a life provide one with such high-level objects and activities? Aristotle himself recognizes that we need easy pleasures that help us relax from work. On the question whether play *(paidia)* is the human good (since we choose it for its own sake and to the detriment of other things), he says, "Play would seem to be relaxation and we need relaxation because it is impossible to be continuously active" (*NE* 10.6 1176b34–35). He also recognizes that sexual pleasure is used to drive out pain: "bodily pleasure expels pain; and due to excesses of pain, people pursue excess and, in general, bodily pleasure as being a cure" (*NE* 7.14 1154a27–29). He does not think, however, that the need for such curative pleasures is very widespread. Bodily pleasure is pursued by those who are unable to pursue other pleasures because, since bodily pleasures are violent, they are easy (*NE* 7.14 1154b2–3). Only youths and people of impulsive nature, however, are always in need of a cure (*NE* 7.14 1154b9–12). Others need not seek curative pleasure to a very great extent, but may seek the pleasures Aristotle calls 'natural' pleasures, that is, pleasures intrinsic to good activity engaged in by healthy and developed faculties, not activities that are pleasurable only or primarily because they expel pain.

The point of this discussion is not to adjudicate fully Aristotle's views on pleasure, for example, to decide whether he is right in claiming that the pleasures intrinsic to activity are as a general rule more valuable than those that expel pain. Instead, it is to thematize and question his view that it is only the lives of youths and naturally excitable people that extensively require techniques for managing, or otherwise adjusting to, pain.

Consider the presence of death in our lives—our own death as well as the deaths of those close to us. Surely, coming to terms with the fact that we will die is a major developmental task for each of us. We do not come to terms with it by learning to take pleasure in it. Instead, acceptance is more to the point, where acceptance does not imply liking, enjoying, or positively evaluating something, but facing it and, by doing so, lessening its power.

Aristotle is aware that facing some pain, rather than eliminating it, is sometimes necessary. In his account of courage, he discusses the necessity of facing, rather than eliminating, fears. Though a courageous man feels fear as little as is humanly possible, he nonetheless is frightened by certain terribly frightening things, as is any sane human being, but still can face his fears. He is frightened no more than is appropriate and then faces his fears (*NE* 3.9 1117a29–35). The most frightening thing, according to Aristotle, is death: "Death is the most frightening thing, for nothing is thought any longer good or bad for one who is dead" (*NE* 3.7 1115a26–27). Alternately, he may have a certain type of death in mind, for example, a brutal death or a slow one. Courage, as understood by Aristotle, is more like continence than other virtues are, we could say, since at least some of the time it is accompanied by pain (fear) rather than pleasure (desire).³

In the case of courage, then, Aristotle accepts that virtue—the best-developed state of the soul—is *not* a harmony of cognition and emotion. In some activities in accord with courage, according to Aristotle, I know what is good and I do not take pleasure in it. However, if it is true in the case of one virtue that the best-developed state of my soul is *not* a harmony of cognition and emotion, then it could be true in other cases as well. Going back to Aristotle's definition of ethical virtue, in some cases, then, virtue will not be a disposition that involves choice, with choice understood as *prohairesis* or deliberate desire, since desire will be lacking.

Courage is different than the other virtues because of the kind of world we live in. We are *not* continually provided only with high-level objects and activities. Nor is it the case that everything we must do is something we can or ought to come to desire. Our lives and the lives of those close to us end inevitably in death. How a person responds to this fact, and to the numerous other frightening situations in life, tells us something central about their character, not something peripheral to it. Do they put the fears in the forefront of their awareness so that they are paralyzed in many of life's activities? Do they put them entirely out of awareness so that when fearful things inevitably occur, they have not developed the capacity productively to deal with them? Or, finally, do they face them in such a way as to be aware of but not paralyzed by them?

This leads to another question about Aristotle's understanding of courage and of virtue in general. According to Aristotle, courage has to do with fearful things that meet two criteria. First, they must be the greatest of fearful things, namely, death. Second, it must not be death in just any circumstance, but in the most beautiful or noble of circumstances, the circumstances of battle, since war involves the greatest and most beautiful dangers. We might ask whether circumscribing courage in this way leaves us with a definition of courage or, rather, with a definition of a certain type of courage. Facing fear in battle is especially laudable, according to Aristotle, because in battle (1) we can show prowess (presumably, agility in battle) and (2) death is noble (presumably because it is for the sake of others, specifically, for the city) (*NE* 3.7 1115b4–5).

Still, what of the death that we all face, even those of us whose deaths involve no acts of prowess and are not for the sake of any higher or greater good? What about facing death from disease or old age? Aristotle considers facing death from disease to be second-order courage since it does not involve prowess and is not noble (*NE* 3.7 1115a34–35).

It is difficult to say which of these is courage to a higher degree. There is certainly something admirable about being able to function at a high level of physical skill in the face of death and when one does not have to do so, in some sense, but does so for others. It is difficult to function well when frightened. On the other hand, one could say that the opportunity for a high level of physical functioning, and the fact that the functioning is for the sake of a higher goal, can make the fearful act easier, for it can take one's mind off of death. A person who faces death through disease does not have this opportunity. The level of physical functioning is low. The death has no purpose. As a result, overcoming one's fears is difficult. Which is more difficult is hard to say. It is difficult to function well when frightened. It is difficult to face one's fears when they are unadulterated. Rather than ranking these, we might instead want to say that the two are, simply, different types of courage, and give each its due.

Our lives are full of painful but mundane activities in which we must engage. There are all the dull things that we must do—doing laundry, waiting in line, finding paper clips, putting caps back on bottles, saving packing boxes, making beds, recycling cans, bagging old newspapers. Then there are the dirty things that must be done—cleaning toilets, changing diapers, mopping floors, wiping the counters, cleaning broiler pans, resurfacing roads, taking out garbage, changing bedpans. Finally, there are dangerous activities—policing the community, putting out fires, bearing children, fighting wars, guarding buildings, walking in dangerous neighborhoods, collecting garbage, putting up beams for tall buildings.[4] Aristotle's idea of virtue is derived from his idea of what human functioning is like, namely, that it is rational or cognitive functioning, whether activity of our cognitive capacities per se or of our cognition-informed emotions, and from his idea of what it is for us to be functioning well—namely, to act in accord with the virtues of our cognitive and affective capacities, namely, intellectual and ethical virtue. As a result, for his account to be consistent and complete, he needs a discussion of how our intellect and emotion must be developed so that we function well in the types of activities I have just described—dull activities, dirty activities, dangerous (but mundane) activities—all the activities that we must do, but need not and perhaps cannot come to desire for their own sakes.

In addition, there is another way in which our lives are painful and we must adjust. We experience pain due to our own lack of virtue. Though we may strive to develop virtues of courage, generosity, wit, justice, and so forth, we often fall short. How do we adjust to this fact? We do not, at least in any ordinary way, come to love our emotional shortcomings—or, for that matter, the emotional shortcomings of others. What is our attitude toward the resulting frustrations? Can we love ourselves despite them? Or, to use the example cited earlier from Aristotle's discussion of friendship, can we live with ourselves despite them? Another claim Aristotle makes clarifies the issue. According to Aristotle, the best type of love is love for the lovable—more specifically, love for someone who has virtue. But, where does that leave all of us? Some other type of love is required, a love that persists despite our lack of virtue.

One could object and point out that Aristotle does discuss another type of love besides love for the lovable, namely, love of one's own (*Pol.* 2.4 1262b22–23). However, there is no virtue pertaining to this kind of love in Aristotle's writings. Does Aristotle think it is natural, rather than developed? Or is it so noncontroversial that it does not occur to him to thematize it? Contemporary psychoanalytic literature is full of discussions of people who have not learned consistently to love others apparently as a result of not having accomplished certain developmental tasks when young. If the literature is correct, then the capacity for persistent love is a developed one. That is, it is a virtue. This is not surprising, given that persistent love is love of something even when it lacks value, a capacity that does not seem simply to be a matter of course. Just as there are some things we cannot or should not desire that we nonetheless must do, so it is true about people that though often there is nothing particularly desirable about them, still often it is both possible and appropriate to love them.

CONCLUSION

What I have done in this section is show an intellectual space that Aristotle leaves open and into which various philosophers and other thinkers have stepped with different theories of virtue. The Stoics stepped into this space, with their idea of the *epochē*, that is, of bracketing or standing back from our passions. Jews and Christians stepped into this space with virtues like love as they understand it (*chesed*, Hebrew; *agapē*, Greek) and, as well, with virtues such as faith (*emunah*, Hebrew; *pistis*, Greek).

Aristotle presents and explains the view that ethical virtue involves shaping or developing emotions rather than eliminating them, suppressing them, or controlling them. It is not clear, however, that this is the whole story about ethical virtue. Human affective development is extraordinarily complicated. It seems more likely that just as we need to learn to shape and develop our emotions, so we need to develop the capacity to distance ourselves from some of them, or to channel them or, in general, to lessen the impact they have on us without changing their cognitive nature. If so, ethical virtue would require two things. It would require that we learn to shape our emotions in accord with our greater and greater recognition of those relationships that can enrich us and of those that can harm or destroy us. It would require, in addition, that we learn to manage those emotions that we cannot or ought not shape.

There is a long and interesting list of ways various people have suggested that we might go about managing emotions that we cannot or should not shape: force against our emotions, channeling our emotions, eliminating our emotions, despising our emotions, repressing our emotions, sublimating our emotions, denying our emotions, dissociating from our emotions, splitting our emotions, not to mention what Buddhists do when they 'are here, now' and what Jews and Christians do when they claim to feel steadfast love (*chesed, agapē*). At some point, virtue theorists need to assess these candidate answers—first, to try to understand them and then to see which among them has an appropriate role to play as part of virtue of character. Good and bad may be yoked together much more than Aristotle realizes. If so, it might not be possible or desirable for us, in every sort of situation, to come to take pleasure in what we must do or experience.

Finally, we need also to consider whether Aristotle's concept of enriching relatedness, the perception of which enables us to shape rather than simply managing our emotions, is the last word on enriching relatedness, and whether Aristotle's concept of wholeness is the last word on wholeness. Aristotle's understanding of each is fundamentally hierarchical. Wherever there is a whole that is not a heap, as we have seen that Aristotle says in the *Politics*, the ruler and the ruled show up.

For Aristotle, I am enriched by that to which I look up. The concept of *telos*, from which Aristotelian enriching relatedness and wholeness derives, is a hierarchical one. *Telos* enriches that which is under it—changes its value, raises it to another level—while it itself remains unchanged. The enrichment is one-way. If there are other, less hierarchical, kinds of enriching relatedness, they, too, might shape our emotions. I suspect that this is one of the implicit teachings of twentieth-century developmental psychology, for example, object relations theory, according to which our sense of our self as a self and of an other as other are coterminous.[5] Self and other, in other words, are mutually constitutive. Each enriches the other. The two together form a whole. If so, developmental theory would be a rich source for thinking about what we have come, somewhat infelicitously, to call 'virtue theory' and for assessing Aristotle's account of the cognitive component of ethical virtue.

NOTES

Introduction

1. My thoughts on God's incomprehensibility were first spurred by Leo Strauss's "Jerusalem and Athens: Some Preliminary Reflections" (in *Studies in Platonic Political Philosophy*, Leo Strauss [Chicago: University of Chicago Press, 1983]); and Albrecht Dihle's *Theory of the Will in Classical Antiquity* (Berkeley: University of California Press, 1982) from which these examples come. Continuing thoughts on the topic have been occasioned by discussions of the tension in the Hebrew *Bible* between God's accessibility and God's incomprehensibility, for example, Richard Elliot Friedman's *Who Wrote the Bible?* (New York: Simon & Schuster, 1987) in which it is argued that the composition of the Hebrew *Bible* out of the now familiar four sources was designed to stress contrasting elements such as near and far, personal and transcendental, and Israel I. Efros's *Ancient Jewish Philosophy* (New York: Bloch Publishing Company, 1964) which describes a fundamental tension in the Hebrew *Bible* between God's glory and God's separateness, between 'immanence' and 'transcendence'.

2. To be more precise, it is not the sort of faculty that other thinkers might call by the name 'will' or by related names, such as 'assent'/'consent' *(synkatathesis)*, a central concept for the Stoics, sometimes thought of as a predecessor concept to the concept of will, though I suggest rather than thinking of it as a predecessor concept to another concept thought of as correct (viz., will) that we would be better off thinking of both assent/consent and will as two members of a family of concepts that have related meanings and functions.

3. In this essay, I have translated *'phronēsis'* as 'practical insight' and *'nous'* as 'theoretical insight' in order to capture the fact that both of them are types of unmediated awareness ('insight') and the fact that one is operative in our theoretical understanding and the other in our understanding of practical affairs.

4. Sometimes, for simplicity's sake, I will speak only of one of them—the good—and then, later, explain and bring in the other—the beautiful. Doing so

will make reading this essay easier and, of course, I do not by this procedure intend to overlook important distinctions.

5. Martha Nussbaum discusses the surprise involved in new situations according to Aristotle as she understands him. My view on this topic is in harmony with hers but adds another dimension to it, namely, the underlying relationality that is responsible for the element of surprise. For Nussbaum's discussion of surprise, see, for example, *The Fragility of Goodness: Luck and Ethics in Greek Tragedy and Philosophy* (Cambridge: Cambridge University Press, 1986b); and the revision of "The Discernment of Perception: An Aristotelian Conception of Private and Public Rationality," in Nussbaum, *Love's Knowledge: Essays on Philosophy and Literature* (Cambridge: Cambridge University Press, 1986a). For the relationality that is responsible for it, see chapter 5, section 7, of this essay.

6. An exception would be Anne Carson in *Eros the Bittersweet* (Princeton: Princeton University Press, 1986). As I understand her, she makes a similar point in her discussion of how the concept of love changes from the one described in lyric poetry to the one discussed in Plato's dialogues, from love as something that melts a person or knocks them out to love as something that causes a person to sprout wings.

7. Or, if one may use the term 'psychologist' more broadly, with Hobbes.

8. For an interesting article that touches on the different understandings of emotion found in Freudian theory and in object relations theory, see Ethel Spector Person, "Sexuality and the Mainstay of Identity: Psychoanalytic Perspectives," in *Women: Sex and Sexuality*, Catharine R. Stimpson and Ethel Spector Person, eds. (Chicago: University of Chicago Press, 1980).

9. Insofar as it involves the assumption of the rejection of the concept of value, our age is best understood as late modern. The early moderns reject value since it does not meet their demand for certainty based on analyticity. Our age is the more pessimistic phase of that rejection after the early modern optimism about its productive possibilities was seen, for a variety of reasons, to be ill-founded. There are also, of course, grounds for applying the term 'postmodern' to this age.

10. I give an extended argument for this claim in Deborah Achtenberg, "On the Metaphysical Presuppositions of Aristotle's *Nicomachean Ethics*," *Journal of Value Inquiry* 26 (1992): 317–340.

11. An object relational account suggests that a large part of the moral teaching Freud claims is learned from the experience of the necessity of sexual repression is actually learned earlier—in the child's recognition that the mother or other nurturing person is not continually available to meet the child's needs. For evaluation of Freud's view, the difference in negotiation of the oedipal stage by the boy and the girl must be taken into account, as well. See, for example, Nancy Chodorow's *Reproduction of Mothering* (Berkeley: University of California Press, 1978).

12. Freud's assumption that heterosexual object choice is basic has been ably criticized by Judith Butler in *Gender Trouble: Feminism and the Subversion of Identity* (New York: Routledge, 1990); and by Chodorow in "Heterosexuality as a Compromise Formation," in *Feminities, Masculinities, Sexualities: Freud and Beyond* (Lexington: University Press of Kentucky, 1994), pp. 33–69.

13. See, for example, the important examples mentioned in N. Gregory Hamilton's useful *Self and Others: Object Relations Theory in Practice* (Northvale, New Jersey: Jason Aronson Press, 1990), pp. 18–19.

14. For discussion of new syntheses, see, for example, Achtenberg, "Replacing the Classics in Today's Curricula: Toward a New Syncretism" (paper presented at the National Endowment for the Humanities Focus Grant series, Temple University, Philadelphia, 1996b); Gloria Anzaldúa, *Borderlands/La Frontera: The New Mestiza* (San Francisco: Aunt Lute Books Company, 1987); Rosi Braidotti, *Nomadic Subjects: Embodiment and Sexual Difference in Contemporary Feminist Theory* (New York: Columbia University Press, 1994).

Chapter One: Valuable Particulars

1. McDowell supports the interpretive claim that, according to Aristotle, a view of how to live is not codifiable by referring to *NE* 1.3. He explains and supports the claim further by referring to and explicating Wittgenstein's account of rule-following according to which action is explained not in terms of being guided by universals or rules but in terms of being guided by shared forms of life. There is no external standard—no standard outside of shared forms of life—from which to demonstrate the rationality of our action.

2. McDowell supports this interpretation of Aristotle by referring to *NE* 5.10 1137b19–34 on equity as a corrective of the universality of law, 1142a23–30 and 1143a25–b5 on practical insight as cognition of particulars.

3. Nussbaum supports this interpretation by referring to *NE* 5.10 1109b18–23 where Aristotle claims that the discrimination or discernment is in the perception of particulars and by referring to Aristotle's discussion of the universality of law in the chapter on equity, 1137b13ff.

4. The argument is based on exegesis of *De An.* 403a5ff., "e.g. getting angry, being confident, desiring appetitively, in general perceiving." I discuss the argument further in chapter 6.

5. Nussbaum translates *'phronēsis'* as 'practical wisdom'. I have followed her practice in passages that refer to her views.

6. Sherman supports her view by referring to what she calls the "celebrated" passage at *NE* 5.10 1109b15–23 on the discernment being in the perception of particulars. In addition, she adduces 1142a23–30 that compares practical wisdom to the perception of a triangle and 1143a35–b5 regarding the *nous* of ultimates.

7. Salkever refers to the passage on the universality of law at *NE* 5.10 1137b11–19. In addition, he supports his interpretation of practical wisdom as a kind of balancing primarily by referring to examples in which Aristotle's decision-procedure in fact involves the balancing of competing goods: friendship duties (*NE* 9), the necessity of slavery, encouraging legal reform, who or what is sovereign in the city, the most desirable human life *(Politics)*.

8. Again, I use 'practically wise' as a translation of *'phronimos'* here since McDowell does.

Chapter Two: Ethics and Moral Theory

1. See especially chapters 3 and 10.

2. Aristotle, of course, does not use the term 'metaphysics' but instead speaks of first philosophy, theology, or the science of being just as being.

3. I do not intend, by using the terms 'ethical' and 'moral' in this way, to correct the ordinary usage of the terms. Only time and culture will tell how we end up using the terms, and philosophers are overblown and somewhat coercive when they try in their writings to determine how language will develop. Still, for the purposes of making some important distinctions, I do in this essay follow a current philosophers' convention of using 'ethics' as the broad term of which 'morality' is one type.

4. Someone might argue against my claim and say that a moral faculty *is* an affective faculty. I would respond by saying that, if so, it is a special kind of affective faculty—for example, a voluntaristic one (in which case we might question whether it ought truly to be called 'affective') or one that is responsive to noncognitive claims (in which case we would have to expand our understanding of emotion). If so, my claim could be rephrased to say that Aristotle does not suppose that we have a moral faculty in addition to our faculties for *ordinary* cognition and affect. The disagreement, in other words, would be a simply terminological one. For a detailed discussion of the view that there is no concept of will in classical Greek thought, see Albrecht Dihle's *Theory of the Will in Classical Antiquity* (Berkeley: University of California Press, 1982).

5. The more complete definition is, of course, "virtue is a disposition regarding choice *(hexis prohairētikē)*, consisting in a mean, the mean relative to us, determined by a *logos*, specifically, by the *logos* by which the person of practical insight would determine it. I justify the shorthand phrase 'developed capacity for good choice' in the following way. In chapter 3, section 3, I argue that a *'hexis'* for Aristotle is a settled disposition to act or be affected well and point out that sometimes he calls such a condition not a *hexis* but a sort of capacity (there is a mere capacity and, in addition, a capacity to act or be affected well). This implies that a *hexis* is a sort of capacity for Aristotle, specifically, a developed capacity to act or be affected well. Virtue is a *hexis* regarding choice consisting in a mean. Choice involves desire and, if one is not impeded, results in action. Thus choice accounts for the affection and action components of a *hexis*. The mean remains and accounts for the evaluatively positive component of a *hexis*. Hence, a virtue is a developed capacity for good choice.

6. For free will as the distinguishing feature, see the Jewish and Christian traditions. For free agency, see Rousseau's *Discourse on Inequality* in *Jean-Jacques Rousseau: The First and Second Discourses Together with the Replies to Critics and Essay on the Origin of Languages* (New York: Harper, 1986), 1.15–16.

7. See also *NE* 3.3, especially 1112b2–3 and 1113a9–10. Along with a number of commentators, I interpret *"tōn pros ta telē"* (1112b11–12) to mean "what is conducive to ends." What is conducive to ends may include both means to ends and components or constituents of ends.

8. According to Anthony A. Long's outline of the history of the term *'enkrateia'* in "Hellenistic Ethics and Philosophical Power," in *Hellenistic History and Culture*, Peter Green, ed. (Berkeley: University of California Press, 1993), *'enkrateia'* does not occur before Plato and Xenophon. The adjective is found earlier, but in reference to physical or political power, not as an attribute of character. In the dialogues, Socrates speaks of *enkratē heautou* (ruling oneself). Evidence for the view that the idea is novel at this time is that Socrates must explain it to an uncomprehending Callicles in the *Gorgias* and that in the dialogues Socrates rarely uses it without the reflexive pronoun. By the time of Aristotle, the psychological sense of 'control' is common enough that the reflexive pronoun can be elided.

9. Aristotle gives not just three, but four, resolutions of the problem of incontinence in *NE* 7.3. However, in two of them (the second and fourth), the same situation obtains, namely that one has universal knowledge but does not have particular knowledge.

10. By 'perceptual knowledge', Aristotle must mean to refer to common perception.

11. Aristotle's view in *De Anima* is the same, namely, that incontinence results when a particular premise conflicts with a universal one, since it is the particular premise that produces movement (*De An.* 3.11 434a19–20). Or, Aristotle says, perhaps both the universal and the particular premise produce movement, but the universal premise tends to stay at rest. That is, we may interpret, it tends in some cases not to be focussed on particulars (3.11 434a20–21). In *De Motu* 7, Aristotle gives a similar account.

12. I shall make note of, rather than analyzing, Aristotle's *De Motu* account of the cause of human action since it gives a similar answer and does not introduce refinements useful to the general topic of this essay.

13. Compare *De Motu* 6 700b18–19: "And all these can be reduced to thought *(nous)* and desire *(orexis)*."

14. An alternative translation would be 'thought that calculates for the sake of something, that is, thought that is practical'. I reject this interpretation for three reasons. First, these two types of thought parallel the two types of non-perceptual imagination Aristotle will soon list, namely, calculative imagination and deliberative imagination. Second, it is not unusual for Aristotle to mention a general category and then mention subcategories that include one with the same name as the name of the general category and meant to specify a narrow sense of the term. For example, in chapter 6, section 8, practical insight is a general category whose subcategories are practical insight, household management, legislation and politics where the subcategory 'practical insight' means 'practical insight in the narrow sense'.

15. In addition, in the *De Motu* 6 700b19–22 discussion of thought and desire as the two causes of animal movement, Aristotle includes perception as a type of thought.

16. Compare *De Motu* 6 700b23–26, 28–29, where Aristotle makes basically the same point when he asserts that it is the end in the sphere of the practical that causes animal movement, then refers to such an end as a type of good

and then counts the apparent good and the pleasant as goods (the pleasant since it is an apparent good).

17. I discuss this passage further, and justify the interpretation of it that I assume here, in chapter 6.

18. Again, I am assuming that Aristotle includes perception as a type of thought in his discussion of the causes of animal movement. He makes it clear that he does so at *De Motu* 6 700b19–22.

19. In *De Motu* 6 700b23–24, Aristotle makes the same point by referring to the first mover as "the object of desire as well as thought" *(to orekton kai dianoēton)*.

20. Other passions (i.e., other desires and aversions) according to Hobbes include love, hate; joy, grief; hope, despair; fear, courage; anger, indignation; confidence, diffidence; benevolence, good nature; covetousness, ambition; pusillanimity, magnanimity; valour, liberality; miserableness; kindness, natural lust, luxury; jealousy, revengefulness; curiosity; religion (superstitious and true), panic terror; admiration, glory, vain-glory; dejection; sudden glory, sudden dejection; shame, impudence; pity, cruelty; contempt, emulation, envy.

21. Hobbes does not use the term 'to value'. For convenience and continuity, I will use it as the general term for calling things either 'good' or 'bad'.

22. See also *Lev.* 1.15, 123: "*Good*, and *evil*, are names that signify our appetites, and aversions. . . ."

23. The desire for glory is basic as well. I leave it out for brevity's sake though including it would strengthen the point I am making.

24. Ego drive, Freud decides in his later writings, is not a drive distinct from sexual drive, but is sexual drive directed to oneself: "the ego is to be regarded as a great reservoir of libido from which libido is sent out *to* objects and which is always ready to absorb libido flowing back *from* objects. Thus the drives of self-preservation were also of a libidinal nature: they were sexual drives which, instead of external objects, had taken the subject's own ego as an object." "The Libido Theory," 1923, in *Freud: General Psychological Theory*, Philip Rieff, ed. (New York: Collier Books, 1963a), p. 182. In the later writings, Freud adds one drive distinct from the sexual drive, an aggressive or death drive that I de-emphasize here for brevity's sake. Bringing it in more fully would strengthen and add detail to the argument I give here.

25. Freud later rejects the generality of the claim that pleasure is elimination or reduction of tension since sometimes tension is pleasurable and reduction of tension painful. He concludes from this that there must be a qualitative factor in pleasure, perhaps of a rhythmic or durational nature. He then assigns pleasure as release to the death drive and the other sort of pleasure to the sexual drive or libido. ("The Economic Problem of Masochism," 1924, in ibid., pp. 190–191).

26. Similarly, "The categorical imperative of Kant is thus a direct inheritance from the Oedipus-complex" (ibid., p. 198; see also, "The Ego and the Id," 1923, in *The Standard Edition of the Complete Works of Sigmund Freud*, James Strachey, ed. Vol. 19. London: Hogarth Press, 1923–1925).

What I describe here is the simple positive oedipus complex in a boy. The more complete oedipus complex involves rivalry and identification both with the mother and with the father and is common, according to Freud (ibid.).

27. It could be objected to my argument that sex drive is basic that Freud sometimes says that the boy identifies with his father prior to feeling hostility toward him. I maintain that, nonetheless, identification is not more basic than drive for Freud takes that original identification to be indistinguishable from object cathexis ("The Ego and the Id," 1923, in ibid., p. 29) or to be "ambivalent from the very first" since it is a derivative of oral libido which involves annihilating what is longed for ("Group Psychology and the Analysis of the Ego," 1921, in ibid., Vol. 18, 1920–22, p. 105). If my response to the objection is inadequate and cannot be made adequate, then my general claim in this section that Freud counsels management not cultivation would have to be narrowed to the claim that the early Freud does so, which would not substantially alter the point in this section of this essay.

28. See also "Instincts and Their Vicissitudes," 1915, in *Freud*, pp. 101–102, where the intimate relation between love and sexual pleasure is discussed.

29. For Freud, then, as mentioned above, emotional development involves two types of emotional management. Drive is basic. It is managed, not cultivated or made reflective.

30. For an initial discussion of the topics discussed in the remainder of this section, see "Aristotelian Resources for Feminist Thinking," in *Ancient Philosophy and Feminism*, Julie K. Ward, ed. (New York: Routledge, 1996), pp. 100–105.

31. Of course, more than just correct beliefs and convictions is involved, since it is *phronēsis* that is the true conviction of the end and *phronēsis* is a type of perception according to Aristotle (*NE* 6.10).

32. The perception of value is common perception.

33. I discuss emotion as a type of perception of value—more precisely, as a type of perception or *phantasia* of value—further in chapter 6.

34. For a general discussion of equivocals including a discussion of the three types of equivocals, see Joseph Owens, *The Doctrine of Being in the Aristotelian 'Metaphysics'* (Toronto: Pontifical Institute of Mediaeval Studies, 1978), pp. 107–135. For an argument that equivocity does not simply reflect the different senses of words, see Terence Irwin, "Homonymy in Aristotle," *Review of Metaphysics* 34, 3 (1981): 523–544. For previous discussions of mine of good as an analogical equivocal, see Deborah Achtenberg, "On the Metaphysical Presuppositions of Aristotle's *Nicomachean Ethics*," *Journal of Value Inquiry* 26 (1992): 320–322; and Achtenberg, "Aristotelian Resources for Feminist Thinking," in *Ancient Philosophy and Feminism*, Julie K. Ward, ed. (New York: Routledge, 1996a), pp. 105–108. The account given here is closest to the one given in "Aristotelian Resources for Feminist Thinking."

35. I prefer 'equivocal' to 'homonymous' as a rendering of Aristotle's point since in English a homonym is a term that has the same pronunciation as another but a different meaning, for example, 'bore' and 'boar'. By using the term 'equivocal', I do not mean to indicate that what is at issue is merely semantic and not ontological. To the contrary, for Aristotle beings are equivocal, that is, appropriately spoken of in different ways.

36. Aristotle's example is not sharp but key *(kleis)* which is merely ambiguous in Greek and means either 'the collarbone' or 'that with which we lock a door'. See also *NE* 1.6 1096b26–27 where Aristotle speaks of chance equivocals and *Met.* 4.2 1003a33–34 where he contrasts focal equivocals with mere equivocals (what I am calling 'merely ambiguous equivocals'). I have altered Aristotle's account of the equivocity of sharp somewhat to utilize the ways in which 'sharp' is equivocal in English, rather than Greek.

37. The term 'focal' applied to *pros hen* equivocity comes from G. E. L. Owen, "Logic and Metaphysics in Some Earlier Works of Aristotle" (1960; reprinted in *Articles on Aristotle*, J. Barnes, J. Schofield, and R. Sorabji, eds. Vol. 3 [London: Duckworth, 1979]), p. 169. I change his "focal meaning" to "focal equivocity."

38. Terence Irwin, *Aristotle: Nicomachean Ethics* (Indianapolis: Hackett Publishing Company, 1985), p. 303, suggests concurrence with the claim that Aristotle's view in this passage is that good is an analogical equivocal.

39. My claim that the passage is an argument for analogical equivocity is qualified ("probably") because the passage stands on its own, contains no explicit questions or comments regarding kinds of equivocity and is part of, not after, an argument that good is equivocal not univocal. Still, I think the claim is probable since one way to argue that good is not univocal would be to show by example that it is equivocal by analogy.

40. Specifically, virtue is completion of something's defining potential. I argue for the claim that virtue is completion of defining potential in Achtenberg, "On the Metaphysical Presuppositions of Aristotle's *Nicomachean Ethics*," *Journal of Value Inquiry* 26 (1992): 329–330. A short version of that argument is: According to Aristotle, the virtue of each thing is relative to its proper *ergon*: "the virtue of each thing is relative to its *ergon*, specifically, to its proper *ergon (to ergon to oikeion)*" (*NE* 6.1 1139a16–17). By '*ergon*', Aristotle means capacity (or, when active, activity), and by 'proper *ergon*', defining capacity: "all things are defined in terms of their *ergon*, that is, their capacity" (*Pol.* 1.1 1253a24). Health, then, is completion of a body's defining potential, that is, of the potential by virtue of which a body is a body. The potential by virtue of which a body—an organic body—is a body is the potential for growth and maintenance. Health, then, is a completion of that potential. That is to say, health is the potential for good growth and maintenance.

41. See also *Met.* 1.2 982b4–7, b10, 1.3 983a31–32, 11.1 1059a35–37.

42. For a confirming interpretation of the first part of this passage, see Hippocrates G. Apostle, trans., *Aristotle's Metaphysics* (Grinnell, Iowa: Peripatetic Press, 1979), p. 356, note 3: "Not everything is definable; and there are principles and attributes of being *qua* being which are indefinable, such as actuality and potentiality."

43. Presumably another reason that *energeia* cannot be defined is that it does not fall in a genus and definitions must be by genus and specific difference.

44. In "Homonymy in Aristotle," Irwin makes a similar, though not identical, point, *Review of Metaphysics* 34, 3 (1981b): 540. It is the case both that there is a single true description of good and that good is multivocal according to him; for "goods are different because they are ends and ends are different."

45. A claim Aristotle makes in the well-known *ergon* argument in the next chapter that "the good and the 'well' is in the *ergon*" supports this interpretation (*NE* 1.7 1097b26–27). I owe the idea that this passage supports my general claim to Irwin, *Aristotle: Nicomachean Ethics* (Indianapolis: Hackett Publishing Company, 1985), p. 303.

46. I discuss *telos* in Achtenberg, "Human Being, Beast and God: The Place of Human Happiness According to Aristotle and Some Twentieth Century Philosophers," *St. John's Review* 38 (1988): 28 from which these comments are derived.

47. I make this proposal first in ibid., pp. 28–29, and discuss it again in Achtenberg, "Aristotelian Resources for Feminist Thinking," pp. 108–109, from which these comments are derived.

48. In order to include not just final but also instrumental ends, *telos* would have to be described more fully in this way: a *telos* is a constitutive (final end) or enabling (instrumental end) limit. Then the distinction drawn in this passage would be between limits that are destructive or harmful on the one hand and limits that are constitutive or enabling on the other. Enabling limits are those that enable what they limit to be, more fully or securely, what it already is. They enable it to flourish. Since instrumental ends are ends because they lead to final ends, and in order to preserve the flow of the argument of this section, I do not here discuss enabling limits.

49. My choice of the example of skiing was originally inspired by Myles F. Burnyeat's "Aristotle on Learning to Be Good" (in *Essays on Aristotle's Ethics*, Amelie Oksenberg Rorty, ed. [Berkeley: University of California Press, 1980], p. 76). I discuss this example further in chapter 5.

50. I make this proposal first in Achtenberg, "Human Being, Beast and God," p. 28, from which this paragraph is derived.

51. Each of these movements, by being together with the others, is more than itself. Or, we could say, each is raised to a higher level. I discuss being raised to a higher level further in chapter 5, section 6.

52. I use the term 'development' to mean positive or successful development and 'maldevelopment' to mean negative development or deterioration.

53. I discuss this example in Achtenberg, "The Role of the *Ergon* Argument in Aristotle's *Nicomachean Ethics*," *Ancient Philosophy* 9 (1989): 38; and in Achtenberg, "Aristotelian Resources for Feminist Thinking," pp. 109–110.

54. I discuss this passage in Achtenberg, "Aristotelian Resources for Feminist Thinking," pp. 109–110.

55. For a concurring interpretation of this example, see Apostle, trans., *Aristotle's On the Soul* (Grinnell, Iowa: Peripatetic Press, 1981), p. 113, note 17. Apostle, too, speaks of 'preservation'. Where I speak of fulfilling or securing, Apostle speaks of reinforcing, strengthening, or stabilizing.

56. In this and the following two paragraphs, I revise the account of *telos* as constitutive limit of plants that appears in Achtenberg, "Aristotelian Resources for Feminist Thinking," p. 110.

57. See also *Phys.* 4.8 215a1–3, 5.6 230a29–30.

Chapter Three: Ethics and Metaphysics

1. In "On the Alleged Metaphysical Foundation of Aristotle's Ethics," *Ancient Philosophy* 8 (1988): 53–54, Timothy Roche makes this objection in his largely successful argument against Irwin's claim that the argument of the ethics requires for its justification appeal outside ethics to the principles of metaphysics and psychology. What Roche is successful in showing is that the ethics utilizes arguments whose premises are reputable opinions *(endoxa)* rather than principles discovered in metaphysics or psychology. I share that view.

For the argument that ethics does not have a metaphysical foundation but, instead, a dialectical one, see, in addition to Roche's article, Alfonso Gomez-Lobo and Sherwin Klein. For Irwin's argument, see Irwin cited in the first paragraph of this section.

2. In this passage, Aristotle gives an ethymematic argument in which the claim that we know better/more fully when we know from what is prior is the unstated premise.

3. Other reasons for greater precision stated in this passage are not being said of something underlying when the other is said of something underlying, depending on fewer items when the other posits more (*Pr. An.* 1.27 87a33–35).

4. He begins to do so, we can surmise, by giving a brief argument by example for the claim that final good is not merely ambiguous (a 'chance equivocal') but, instead, an analogical equivocal.

5. I quote this and related passages regarding the equivocity of *energeia* in Achtenberg, "Role of the *Ergon* Argument in Aristotle's *Nicomachean Ethics*," p. 39.

6. For relational realism about the good, see Achtenberg, "What Is Goodness? An Introduction" (Ph.D. diss., Graduate Faculty, New School for Social Research, 1982).

7. I prefer to translate '*krisis*' as 'decision' because I see the process of coming to a choice *(prohairesis)* as involving, for Aristotle, four stages: perception *(aisthēsis)*, deliberation *(bouleusis)*, decision *(krisis)*, and choice *(prohairesis)*. First we perceive, then we deliberate between different means/end or constituents/end alternatives, then we decide on one of them, and then, if we have virtue, we choose it. (If we are incontinent, we might decide on the appropriate alternative, but not desire it, and so not choose it, since choice involves desire.) I discuss this process of coming to choice further in chapter 4, section 3.

8. See also *EE* 1.8 1217b32, *Top.* 1.15 107a8–10. I discuss the appropriate as the good further in chapter 4, section 3.

9. The statement is a negative, but the affirmation of the positive can be inferred from the context.

10. In the *Met.* 8.3 1043b23–25 example, a philosophical *aporia* raised by Antisthenes and other uneducated people is said to have a certain appropriateness *(echei tina kairon)*.

11. In *NE* 1.2 1094b6–7, 1.13 1102a7–10, and 10.9 1179a35–b2, Aristotle probably makes the same point, but caution prohibits citing these passages as

support since one could argue that they are about the practitioner of politics not the student of politics.

12. See note 3.

13. I take the point of this sentence from an unpublished paper by Mark Gifford who points out that W. F. R. Hardie and Irwin import temporal clauses into Aristotle's statement itself: "he will not *at the start* need the reason as well" (Hardie); "we will not, *at this stage*, need the reason why it is true in addition" (Irwin) (Gifford's emphases). "A Fallacy in Aristotle's Ethics?" (Department of Philosophy, Virginia Polytechnic Institute and State University, photocopy), p. 6.

14. I have simplified Aristotle's argument here—for reasons similar to his reason for simplifying them in the ethics.

15. Following Irwin, *Aristotle's First Principles* (Oxford: Oxford University Press, 1988), p. 287.

16. See chapter 5, section 3, for further discussion of this passage.

17. According to *Posterior Analytics*, as we have seen, the more precise knowledge would be the knowledge of both the 'that' and the 'why': Chicken is light meat. Light meats are healthy because they are digestible. Thus, chicken is healthy. This additional point is not needed for the argument, however.

18. Irwin, too, sees this as problematic for his assertion of the claim that the ethics has a metaphysical foundation ("Homonymy in Aristotle," *Review of Metaphysics* 34, 3 [1981b]: 222–223).

19. When Aristotle says in 6.8 that practical wisdom concerns the ultimate (by which, in context, he means the particular) and that the ultimate is the object of perception, he goes on to say that he does not mean perception like that of the special senses but perception similar to that by which we perceive that the ultimate is a triangle. So, he does not mean perception by what Aristotle calls the 'special senses' but perception by multiple senses of the common sense-objects. I can see that a figure is a triangle and I can feel that a figure is a triangle. And, in that sense, he is not referring to the analogical meaning closest to the special senses, but to 'this is X'. I discuss this further in chapter 5, section 3.

20. What level is needed will be discussed further in chapter 5, sections 2–6.

Chapter Four: The Mean

1. For an interesting contemporary account of ethical virtues pertaining to thinking, see Linda Trinkaus Zagzebski, *Virtues of the Mind: An Inquiry into the Nature of Virtue and the Ethical Foundations of Knowledge* (Cambridge: Cambridge University Press, 1996).

2. David Ross, *Aristotle* (London: Methuen and Company, 1971) makes a similar point.

3. I follow Irwin's translation here (*Aristotle: Nicomachean Ethics*, p. 93).

4. The other candidate for highest ethical virtue is justice. Aristotle says the just as the lawful is "virtue entire" (*NE* 5.1 1130a8–9; cf. 1129b25–27). However, presumably he means it is the highest of the virtues other than the one

virtue that is an ornament *(kosmos)* on the virtues, namely, pride, since he says that pride requires and is in addition to all the others.

5. Compare *De Cael.* 3.3 302a21: "For in flesh and wood and all bodies of this sort, fire and earth are present potentially, for being separated out they are apparent."

6. For 'well or badly off', see Irwin's translation (*Aristotle: Nicomachean Ethics*, p. 41).

7. One could object to this on the grounds that the capacity to feel pleasure is a mean between extremes, namely, the perceptual mean between what is good or bad as such. However, in that case, the mean is not a state of soul that has two other states as its two opposites. Instead, it is a state of soul that is a mean because it can achieve two opposites.

8. That by *'t'anankaion'* Aristotle mean 'the inevitable' is clear from the context.

9. In another context, John Burnet gives a similar interpretation of *'dei'* for Aristotle, "The verb *dei* means *agathon esti*," he says (*The Ethics of Aristotle* [London: Methuen, 1900], p. 302).

10. Ross translates "what is appropriate to the occasion" (*Aristotle: The Nicomachean Ethics*, rev. ed. [Oxford: Oxford University Press, 1980], p. 30); Irwin, "what the opportune action is" (*Aristotle: Nicomachean Ethics* [Indianapolis: Hackett Publishing Company, 1985], p. 36); Apostle, "what is proper to the occasion" (*Aristotle's Nicomachean Ethics* [Grinnell, Iowa: Peripatetic Press, 1975], p. 23).

11. See also *EE* 1.8 1217b32, *Top.* 1.15 107a8–10.

12. The statement here is in the negative, but Aristotle's affirmation of the positive can be inferred from the context.

13. See *Met.* 8.3 1043b25 for another example of this.

14. I discuss these examples first in Achtenberg, "Aristotelian Resources for Feminist Thinking."

15. We must not here assume the *De Anima* 3.3 categorization of *hypolēpsis* into three types—knowledge *(epistēmē)*, opinion *(doxa)*, and practical insight *(phronēsis)*—since *NE* 6.5 1040b8–13 indicates that *hypolēpsis* is a type of *theōria*. Or, put differently, we must not assume the 3.3 categorization unless we understand *phronēsis* to be like *theōria* (or, to have a *theōria*-like component).

16. He also, of course, refers to the practically wise person as one who deliberates well. This kind of terminological usage, though confusing to readers, is not unusual in Aristotle's writings. It is common for him to distinguish A and B and then give A as the more general categorical name both for A and B. We have seen an example above. Correct deliberation is distinguished from good deliberation (deliberating well) (the former being about what conduces to ends and the latter also about the ends themselves). Then, 'correct deliberation' is used as the umbrella term for them both. In the narrow sense, correct deliberation is about what conduces to ends. In the broad sense, correct deliberation is about both what conduces to ends and about ends themselves.

Aristotle makes a similar move with regard to practical wisdom and deliberation. In some places, he distinguishes practical wisdom from deliberation, specifying that the former is about the end and the latter about what conduces to the end (*NE* 6.9). In other places, he speaks of practical wisdom as about both the end and what conduces to the end (6.5).

17. See chapter 2, section 1, on *De An.* 434a5–10.

Chapter Five: Analogy, Habit, Beauty, Unexpectedness

1. For simplicity's sake, I shall refer to the author(s) of the *Iliad* and the *Odyssey* as 'Homer'.

2. Clearly, full argument for these claims regarding Plato would require a longer account.

3. Norman O. Dahl, *Practical Reason, Aristotle, and Weakness of the Will* (Minneapolis: University of Minnesota Press, 1984), p. 278 makes a similar point. According to him, for Aristotle, the practically insightful person sees that actions like this one in situations like this one are good.

4. It is the constitutive not the instrumental that is important and new in Aristotle. Odysseus, in the examples I have mentioned, sees the instrumental relation. He sees enduring different types of pain and shame as desirable because they are instrumental to achieving different ends. What is new in Aristotle is the idea of seeing different actions or states of affairs as constitutive of different ends or completions. The brutality of the slaughter of the suitors often leads contemporary readers of the *Odyssey* to remark on the instrumental nature of Odysseus' virtue.

5. See chapter 5, note 10.

6. Though the best life is the contemplative life according to Aristotle in the *Nicomachean Ethics*, this passage suggests that the contemplation involved includes contemplation of (the universal aspect of certain) particulars as well as of unchanging universals.

7. I discuss this topic first in Achtenberg, "What Is Goodness?" pp. 109–120. The discussion in this section is the same as that discussion with substantial revisions.

8. See also *De An.* 2.1 412b7–9.

9. I discuss this first in Achtenberg, "What Is Goodness?" pp. 120–128. The discussion that follows here is substantially the same as that discussion but revised and shortened (due to the discussion of good as end in 2.3).

Chapter Six: Emotions as Perceptions of Value

1. It is no objection to Nussbaum and Putnam's argument, or my own, that 'emotion' translates *'pathos'* and *pathos* is something suffered not something done while perception or *aisthēsis* is an activity or *energeia*. For regarding both *pathos* and *aisthēsis*, there are two stages: *dynamis* and *energeia*. There is potential to suffer and potential to perceive; there is activity of suffering and activity of perceiving.

2. Since according to my interpretation, emotions are types of pleasure or pain, we can carry the point further and say that for Aristotle emotions are not

a type of assertion or denial but are a type of perception. The importance of this for contemporary discussions is clear. On this interpretation, Aristotle is not one who thinks that emotions are types of judgment (whether assertion or denial) but instead thinks emotions are types of perception, specifically, types of perception of value.

3. Smith, Hett, and Apostle read the object of the second clause to be 'images'. Smith, for example, translates "when it asserts or denies them [images] to be good or bad it avoids or pursues them." However, Aristotle cannot mean to say that the soul pursues or flees images. Instead, Aristotle must mean that when the thinking soul asserts that something (or things) is good (are good), it pursues or flees them (Smith, "*Tode Ti* in Aristotle," *Classical Review* 35 (1921): 19; Hett, ed. and trans., *Aristotle VII: On the Soul, Parva Naturalia, On Breath* [Cambridge: Harvard University Press, 1975], p. 177; Apostle, *Aristotle's On the Soul*, p. 53).

4. In the *Meno*, Socrates uses 'accompanies' to denote an intimate relation—the intimate relation between shape and color: shape is "that which alone among beings in fact always accompanies color" (*Meno* 75b10–11).

5. Sarah Broadie makes a similar point in *Ethics with Aristotle* (Oxford: Oxford University Press, 1991), pp. 181–182.

6. Aristotle says 'due to' not 'experienced by' (*Rhet.* 2.4 1381a5). 'Experienced by' is justified by the fact that he goes on to say that the pain and pleasure is a sign of the wish (presumably, one's wishing good things for one's friend) (1381a7).

Conclusion: Imaginative Construction

1. I cite this passage in a different but related context in Achtenberg, "Human Being, Beast and God," p. 27. As I say there in note 14, 'superficial ornament' is an interpetive translation. Aristotle says pleasure '*hōsper periaptou tinos*' (*NE* 1.8 1099a16 which Ross translates as pleasure 'as a sort of adventitious charm' and Irwin translates as pleasure 'as some sort of ornament').

2. Aristotle says that horses and spectacles are not by nature pleasant. Presumably, however, he means that they are not by nature *very* pleasant. They provide some small amount of pleasure due to their own nature. They come to seem highly pleasurable to those who use them to compensate for lack of pleasure in the rest of their lives. The lover-of-horses uses horses in this way, the lover-of-spectacles uses spectacles in this way, and so on. The use of 'x' to mean 'very x' is not unusual in Aristotle. In numerous passages, for example, he says 'the good' and means 'the best good', for example, in his discussion of whether politics or contemplation is the good.

3. This is contradicted by Aristotle's claim in *NE* 2.3 1104b5–8 that "the one who endures what is terrible and delights in doing so, or at least is not pained by doing so, is courageous while the one who is pained by doing so is cowardly." It is also contradicted by his claim in 3.6 1115a32–35, that "A person is called courageous in the strict sense who is fearless in face of a noble

death, and of all immediate circumstances that bring death, and the circumstances of war are most of all of this sort." Nonetheless, it is true to what Aristotle says in 3.7 which is probably a revision of the views of 3.6.

4. For an interesting discussion of dirty work and dangerous work—specifically, of the justice issues they involve—see Michael Walzer's *Spheres of Justice: A Defense of Pluralism and Equality* (New York: Basic, 1983), pp. 165–183.

5. See, for example, Hamilton, *Self and Others*.

BIBLIOGRAPHY

Achtenberg, Deborah. "What is Goodness? An Introduction." Ph.D. diss., Graduate Faculty, New School for Social Research, 1982.

———. "The Role of the *Ergon* Argument in Aristotle's *Nicomachean Ethics*." *Ancient Philosophy* 9 (1989): 37–47. Reprint in *Essays in Ancient Greek Philosophy IV: Aristotle's Ethics*, John P. Anton and Anthony Preus, eds. Albany: State University of New York Press, 1991.

———. "On the Metaphysical Presuppositions of Aristotle's *Nicomachean Ethics*." *Journal of Value Inquiry* 26 (1992): 317–340.

———. "Human Being, Beast and God: The Place of Human Happiness According to Aristotle and Some Twentieth Century Philosophers." *St. John's Review* 38 (1988): 21–47. Reprint in *The Crossroads of Norm and Nature: Essays on Aristotle's 'Ethics' and 'Metaphysics'*, May Sim, ed. Lanham, Maryland: Rowman and Littlefield Press, 1995.

———. "Aristotelian Resources for Feminist Thinking." In *Ancient Philosophy and Feminism*, Julie K. Ward, ed. New York: Routledge, 1996a.

———. "Re-placing the Classics in Today's Curricula: Toward a New Syncretism." Paper presented at the National Endowment for the Humanities Focus Grant series, Temple University, Philadelphia, 1996b.

Anagnostopoulos, Georgios. *Aristotle on the Goals and Exactness of Ethics*. Berkeley: University of California Press, 1994.

Annas, Julia. "Virtue as a Skill." Paper presented at the Sixth Leonard Conference, Contemporary Perspectives on Ancient Greek Thought, Department of Philosophy, University of Nevada, Reno, 1991.

———. *The Morality of Happiness*. Oxford: Oxford University Press, 1993.

Anton, John P., and Anthony Preus, eds. *Essays in Ancient Greek Philosophy IV: Aristotle's Ethics*. Albany: State University of New York Press, 1991.

Anzaldúa, Gloria. *Borderlands/La Frontera: The New Mestiza*. San Francisco: Aunt Lute Books Company, 1987.

Apostle, Hippocrates G., trans. *Aristotle's Nicomachean Ethics*. Grinnell, Iowa: Peripatetic Press, 1975.

———, trans. *Aristotle's Metaphysics*. Grinnell, Iowa: Peripatetic Press, 1979.
———, trans. *Aristotle's On the Soul*. Grinnell, Iowa: Peripatetic Press, 1981.
Barnes, Jonathan, ed. *The Complete Works of Aristotle. The Revised Oxford Translation*. Princeton: Princeton University Press, 1984.
Barnes, J., J. Schofield, and R. Sorabji, eds. *Articles on Aristotle*. Vol. 3. London: Duckworth, 1979.
Braidotti, Rosi. *Nomadic Subjects: Embodiment and Sexual Difference in Contemporary Feminist Theory*. New York: Columbia University Press, 1994.
Broadie, Sarah. *Ethics with Aristotle*. Oxford: Oxford University Press, 1991.
Burnet, John, ed. *The Ethics of Aristotle*. London: Methuen, 1900.
———, ed. *Platonis Opera*. Vol. 2. Oxford: Clarendon Press, 1973.
———, ed. *Platonis Opera*. Vol. 3. Oxford: Clarendon Press, 1974a.
———, ed. *Platonis Opera*. Vol. 4. Oxford: Clarendon Press, 1974b.
Burnyeat, Myles F. "Aristotle on Learning to Be Good." In *Essays on Aristotle's Ethics*, Amelie Oksenberg Rorty, ed. Berkeley: University of California Press, 1980.
Butler, Judith. *Gender Trouble: Feminism and the Subversion of Identity*. New York: Routledge, 1990.
Bywater, I., ed. *Aristotelis: Ethica Nicomachea*. Oxford: Clarendon Press, 1975.
Calhoun, Cheshire, and Robert C. Solomon. *What Is an Emotion? Classic Readings in Philosophical Psychology*. Oxford: Oxford University Press, 1984.
Carson, Anne. *Eros the Bittersweet*. Princeton: Princeton University Press, 1986.
Chodorow, Nancy. *The Reproduction of Mothering*. Berkeley: University of California Press, 1978.
———. *Feminities, Masculinities, Sexualities: Freud and Beyond*. Lexington: University Press of Kentucky, 1994.
Clark, S. L. R. *Aristotle's Man: Speculations upon Aristotelian Anthropology*. Oxford: Oxford University Press, 1975.
Crisp, Roger, and Michael Slote, eds. *Virtue Ethics*. Oxford: Oxford University Press, 1997.
Dahl, Norman O. *Practical Reason, Aristotle, and Weakness of the Will*. Minneapolis: University of Minnesota Press, 1984.
Dihle, Albrecht. *The Theory of the Will in Classical Antiquity*. Berkeley: University of California Press, 1982.
Dillon, J. M., and A. A. Long. *The Question of "Eclecticism": Studies in Later Greek Philosophy*. Berkeley: University of California Press, 1988.
Efros, Israel I. *Ancient Jewish Philosophy*. New York: Bloch Publishing Company, 1964.
Engstrom, Stephen, and Jennifer Whiting. *Aristotle, Kant, and the Stoics: Rethinking Happiness and Duty*. Cambridge: Cambridge University Press, 1996.
Forster, E. S., and D. J. Furley, eds. and trans. *Aristotle III: On Sophistical Refutations, On Coming-to-Be and Passing Away, On the Cosmos*. Cambridge: Harvard University Press, 1978.
Fortenbaugh, W. W. *Aristotle on Emotion: A Contribution to Philosophical Psychology, Rhetoric, Poetics, Politics and Ethics*. New York: Harper and Row, 1975.

P. A. French et al., eds. *Studies in Ethical Theory.* Vol. 3, *Midwest Studies in Philosophy.* Morris: University of Minnesota Press, 1978.

Freud, Sigmund. *Three Essays on the Theory of Sexuality,* 1905. In *Sigmund Freud: Three Essays on the Theory of Sexuality,* James Strachey, ed. New York: Basic Books, 1962.

———. "On Narcissism: An Introduction," 1914. In *Freud: General Psychological Theory,* Philip Rieff, ed. New York: Collier Books, 1963.

———. "Instincts and Their Vicissitudes," 1915. In *Freud: General Psychological Theory,* Philip Rieff, ed. New York: Collier Books, 1963.

———. "Mourning and Melancholia," 1917. In *Freud: General Psychological Theory,* Philip Rieff, ed. New York: Collier Books, 1963.

———. "Group Psychology and the Analysis of the Ego," 1921. In *The Standard Edition of the Complete Works of Sigmund Freud,* James Strachey, ed. Vol. 18. London: Hogarth Press, 1920–1922.

———. "The Ego and the Id," 1923. In *The Standard Edition of the Complete Works of Sigmund Freud,* James Strachey, ed. Vol. 19. London: Hogarth Press, 1923–1925.

———. "The Libido Theory," 1923. In *Freud: General Psychological Theory,* Philip Rieff, ed. New York: Collier Books, 1963.

———. "The Economic Problem of Masochism," 1924. In *Freud: General Psychological Theory,* Philip Rieff, ed. New York: Collier Books, 1963.

Friedman, Richard Elliot. *Who Wrote the Bible?* New York: Simon & Schuster, 1987.

Gifford, Mark. "A Fallacy in Aristotle's Ethics?" Department of Philosophy, Virginia Polytechnic Institute and State University. Photocopy.

Gomez-Lobo, Alfonso. "The Ergon Inference." *Phronesis* 34 (1989): 170–184.

Gourevitch, Victor, ed. and trans. *Jean-Jacques Rousseau: The First and Second Discourses Together with the Replies to Critics and Essay on the Origin of Languages.* New York: Harper, 1986.

Grant, Alexander, ed. *The Ethics of Aristotle.* Vols. 1 and 2. London: Longmans, Green and Co, 1874.

Green, Peter, ed. *Hellenistic History and Culture.* Berkeley: University of California Press, 1993.

Gregor, Mary, trans. *Immanuel Kant: The Metaphysics of Morals.* Cambridge: Cambridge University Press, 1996.

Grube. G. M. A., trans. *The Meditations of Marcus Aurelius.* Indianapolis: Hackett Publishing Company, 1983.

Guthrie, W. K. C., ed. and trans. *Aristotle VI: On the Heavens.* Cambridge: Harvard University Press, 1971.

Hamilton, N. Gregory. *Self and Others: Object Relations Theory in Practice.* Northvale, New Jersey: Jason Aronson Press, 1990.

Hardie, W. F. R. *Aristotle's Ethical Theory.* Oxford: Oxford University Press, 1968.

Hett, W. S., ed. and trans. *Aristotle VII: On the Soul, Parva Naturalia, On Breath.* Cambridge: Harvard University Press, 1975.

Irwin, Terence. "First Principles in Aristotle's Ethics." In *Studies in Ethical Theory.* Vol. 3, *Midwest Studies in Philosophy.* P. A. French et al., eds. Morris: University of Minnesota Press, 1978.

———. "The Metaphysical and Psychological Basis of Aristotle's Ethics." In *Essays on Aristotle's Ethics*, Amelie Oksenberg Rorty, ed. Berkeley: University of California Press, 1980.

———. "Aristotle's Methods of Ethics." *Studies in Aristotle*, Dominic J. O'Meara, ed. Washington, D.C.: Catholic University Press, 1981a.

———. "Homonymy in Aristotle." *Review of Metaphysics* 34, 3 (1981b): 523–544.

———. *Aristotle: Nicomachean Ethics*. Indianapolis: Hackett Publishing Company, 1985.

———. *Aristotle's First Principles*. Oxford: Oxford University Press, 1988.

Jaeger, W., ed. *Aristotelis: Metaphysica*. Oxford: Clarendon Press, 1978.

Jewish Publication Society (JPS). *Tanakh: A New Translation of the Holy Scriptures According to the Traditional Hebrew Text*. Philadelphia: Jewish Publication Society, 1985.

Kahn, Charles. "Discovering the Will: From Aristotle to Augustine." In *The Question of "Eclecticism": Studies in Later Greek Philosophy*, J. M. Dillon and A. A. Long, eds. Berkeley: University of California Press, 1988.

Kaufmann, Walter, trans. *Friedrich Nietzsche: Beyond Good and Evil: Prelude to a Philosophy of the Future*. New York: Vintage, 1966.

Klein, Sherwin. "An Analysis and Defense of Aristotle's Method in *Nicomachean Ethics* i and x," *Ancient Philosophy* 8 (1988): 63–72.

Lattimore, Richmond, trans. *The Iliad of Homer*. Chicago: University of Chicago Press, 1951.

———, trans. *Greek Lyrics*. Chicago: University of Chicago Press, 1960.

———, trans. *The Odyssey of Homer: A Modern Translation*. Chicago: University of Chicago Press, 1965.

Lear, Jonathan. *Love and Its Place in Nature: A Philosophical Interpretation of Freudian Psychoanalysis*. New York: Farrar, 1990.

Leighton, Stephen R. "Aristotle and the Emotions," *Phronesis* 27 (1982): 144–174.

———. "Eudemian Ethics 1220b11–13." *Classical Quarterly* 34 (1984): 135–138.

Liddell, Henry George, Robert Scott, and Henry Stuart Jones. *A Greek-English Lexicon*. Oxford: Clarendon Press, 1983.

Long, Anthony A. "Hellenistic Ethics and Philosophical Power." In *Hellenistic History and Culture*, Peter Green, ed. Berkeley: University of California Press, 1993.

———, ed. *Stoic Studies*. Cambridge: Cambridge University Press, 1996.

———. "Representation and the Self in Stoicism." In *Stoic Studies*, Anthony A. Long, ed. Cambridge: Cambridge University Press, 1996.

Lord, Carnes, trans. *Aristotle: The Politics*. Chicago: University of Chicago Press, 1984.

Macpherson, C. B., ed. *John Locke: Second Treatise of Government*. Indianapolis: Hackett Publishing Company, 1980.

McDowell, John. "Virtue and Reason." *Monist* 62 (1979): 331–350.

———. "Deliberation and Moral Development in Aristotle's Ethics." In *Aristotle, Kant, and the Stoics: Rethinking Happiness and Duty*, Stephen Engstrom and Jennifer Whiting, eds. Cambridge: Cambridge University Press, 1996.

Metzger, Bruce M., and Roland E. Murphy, eds. *The New Oxford Annotated Bible with the Apocryphal/Deuterocanonical Books*. New York: Oxford University Press, 1991.
Minio-Paluello, L., ed. *Aristotelis: Categoriae et Liber De Interpretatione*. Oxford: Clarendon Press, 1986.
Modrak, Deborah K. W. *Aristotle: The Power of Perception*. Chicago: University of Chicago Press, 1987.
Nussbaum, Martha. *Aristotle's 'De Motu Animalium'*. Princeton: Princeton University Press, 1978.
———. "The Discernment of Perception: An Aristotelian Conception of Private and Public Rationality," 1985. Reprint and revision in *Love's Knowledge: Essays on Philosophy and Literature*. Cambridge: Cambridge University Press, 1986a.
———. *The Fragility of Goodness: Luck and Ethics in Greek Tragedy and Philosophy*. Cambridge: Cambridge University Press, 1986b.
———. *Love's Knowledge: Essays on Philosophy and Literature*. Oxford: Oxford University Press, 1990.
Nussbaum, Martha, and Hilary Putnam. "Changing Aristotle's Mind." In *Essays on Aristotle's 'De Anima'*, Martha Nussbaum and Amelie Oksenberg Rorty, eds. Oxford: Oxford University Press, 1992.
Nussbaum, Martha, and Amelie Oksenberg Rorty. *Essays on Aristotle's 'De Anima'*. Oxford: Oxford University Press, 1992.
Oakeshott, Michael, ed. *Leviathan: On the Matter, Forme and Power of a Commonwealth Ecclesiasticall and Civil*. New York: Collier Books, 1962.
O'Meara, Dominic J., ed. *Studies in Aristotle*. Washington, D.C.: Catholic University Press, 1981.
Owen, G. E. L. "Logic and Metaphysics in Some Earlier Works of Aristotle." 1960. Reprint in *Articles on Aristotle*. Vol. 3, J. Barnes, J. Schofield, and R. Sorabji, eds. London: Duckworth, 1979.
Owens, Joseph. *The Doctrine of Being in the Aristotelian 'Metaphysics'*. Toronto: Pontifical Institute of Mediaeval Studies, 1978.
Paton, H. J., trans. *Immanuel Kant: Groundwork of the Metaphysic of Morals*. New York: Harper, 1956.
Person, Ethel Spector. "Sexuality and the Mainstay of Identity: Psychoanalytic Perspectives." 1980. In *Women: Sex and Sexuality*, Catharine R. Stimpson and Ethel Spector Person, eds. Chicago: University of Chicago Press, 1980.
Rackham, H., ed. and trans. *Aristotle: The Athenian Constitution, The Eudemian Ethics, On Virtues and Vices*. Cambridge: Harvard University Press, 1971.
Rieff, Philip, ed. *Freud: General Psychological Theory*. New York: Collier Books, 1963a.
———. *Freud: Sexuality and the Psychology of Love*. New York: Collier Books, 1963b.
Roche, Timothy. "On the Alleged Metaphysical Foundation of Aristotle's Ethics." *Ancient Philosophy* 8 (1988): 49–62.
Rorty, Amelie Oksenberg. *Essays on Aristotle's Ethics*. Berkeley: University of California Press, 1980.

Ross, David. *Aristotle*. London: Methuen and Company, 1971.
———, ed. *Aristotelis: Physica*. Oxford: Clarendon Press, 1973.
———, ed. *Aristotelis: Ars Rhetorica*. Oxford: Clarendon Press, 1975.
———, ed. *Aristotelis: Analytica Priora et Posteriora*. Oxford: Clarendon Press, 1978.
———, trans. *Aristotle: The Nicomachean Ethics*. Rev. ed. Oxford: Oxford University Press, 1980.
———, ed. *Aristotelis: Topica et Sophistici Elenchi*. Oxford: Clarendon Press, 1984.
———, ed. *Aristotelis: De Anima*. Oxford: Clarendon Press, 1986.
———, ed. *Aristotelis: Politica*. Oxford: Clarendon Press, 1988.
Salkever, Stephen G. *Finding the Mean: Theory and Practice in Aristotelian Political Philosophy*. Princeton: Princeton University Press, 1990.
Sherman, Nancy. *The Fabric of Character: Aristotle's Theory of Virtue*. Oxford: Oxford University Press, 1989.
———. *Making a Necessity of Virtue: Aristotle and Kant on Virtue*. Cambridge: Cambridge University Press, 1997.
Sim, May, ed. *The Crossroads of Norm and Nature: Essays on Aristotle's 'Ethics' and 'Metaphysics'*. Lanham, Maryland: Rowman and Littlefield Press, 1995.
Slote, Michael. "Agent-Based Virtue Ethics," 1995. In *Virtue Ethics*, Roger Crisp and Michael Slote, eds. Oxford: Oxford University Press, 1997.
Smith, J. A. "*Tode Ti* in Aristotle." *Classical Review* 35 (1921): 19.
Smith, Norman Kemp, trans. *Immanuel Kant's Critique of Pure Reason*. New York: St. Martin's, 1965.
Stimpson, Catharine R., and Ethel Spector Person. *Women: Sex and Sexuality*. Chicago: University of Chicago Press, 1980.
Strachey, James, ed. *The Standard Edition of the Complete Works of Sigmund Freud*. Vol. 18. London: Hogarth Press, 1920–1922.
———, ed. *The Standard Edition of the Complete Works of Sigmund Freud*. Vol. 19. London: Hogarth Press, 1923–1925.
———, trans. *Sigmund Freud: Three Essays on the Theory of Sexuality*. New York: Basic, 1962.
Strauss, Leo. "Jerusalem and Athens: Some Preliminary Reflections," 1967. In *Studies in Platonic Political Philosophy*, Leo Strauss. Chicago: University of Chicago Press, 1983.
———. *Studies in Platonic Political Philosophy*. Chicago: University of Chicago Press, 1983.
Taylor, Charles. *Sources of the Self: The Making of the Modern Identity*. Cambridge: Harvard University Press, 1989.
Tracy, Theodore James. *Physiological Theory and the Doctrine of the Mean in Plato and Aristotle*. The Hague: Mouton, 1969.
Urmson, J. O. "Aristotle's Doctrine of the Mean," 1973. In *Essays on Aristotle's Ethics*, Amelie Oksenberg Rorty, ed. Berkeley: University of California Press, 1980.
Walzer, Michael. *Spheres of Justice: A Defense of Pluralism and Equality*. New York: Basic, 1983.

Walzer, R. R., and J. M. Mingay, eds. *Aristotelis: Ethica Eudemia*. Oxford: Clarendon Press, 1991.
Ward, Julie K., ed. *Ancient Philosophy and Feminism*. New York: Routledge, 1996.
West, M. L. *Iambi et Elegi Graeci ante Alexandrum Cantati, Volumen I: Archilochus, Hipponax, Theognidea*. Oxford: Clarendon Press, 1971.
Williams, Bernard. *Ethics and the Limits of Philosophy*. Cambridge: Harvard University Press, 1985.
Woods, Michael. *Aristotle's 'Eudemian Ethics' Books I, II, and VIII*. Oxford: Oxford University Press, 1982.
Zagzebski, Linda Trinkaus. *Virtues of the Mind: An Inquiry into the Nature of Virtue and the Ethical Foundations of Knowledge*. Cambridge: Cambridge University Press, 1996.

INDEX

Achilles, 123–24
Achtenberg, Deborah, 192n10, 193n14, 197n34, 198n40, 199nn46,47,53,54,56, 200nn5–6, 202n14, 204n1
Action, causes of, 26–30
Akrasia. See incontinence
Anagnostopoulos, Georgios, 74, 86–90
Analogy, 123–28; analogical equivocal, 45–48; *logos* and, 127–28; practical perception of, 125, 126–27
Annas, Julia, 97, 99–100, 110, 111, 114
Anzaldúa, Gloria, 193n14
Apostle, Hippocrates G., 198n42, 199n55, 202n10, 204n3
Appropriate, as the good, 71–72, 116–17, 127
Archilochus, 125

Beautiful, 9, 129–30, 130–32, 133, 142–49, 151–56; as form, formal cause, substance, 142–49; awareness of, insight into, 130–32, 133, 151–56; lovers of, 129–30; meaning, 142–49; principle of wholeness, completeness, 9, 142–49
Braidotti, Rosi, 193n14

Broadie, Sarah, 167, 204n5
Burnet, John, 103, 106, 202n9
Burnyeat, Myles F., 73, 128–30, 135, 152–54, 199n49
Butler, Judith, 192n12

Calhoun, Cheshire, 14–15
Carson, Anne, 192n6
Chodorow, Nancy, 192nn11,12
Choice, 22–23
Clark, S. L. R., 100–1

Dahl, Norman O., 135–41, 203n3
Dihle, Albrecht, 191n1, 194n4

Efros, Israel I., 191n1
Emotional, ethical development: as channeling of emotion, 6–7, 30–44, 189; as decrease in or suppression of intellect, 5, 6, 7, 10; as development of intellect and emotion, 7, 10, 30–44; as elimination of emotion and decrease in or suppression of intellect, awareness, 3–6, 9, 10,189; as emotional management, 32–41, 43–44; as involving imaginative construction or deconstruction of wholes, 9–10, 179–90
Emotions: appropriate, 114–15, 164; as cognition of value of particu-

Emotions *(continued)*
lars, 1–3; as perceptions, 159; as perceptions and pleasure or pain, 162; as perceptions of value, 159–77, 160, 161–62; as perceptions or appearances of particular persons, 168–69; as perceptions or appearances of particulars, 161, 167–68; as states or types of pleasure or pain, 165–67; as types of pleasure or pain, 160, 165, 167; cognitive component of, 1–3, 159, 177; deliberation and, 164–65; development, shaping of, 159, 177; ethical virtue and, 165; *Eudemian Ethics* definition of, 174–76; following, 129; hate as borderline case of, 174; hate as case of in *Rhetoric*, 176–77; leading to good, 115; Nussbaum and Putnam on, 159–176; suppression, channeling of, 159–177; 'usually' in definition of, 176

Emotivism, 1

Energeia, entelecheia. See telos

Equivocity, 16, 18, 45–48, 63, 70–72, 197nn34, 35, 198nn36, 37, 38, 39

Ethical cognition, as cognition of value, 1–3

Ethical virtue: Aristotle's account of, strengths and weaknesses, 10–11, 182–90; as settled disposition to feel a certain type of feeling, do a certain type of action when it is what is appropriate or needed, 113–14; awareness of balance of particulars the cognitive component (Salkever), 15; awareness of particulars the cognitive component of, 13–18; awareness of salient particulars the cognitive component of, 15–18; awareness of universals, rules, codes the cognitive component of, 15, 127–28; awareness of value the cognitive component of, 1–3, 117–18, 118–21; blueprint and (McDowell), 17; definition of, 110–13; deliberation as awareness of value in, 118; *hexis* in definition of, 111–13; nondetachability and (McDowell), 17; perception as awareness of value in, 120; person of excellence as standard of (Nussbaum), 18; practical insight as awareness of value in, 119; uncodifiability and (McDowell), 15–16; Wittgenstein and, 16, 140

Ethics and metaphysics: Charles Taylor and, 63; dialectical ground of Aristotle's ethics, 61–62, 93–94; experience-near account and, 90–95; metaphysical foundation of Aristotle's ethics (Irwin), 61, 62, 93–94; metaphysical foundation of ethics, 61–65; metaphysical principles and Aristotle's ethics, 61–65, 95–96; metaphysics and full articulation, 63, 65, 90–95; sciences under another and, 91–94; 'that' and 'what' in, 64, 84–86; 'that' and 'why' in, 64, 75, 76–84, 91–94, 131–32, 133–42

Ethics and moral theory, 21–59; constraint, channeling, force, 30–44; metaphysics and moral theory, 19–21; special moral faculty, 21–30; special moral object, 44–58

Ethics, Aristotle's: goal of, 63; interpretive problems in, 11, 127; strengths and weaknesses of, 10–11, 182–90; two-level reading of, 63

Experience, 90–95, 128–32, 138

'For the most part', 15, 16–17, 67–70; Aristotle's ethics and, 68; Aristotle's politics and, 67–68; McDowell on, 15, 16–17; wealth, courage and, 67–70

Formalism, 1

Foundationalism, 61, 62
Freud, Sigmund, 4–5, 8, 10, 32, 37–41, 43, 44, 183
Friedman, Richard Elliot, 191n1

Gifford, Mark, 201n13
Gomez-Lobo, Alfonso, 61, 200n1
Good, 8–9; appropriate as, 71–72, 116–17, 127; as analogical equivocal, 16, 18, 45–48, 70–72; as end or final cause, 149–51; as *telos*, *entelecheia*, *energeia*, 8, 44; as transcategorial, 9
Government: as constraint (Hobbes, Locke, Rousseau), 56–57; as development (Aristotle), 57–58
Grant, Alexander, 171–72

Habit, 128–32
Hamilton, N. Gregory, 193n13, 205n5
Hardie, W. F. R., 103, 201n13
Harmonious life, 10
Hebrew *Bible*, 5–6, 10, 12, 23
Hesiod, 132, 156
Hett, W. S., 204n3
Hexis, 111–13; as disposition, 111; as good or bad disposition, 111–12; as settled disposition, 111; ethical, 112–13
Hobbes, Thomas, 6–7, 32, 35–37, 41, 43–44, 56, 58, 182, 192n7

Iliad, 123–24, 203n1
Imaginative construction, 9, 179–90; Marcus and, 182
Incontinence, 23–26
Insight, 133, 135
Irwin, Terence, 61, 62, 73, 197n34, 198nn38,44, 199n45, 201nn3,13,15,18, 202n6,10, 204n1

Kairos. See Apppropriate
Kant, Immanuel, 7, 10, 19–21, 22, 32–35, 41, 43, 58, 99
Klein, Sherwin, 61, 73, 200n1

Lear, Jonathan, 15
Leighton, Stephen R., 174–75
Locke, John, 56, 182
Logos, 11, 127–28
Long, Anthony A., 23, 195n8

Marcus Aurelius, 3–4, 5, 9, 10, 181–82
McDowell, John, 13, 15–18, 140
Mean: aesthetic mean, 106–8; ethical mean, 109–10; ethical mean and other types of mean, 102–10; flexibility implied by, 118, 121–22, 123, 158; heuristic for not component of ethical virtue, 97–98; hyletic mean, 104–6; meaning of, 98; middling amount interpretation of, 98–102; middling amount interpretation, successful and unsuccessful refutations of, 100–2; mixture of opposites intepretation, 103; non-specification of amount, degree, 99, 100, 114; point of discussion of, 98; somatic proportion of opposites, 108–9; trivial, 97, 99, 100, 110; uninspiring, 97, 99, 100
Modrak, Deborah K. W., 170–71, 172

Needed, as the good, 115–16
Nietzsche, Friedrich, 7, 10, 12, 100, 101
Nous. See theoretical insight
Nussbaum, Martha, 13–14, 15, 18, 127–28, 159–76, 192n5, 203n1

Odysseus, 124–25, 126, 132, 203n4
Odyssey, 124–25, 203nn1,4
Opposites, two, 113
Owen, G. E. L., 198n37
Owens, Joseph, 197n34

Parmenides, 4
Paul, 23
Perception, 179–82
Pericles, 134

Person, Ethel Spector, 192n8
Plato, 4, 8, 125
Pleasure and pain: Aristotle's antihedonism, 183–85; as common perception, 172; as perception of particulars as good or bad, 161–62, 170–72; as perception of value, 161–62; as perception or appearance, 162–64; management of, adjustment to, pain, 185–88; perceptual, 175–76; subtypes of, 170; types of, 169–70; why perception of something as good is pleasure, 172–74
Practical decision-making, progression of, 118–20
Practical insight, 179–82
Precision in ethics, 62–65; being an instance and, 63; coarse, outline quality, 67–70; eliminability/ineliminability of imprecision, 63, 65–90; imprecision of ethics, 62, 63, 141; inquiry imprecision, 63–64, 65–72; metaphysics and, 63; more precise account of human good, 91; precise as prior, fundamental, 62; precision of metaphysics, 62; subject matter imprecision, 63–64, 72–86; two types of, 63, 141
Putnam, Hilary, 14, 159–76, 203n1

Relatedness, enriching, 11, 189–90
Roche, Timothy, 61, 62, 73, 74, 93–94
Ross, David, 77, 201n2, 202n10, 204n1
Rousseau, Jean-Jacques, 5, 10, 12, 22, 56–57, 101, 194n6

Salient, 1–2; as conducive to or component of value, 2
Salkever, Stephen G., 6, 13, 14, 15, 73, 97–98
Sherman, Nancy, 13, 14, 15, 32, 97–98
Smith, J. A., 145, 204n3
Socrates, 23–24, 125
Solomon, Robert C., 14–15
Strauss, Leo, 191n1

Taylor, Charles, 63
Telos: analogy, 9; as completion, development, fulfillment, 51, 54–58; as constitutive limit, 49–54; good as, 8, 44; mutually constitutive relationships and, 57–58; relationship, 8
Theoretical insight, 133–42; Dahl on, 135–41; of particulars, 133–34; practical, 133–34
To ti ēn einai, 50
Tode ti, 145–46
Tracy, Theodore James, 74
Truth, two kinds of, 88

Unexpectedness, 156–58
Upbringing, 129
Urmson, J. O., 100

Value, 7–9; as umbrella term, 7; cognition of (intellectual insight, practical insight), 44

Walzer, Michael, 205n4
Williams, Bernard, 19, 97, 99, 110
Wittgenstein, Ludwig, 16, 140
Woods, Michael, 174–75